"I was insane the way an animal is insane because I'd lost everything."

"Anything done supremely well is an act of sex."

"I was alone and I was terrified. . ."

William Shatner

The intimate personal story of William Shatner's life, work, divorce, marriage, and his encounter with the legend of STAR TREK—comes alive in the words of the man who is both actor and writer. Candid, provocative exchanges with co-authors Marshak and Culbreath—boldly go where no biography has gone before. . .

The legend of STAR TREK lives again.

For the first time together for publication since STAR TREK: William Shatner and Leonard Nimoy

"Kirk Meets Spock"—startling answers to what made the chemistry between them work.

Shatner and Gene Roddenberry

STAR TREK: THE MOTION PICTURE

How is it different? The creator of the old and new STAR TREK:

What fantasies and realities lay behind their Camelot to the stars?

THE STAR TREK CAST: "Is he Kirk?"

Marcy Lafferty Shatner:

Their marriage; the revolutions of a decade.

This, then, is the story of our voyage into that mystery. It is biography, autobiography and a report from the revolution.

ABOUT THE CO-AUTHORS

"I'll need a whole file drawer just for you two"—was the first comment of co-authors Marshak's and Culbreath's agent at the William Morris Agency.

That file drawer now includes six published and several more forthcoming books, scripting and co-writing projects with various celebrities, consulting work, etc. They are also moving into television scripting and concept development. In progress are several novels (Their first was written in two weeks). One focus of their fiction is on new themes coming out of the "revolutions" of the decade and new concepts of sexuality, human nature, etc.

Sondra's B.A. and M.A. are in history. Myrna's B.A. is in psychology and philosophy. At nineteen, Sondra organized lecture series in psychology, philosophy, economics, fiction. Myrna founded the Culbreath Schools, developed a method of teaching reading by phonics which is published nationally, and edited a political journal.

Myrna moved from Colorado to Baton Rouge, Louisiana, where Sondra lives with her husband Alan, a professor of electrical engineering at LSU, their son Jerry, eight, and Sondra's mother Mrs. Anna Tornheim Hassan. Jerry was "discovered" landing roles in DIFFERENT STROKES, SUPERTRAIN, VEGAS, etc.—causing the family to set up a second base in Los Angeles.

SHATNER:
WHERE NO MAN...

THE
AUTHORIZED
BIOGRAPHY
OF WILLIAM
SHATNER

By William Shatner,
Sondra Marshak and Myrna Culbreath

A Tempo Star Book

Distributed by Ace Books
Grosset & Dunlap, Inc., Publishers
New York, N.Y. 10010
A Filmways Company

For my family

WILLIAM SHATNER

Copyright © 1979 by William Shatner, Sondra Marshak,
and Myrna Culbreath
All Rights Reserved
Published simultaneously in Canada
ISBN: 0-441-88975-1
Tempo Books is registered in the U.S. Patent Office
Printed in the United States of America

Cover photo by Ann C. Teipen

WILLIAM SHATNER: WHERE NO MAN...

INTRODUCTION
Voyage Into Legend

On any Monday a working actor may be called upon to play a man who became legend in his lifetime: Alexander the Great, Captain James T. Kirk.

But it is not on any Monday that an actor sails into the trackless regions of legend himself—evoking not merely the response to a lifetime of workmanship, but an overwhelming, almost inexplicable response to the chemistry of that actor's interaction with one particular role.

It may not happen in a lifetime.

It began to happen for an actor who has played everything from Shakespeare to farce on some Monday when he signed on to say: "These are the voyages of the starship *Enterprise*. . ."

That actor could not have known that he was signing on for a voyage into legend. It has taken these dozen years to reveal just how fully he did sail where no man has gone, and what an uncharted voyage it still is, to what strange new worlds—not least our own.

In that world a President of the United States changed the name of man's first Orbital spaceship to honor that legend. The *Enterprise* has flown in the real skies of earth.

And now it flies again—to the stars. Shatner was called back to command that flight, too: recreating the role of Kirk in the new STAR TREK movie—which became the pre-release blockbuster of all time.

The impact of such a close encounter with legend is not something an actor can fully recognize for himself.

He can see, objectively, that the response was unprecedented. He knows that he has had many kinds of recognition and much critical acclaim in his career before and since. But this is something else again in sheer power, intensity, depth—even numbers. He can see the tens of thousands turning out to STAR TREK conventions, feel the electric quality of their response—something crackling in the air, indefinable. The first time he tries a STAR TREK convention appearance, it makes him vaguely uneasy. Maybe not so vaguely. He does not in truth know why these people are here—ten thousand strong, to his one. They are friendly, even loving—but what makes them tick?

And what's a nice working actor doing in a place like this?

But He's a pro who has come to give a performance. He offers to answer questions "with a minimum of crap." The audience loves it. But there are still his questions: What *are* they doing here?

Is this just the response to STAR TREK—itself an unprecedented phenomenon—or is it to *him?* to both? If to him—is it to Kirk or to Shatner? Both? Or is it to some improbable alchemy which made him the right man for the right role at the right time? Did it, perhaps, touch some important nerve in our culture?

In some sense, he is the last man who can know, and certainly the last man who can say.

He is the last man to whom anyone will dare or presume to say certain things about it. And for him to say certain things might be regarded as presumption, especially by *him*.

Yet he is the man in whom the answer is to be found, and the answer to what has moved so many people to preserve and preside over the rebirth of a legend, is worth digging for. What turned them on? What does that reveal about this strange world? What did they learn? What did *he* learn? Would he be willing to sign on to explore *that* unchartered world?

But the man is also more than the legend. People have watched him, boy and man, through the media which have made us a global village. Yet the private man has remained essentially unknown.

In the role of Kirk—many people did feel that they saw the man coming through: not merely the captain, but the actor. It was hard to tell where Kirk left off and Shatner began. Even for Shatner.

And there was something in both which touched people.

Nor was it merely the role.

As if in a laboratory experiment, the first unsold pilot of STAR TREK was filmed with Jeffrey Hunter playing the captain. Everything which the writing and script could give the role and the series was there. The alchemy was not. Most viewers agree that it *was* there from the first moment of Shatner's Kirk in the second pilot which sold STAR TREK: "Where No Man Has Gone Before."

If Shatner were to say that, it would be presumption. Moreover, he might not even know of the difference in response. As an actor he can know how he judges another performance, or his own—but to know really how it was received is much tougher. Even if someone tells him it was great, it is fact, flattery? By what standards are they judging?

That is, roughly, where we came in.

We are judging on the basis of a years-long study which finally incorporated probably the largest in-depth mass communication study ever done of the mass impact of a television series.

Through responses to our books on STAR TREK* we collected a body of data. Many thousands of letters, manuscripts, personal communications and questionnaires show that the response to Kirk and Shatner was not merely a matter of fandom or fantasy, although there was certainly plenty of *that*—often of the most unexpurgated kinds.

It turns out that the very things which Shatner brought to the role of Kirk were exactly what most people say brought the chemistry of the role—and of STAR TREK—alive for them.

Shatner himself, if asked, will mention first of all: "Humor—I figured everyone else took the Captain seriously. *I* didn't have to take myself so seriously."

And, indeed, many people were very much turned on by the humor and the down-to-earth quality Shatner brought to the role.

Of course, some people were even more turned on, sometimes literally, by things which might make a starship captain blush—possibly even an actor. Countless letters indicate that the flesh which he gave the role was solid enough, especially in all the more interesting portions of his interesting anatomy. Not least the one which all the recent surveys show is the piece of male anatomy which turns women on most. (Have you followed them? It's "Gentlemen, guard your rear," time. And Kirk's is generally regarded as gorgeous.)

But there is more to the anatomy of a legend than anatomy.

STAR TREK was itself legend for its projection of a future in which man prevailed. And within it Kirk was

---

Star Trek Lives! (Marshak, Lichtenberg, Winston), *Star Trek: The New Voyages I & II* (edited by Marshak & Culbreath), *Star Trek* novels: *The Price of the Phoenix, The Fate of the Phoenix* (by Marshak & Culbreath), etc. published by Bantam Books.

the projection of the man who would prevail—in some sense, the future of us all.

If he had been played as less than he was—a man who, in many respects, *was* a new ideal—there is every chance that the emotional chemistry of his relationship with his alien friend, Spock, and the rest of his diverse crew would never have caught fire. And the *Enterprise* would not fly today. Not in our NASA program. And not on seven sound stages—with the same captain and crew.

The facts of the legend almost explode in Shatner's face. He goes to STAR TREK conventions which draw up to 30,000 people—in almost every major city.

A million-letter campaign revived STAR TREK when it was first cancelled on network. Paramount continued to be bombarded with letters, demonstrations, etc. for ten years. A four hundred thousand letter campaign got President Ford to change the name of the first Orbiter to *Enterprise*.

Those numbers alone indicate a staggering effect.

But of what kind? Our questionnaire on the mass impact of STAR TREK and Shatner reached more than 40,000 people; not only STAR TREK fans but the general public.

We got a rate of return which outdrew the Hite Report.

Some of it was as unexpurgated.

But also it was as serious: people's gut-level reactions to questions about the revolutions of this decade: acceptance of diversity, greater acceptance of changes in male-female roles, greater acceptance of emotional openness, especially in men.

Did STAR TREK or the way Shatner played Kirk change people's attitudes on those questions?

The results of that study will have to be published in more detail than can be included here. But the overwhelming answer was Yes. On all counts. But especially on the impact of Shatner's Kirk.

Thirteen-year-old boys write that they are not afraid
to be emotionally open (using those words), that they
know it's not unmanly to cry—because of the way
Shatner played Kirk.

A male physician writes us a curt note on his MD
letterhead about a story emphasizing that aspect of
Kirk: "You have the honor, if one can call it that, of
being the first to make me cry."

There was a blockbuster in Shatner's Kirk—a sleeper
effect, valued then, becoming more devastating as the
world caught up with it.

Shatner played Kirk as a strong, profoundly
masculine man who was able and willing to express the
most profound and most tender emotions—even those
which a man is not supposed to express: fear, uncertainty, vulnerability, pain.

That was a time bomb. It is still going off. It touched
a raw nerve in our culture, where men have been taught
to suppress, repress, deny: "men don't cry."

Set against the character of the Vulcan Spock, who
was the archetype of emotional control, Kirk showed
people a new archetype: a kind of control which was not
denial.

While many identified, at least in the beginning, with
Spock's tendency to deny emotions—and some still do,
most saw eventually that Spock did have emotions—and
that to deny it was part of the problem—of which Kirk
was part of the solution.

That was so rare a thing that people barely knew how
to take it in at the time.

This was in a world where no one yet spoke of "emotional openness in men."

The impact of Kirk registered in ways for which people had no words. It virtually had to create its own audience. But when people did begin to register it fully, it
was like an earthquake.

Kirk shock.
Off the Richter scale.

Now—consider the difficulty when we approached William Shatner with the idea of this book.

Can you possibly walk up to William Shatner and *say* that?

Even after phone interviews for *Star Trek Lives!*, can you walk up to him and say, "Listen, we have boxes and bales of letters and manuscripts, some of them exceedingly unexpurgated, which show that people lost their minds over the way you played Kirk."

Nor, of course, is the appreciation strictly philosophical.

Can you look a working actor in the eye and say, "Listen, they love your gorgeous rear. Did you know that millions of poeple have noticed that you always put it up first when you get up from a fight?"

Would Shatner shock register off the Richter scale?

Would you prefer maybe to say: "You have become an object of sexual fantasy—not merely as you might have in other roles, but as Kirk—an unconventional man who has really been where-no-man has gone: confronting women who can command a Romulan fleet—or a planet—or possibly even *him;* finding himself in a woman's body; or a captive, a slave; a stranger among aliens with alien ways, even alien 'biology' and physiology—some of them female, some male, some enemies, some friends, one a friend who is closer than a brother."

Can you say: "Some of those fantasies would raise a Vulcan's eyebrow—and possibly a Captain's hair, but there they are, and they reveal 'fascinating' things about the nature of human beings."

And especially, can you say to a hard-boiled working actor who resists taking himself too seriously: "We think this is important. We have evidence that the way you played Kirk has changed minds, changed lives. The emotional openness in Kirk touches on, or perhaps has even helped to touch off many of the revolutions of the decade—from women's fight for emotional openness in men, to encounter movements to get in touch with real emotions, to re-thinking of male-female role stereotypes, to studies of male and female sex fantasies which have been coming out, to a more adult attitude about sex. There's a mine of information in our files to show that STAR TREK and especially the impact of Kirk are intimately tied in, in many people's minds, with this on-going 'revolution.' "

And then can you say: 'We'd like to do a book with you that would tackle these kinds of questions, including the sex fantasies, more or less no-holds-barred—subject to your approval, of course, but with the basic understanding that it's to be a where-no-man kind of book?'

Obviously you would say that at your own risk. That actor may easily throw you out on the more interesting portions of your own anatomy. Politely, of course, but very firmly.

Except that just possibly you *can* say that—not all in one breath, but with evidence, and examples and some intriguing ideas to hook the curiosity of a mind alive to ideas. And with a chuckle or two.

And just possibly the man who could play Kirk will not throw you out.

We did. And he didn't.

Witness this book. That man had the where-no-man nerve to sign on for that voyage, too.

And if you think about that, you will begin to know why the millions could believe in a captain who went where no man had gone before.

There was a man behind him.

What do you do if you are Shatner and writers come to you not only with some of the above, but with the news item that you have become—a sex object? ("Sex symbol" is only the most polite name for it.)

You are immortalized in fantasy.

Indeed, you are enshrined in pornography.

At least, Kirk is. And he has become a sex object for practically everybody. His "secret garden" has sprouted a remarkable collection of thorns.

Or is it so remarkable? Studies are beginning to show that some of the darker or thornier kinds of fantasies are common.

If you were Shatner would you have the nerve to let your co-authors open their secret files and discuss some of these fantasies with you for this book? True, Shatner is not Kirk. But Kirk bears a remarkable resemblance to Shatner.

It takes a rare man to agree that, and one capable of thinking completely outside the square, as in the puzzle which can only be solved by going outside the square of dots which limits most people's thinking.

It might interest you to know that was the *first* thing which William Shatner agreed to about the book.

It's another one of those things which you say at your own risk. In fact, it's several of them.

We sat for five hours in a Kansas City steakhouse saying them with illustrations and examples and animated feedback and forth with a William Shatner who looked alive, fascinated, quick, thinking very fast, engaged by ideas.

It was by no accident that Kirk looked like that.

That set of ideas can only be sketched here.

The fuller picture will emerge throughout the book.

Briefly, it goes like this:

The past ten years have seen a transformation in the world: self-awareness movements, women's lib, men's lib, everybody's lib, the revolution of rising sexpectations. People have learned more in a decade than we ever learned in millennia. There's the Masters and Johnson research—a real where-no-scientist effort. There's more. Ten years ago *nobody* admitted to sex fantasies. Psychiatrists and experts, denied, especially, that *women* ever had them. (Those were *male* experts, of course.) One woman broke the ground with *My Secret Garden.* Now studies are coming out which casually discuss such subjects in a matter-of-fact way which would have been impossible a decade ago. And almost nobody blinks an eye. *Playboy,* the great liberator of two decades ago is almost passé, because it has not moved quite so far. If there are people who are offended by any of this, there are also millions more who feel grateful, liberated, delighted—under the heading of "You shall know the truth and the truth will set you free."

Not a bad truth itself.

Meanwhile, what is most needed is a certain integration of all this new truth. Are there some principles which make sense of it?

Are there in fact really two halves of each of us, male or female—two sides to our nature: an aggressive, dominant side and a side which wants to yield—but not easily?

Tradition has expected the male to be dominant and the dominant to be male. But in fact it just doesn't work out that way. Yielding is neither feminine nor effeminate, but a potential also of the strongest male. It may even be a need. Further study may show that to be fully happy we need to actualize both potentials, experience both halves.

It is not only or even primarily a question of sex. It permeates our lives—from male-female relationships, to sex roles, to office confrontations, to—possibly—war and peace.

It may well tie in with another line of study—of our animal origins and what we may retain from them—which has been pursued lately by anthropologists, zoologists, and ethologists who study animal behavior and its possible relation to human behavior. It has been interpreted and popularized by people like Robert Ardrey, Conrad Lorenz, Lionel Tiger. *(African Genesis, On Aggression, Men in Groups,* etc.) Some of the interpretation is, of course, open to question, but the data and even the speculations are interesting.

Does it make any sense to believe that we, of all living beings, are suddenly free of instincts which are a billion years deep? And if not, what do we retain of baboons and breast-beating—or more pacific chimpanzees—or some other kind of primate ancestor entirely: a predator?

Does the concept of the "alpha" male—the dominant male of a primate group (with the second most dominant being "beta," etc.) apply to man? Do men strive for dominance in that way? Do women? Is there such a thing as an "alpha female?

If there are men who are alpha males—do they still experience the need to yield? And to whom would or could they yield? An alpha female? But in an Earth context, while that is intellectually possible, it is physically not very convincing. There is a certain issue of plain strength. Muscle.

What about an alien woman now? Say, a Romulan fleet commander? Say, a Vulcan woman? Vulcans are, after all, stronger than humans. Even alpha male male starship captains.

And that, of course, is where STAR· TREK came in. There has never been a study of the fullest potential of human fantasies. It simply can't take place within the limits of this planet, this place, this time, these limitations. The imagination is not limited, and the needs we have never fully known we had are not limited. By exploring the outer limits we can not only find enjoyment —which would be reason enough in itself—but we can learn more about our real natures and what really is important to us in our actual lives.

Ultimately it may be through that kind of creative fantasy that revolutions are born, and made.

STAR TREK was an absolute mine of such ideas; the first such real paydirt strike in our history. And the gold rush is still on.

But it is more than a matter of fantasy. In some way STAR TREK managed to anticipate much of what we have since learned about human nature. How? Why? With what effect? Had the leading actor who created some of those effects known what he was doing? Was he willing to explore such ideas now?

You will find in "Savage Interlude," "Male and Female," "The House on the Hill," "The Chameleon Effect," and elsewhere more of the ideas we first discussed at the beginning of plans for this book—and a few skirmishes along the final frontier of the revolution.

Among other things, we all three had fun.

We sat down with a prime male who had played a new male archetype in the midst of a fermenting revolution.

The irony of Shatner's position, let alone Kirk's, was lost on none of us.

Master's theses and doctoral dissertations analyze STAR TREK and dissect Kirk's philosophy, psychology, and sex role stereotypes—or breaking of stereotypes.

Women's lib groups damn Kirk as a male chauvinist pig.

Women's lib groups hail Kirk as a liberator.

Then you notice that the "damners" are damning Kirk by standards which he and STAR TREK helped to *set*.

The "hailers" are recognizing an almost explosive interaction between Shatner's Kirk and women. Singly or in groups, in or out of the women's movements, many women have recognized that what they want most from a man—or for their sons—is emotional openness.

Many write us that they recognized that first through

Kirk—and fought a years-long battle to free reserved Spock-like husbands, sons, lovers. And—themselves. The story is legend, and legion. It is matched only by boys and men who write that Kirk has been crucial in their own efforts to liberate themselves from what they learned in a hard school: men don't cry. Sometimes, now, they *do*.

Shatner's Kirk became for many the symbol of their fight for a liberation which had no name.

Ultimately that revolution returned to affect the life of the living man who had never intended to be a revolutionary: the professional actor, William Shatner; and the private man—whose own fight was known to no one.

Finally ours became a voyage into a still less explored unknown: that man.

He has long been known as a very private man, whose personal life—divorce and a black period following it—has been a closed book.

In the end there was a building of trust, so that the private man was ultimately willing to reveal much more of his inner self, his life, his marriage, his hopes and doubts than he had ever really contemplated.

And finally, in a house on a hill, we found the other half of a love story, and a story which may be the other side of "men don't cry."

You will detect in the book some of the bare bones of the process by which that trust was built. We've chosen to leave it that way, for the process itself is revealing. Many collaborations with celebrities are polite fictions. This one with Shatner is not. In the process of such a collaboration ideas are sparked back and forth and feedback intermingled until the whole effort is genuinely by the three of us. But since he is also the subject, it is convenient to say "he" and "we." Shatner himself is a writer whose scripts have been performed on Canadian and American television, and that quality often comes through even when he speaks. You will find, therefore, a great deal of the book, in one form or another, in his own words—including the whole of the "Landmarks" chapter.

And you must take the evalutations of his anatomy or destiny as being in the words of the distaff side.

We found, among other things, a man who was intrigued by ideas. Not merely a performer of parts who said his lines, shut up, and went home. This was and is a man who consciously shaped every aspect of what he did. (Even the anatomy itself, which he reshaped by nine months of packing on muscle for the part of Alexander. If he was going to ride bareback—which he learned to do for the part—not to mention bare-armed, bare-thighed—then he would *look* like a warrior king.)

Consider the professionalism of that. Kirk also was the beneficiary of that kind of effort. But also: one of the first things we learned about Shatner was that he had made the intellectual leap of playing Kirk as Alexander to the stars.

What kind of actor does it take to see Alexander as a civilizing influence, who even respected the customs of others, and to play a starship captain dedicated to peace on the model of a warrior-king?

What does it take to create something of Alexander's immortal friendship with Hephaestion in Kirk's friendship for the alien Spock who became the brother of his heart?

Whatever kind of actor that took, it was Shatner.

The role found him, and he it. The meeting set off an explosive alchemy which by some touch of the philosopher's stone and the actor's magic transmuted an idea into a living creation not of gold, but of mind and flesh, wearing the face of Kirk, and of Shatner.

Now the man goes out to confront his legend, alone.

And the legend comes out to confront him—in droves. More than 100,000 come to see him as Shatner, alone, on his one man tour. Some of them seven or eight

years old and yet unborn when the *Enterprise* last flew:
the rerun generation.

Now—he faces an awesome actor's challenge. To
create alchemy once is tough. Twice—is tougher.

A ten-year fan campaign would settle for nothing less.
One of the most expensive productions of all time says
that the campaign has won, and is the ultimate review
on a performance.

Shatner, and the entire original cast of STAR TREK,
creator Gene Roddenberry, director Robert Wise, have
undertaken to make the legend which would not die—
live again.

As it happened, another project with Shatner spanned
the seven-month filming of the new STAR TREK movie.

And new where-no-actor projects conceived by
Shatner were also writing new endings to this book.

How Shatner created and re-created the legendary
role, how the professional who was Shatner was ready
for it, how he has moved beyond it, what he brings to it
now, and how he has survived a close encounter with
legend are part of that story.

There is a smorgasbord of Shatner—his career, his
wide ranging skills—from flying to bow hunting, by way
of ten other ways to endanger interesting anatomy. His
ideas. Where he's from. Where he's at. Where he's
going.

There's a rather different smorgasbord of Kirk, who
is served up neatly in a variety of predicaments which
shouldn't happen to a starship captain, but do.

Beyond that, what emerged more and more strongly
was: the man, his life, his love story, his own confrontation with loneliness and longing, his walk through fire.

And at the bottom of it all we found a mystery which
in some sense, perhaps is the story of us all.

This, then is the story of our voyage into that mystery.

It is biography, autobiography, and a report from the
revolution. . .

Shatner: Where From?

You have this stick between your legs and you're turning, and the centrifugal force is forcing the blood down. . . I mean, it's all sexual. . .
William Shatner

Which doesn't exactly describe fear of flying. . .

Shatner's eyes glint with amusement—an expression which would have been at home on the face of a starship captain.

In fact, it's a straight answer to a straight question. The actor has risked his expensive anatomy on a dozen-odd sports—even in the STAR TREK years when he had to be on camera 10, 12, 14 hours a day, six days a week.

And on the seventh day he—Motorcycled? Flew? (Soloed after an incredible eight hours.) Scuba dived? Went bow hunting? (Once after Alaskan Kodiak bear, the largest carnivore on earth, standing nine feet tall against his single arrow—and dying.)

Much later, in the upstairs study of his house on the hill, Shatner does for us the daring performance he will do for a STAR TREK convention drawing 18,000 people—a dramatic, even erotic poem by D. H. Lawrence: "Whales Weep Not." It is perhaps the last poem an actor would dare to do for a STAR TREK convention. Shatner uses it to call attention to the plight of whales being slaughtered in our seas—perhaps the intelligent, loving aliens of our own home seas.

It is his own idea, and he is moved by that plight.

And on the floor of the study is the bearskin which is also a part of what William Shatner is, or was.

Today he tells us that he regrets killing it, would not do it again. And he has since hunted Iranian snow leopard—with a camera.

Nevertheless, the bear and the fact of having faced it from within bowshot are still a part of the man. It is not as if he killed it with an express rifle.

Karate, more recently akido, car racing, canoeing, just plain archery—the list does not seem to end.

And now in a New York hotel suite, the man who is both the civilized William Shatner and the man who hunts bear is cataloging the satisfactions of sports, and saying cheerfully, "Just plain archery. But what could be more sexual than archery as a phallic symbol? The arrow and the bow as you draw it taut, gathering the tension—your strength, your power pumped into it, behind the thrust, and then the release—like an ejaculation, thrusting the arrow forward to impale the target. The arrow arcs up and flies straight home and penetrates the center of the bull's-eye . . . I mean, it's like an act of sex."

He pauses and the thoughtful hazel eyes gaze at some distance, without losing the glint of humor, but with the look of pursuing a thought. "And that, I think, is the essence of doing anything like that. It's the same with any athlete—with the athlete, and the artist. Anything in life that's done supremely well is an act of sex."

It's a startling statement from a man who is both athlete and artist.

It's surprising on another level. This is the man who is, with some justice, reported to be the Aldebaran shellmouth of the galaxy—tight-lipped enough to make a Vulcan green with envy.

He has charmed interviewers more or less from one end of the galaxy to the other—and very little of the private man has emerged.

He's saying: "That act of sex just doesn't happen to be with someone else—I mean with some individual. It may be with a whole audience. I have had visions, dreams, before an opening night of actually—encompassing—a whole audience. . ."

He smiles thoughtfully, for a moment conscious of the choice he is making for this book and of the tape recorder in the New York hotel suite.

But he goes on:

". . . of actually making love to a whole audience—and making them my lover, and I theirs."

A building of trust in private conversation is one thing. How open the working actor and private man would be willing to be with the tape recorder cranking over in a joint working session for this book remained an open question.

It was being answered:

". . . but the point was, I was on stage and I was in rhythm with them, and finally—the moment culminated—with the audience."

Which gives you some idea what the man is doing on a stage besides playing Shakespeare. It may even be that he is doing much the same thing hunting nine-foot bear with a two-foot arrow.

He looks as if writing a book is also an act of the same kind.

He strolls in looking like a truant schoolboy in blue jeans and body shirt, prowling the hotel suite overlooking Central Park with the energy which cannot be still for long.

Schoolboy? He's been on the road more than a month on a man-killing schedule, making a movie, preparing a two-hour one-man-show on airplanes *while* flying all over the country to make the movie. Then doing one, sometimes two, performances a day —every day, except that he just managed to have the flu on his one day off.

He'd have every right to look like death warmed over. He looks as if an all-day and into the night working session is tantamount to playing hooky.

Maybe it is. This is a man who works fifty-two weeks a year, every year. He is that rarity among actors: a working actor. Also: employed. He has been that essentially since the beginning of his career in his native Montreal, Canada, where the son of a middle-class clothing manufacturer began to diverge from his father's dream for him—acting on radio to put himself through college; writing, acting, and producing college productions at McGill University; graduating to Shakespearean repertory theater; then to New York: Broadway and live television in its great years, movies, more television. Finally—legend. The television series which died prematurely, became an American and world institution. The model of STAR TREK's *Enterprise* was enshrined in The Smithsonian Institution in Washington, D.C. The starship's captain became known worldwide, not only as actor but as the face on medallions, artwork, merchandising, comic books, fan magazines, professional magazines, and books of both fiction and nonfiction whose combined sales now run probably in excess of thirty million copies, world wide. STAR TREK reruns play almost four hundred times a week in one-hundred-fifty American cities and in more than sixty-seven foreign countries—almost fifteen years after the first filming by Shatner.

What do you do after the legend?

If you are Shatner, you dig in, not complaining of the possibly fatal effects of typecasting or the mixed blessings and hazards of legend.

There are undeniable benefits. It is one thing to be recognized as an excellent craftsman and artist in your field. It is another to win more of an immortality than most men earn in a lifetime—and for something which he loved. Of the hazards he does not speak, until now. But the man is not the legend. The actor is not the role. And the man who hunts bear with a bow is not inclined to sit on his anatomy nor to rest on his laurels or his legend.

He goes to work. If it is not always the work he would choose, he still makes it the practice of his craft and his art.

Of the rebirth of legend there is no glimmer for years—even when tens of thousands turn out to conventions. Then the STAR TREK movie becomes a five-year mission of stops, starts, reverses and holding patterns for which Shatner pays a heavy price in other opportunities. The hit show he cannot take to Broadway is a cost he can count. (*Tricks of the Trade* with Yvette Mimieux was cancelled soon after he left to film STAR TREK: THE MOTION PICTURE.) So are the roles he must turn down to keep the time open. Of the costs he cannot count—decisions made or not made in offices he may not know—he also does not speak, until now.

But this is a man who lives on challenge.

The sports and the acting are not, perhaps, two different things for him.

Take that man, who has thrived on the toughest acting challenges in show business—from Shakespeare to classic live television drama to STAR TREK, shoot his personal life out from under him at the same time as the legend is cancelled for greatness —and you begin to get a man who must rebuild his

life, create his own challenges, find his own way
through what is sometimes the fire of legend.

"I had to take an animal audience last night and
tame it."

Those were William Shatner's first words for this
book.

No elaboration. As if that were sufficient explanation of what he is doing on a man-killing schedule on
a one-man tour of 43 cities.

Perhaps it is:

"There's a kind of primitive fear—you have to be
afraid of facing an audience as naturally as you fear
heights, like those marvelous Indian steelworkers
from Quebec who can walk the high steel, build the
skyscrapers, because their fear of heights has gone.
Well, I'm a pilot, and *I* get dizzy looking down from
three floors up unless I'm enclosed in a cockpit.

"You have to put yourself into that kind of fear, of
heights, say, or of a snake, some basic, primitive fear
that everyone can identify with to realize what can go
on in an actor's mind when he faces an audience.

"What is this audience going to do that I have to
overcome? What is going to happen to that 'animal'
that Richard Rodgers talks about? How am I going
to have to subdue that animal? Can it be led, gently,
by the muzzle, my hand in its mouth? Do I have to
beat it on the head? Approach it from behind? Whip
it?

"I mean—there is . . . Last night there was close to
being a *mob*.

"God!"

His voice drops to a tone of astonishment.

"It's—an actor's art. And I'm suddenly thinking,
'My God, look what I'm *doing*! It—comes as a
revelation.'"

Is there some basic, elemental, very primitive

challenge in doing that—especially since there are very few challenges today which can make a man experience the primitive self?

His look confirms that that hits a nail on the head: "I'll *tell* you what it is. The man who walks the wire between skyscrapers says: It's because when I'm on that wire, I'm *alive*.

"Now, I'm doing this tour, which I had no need to do—not financial, professional, social—none of those have any bearing on what I'm doing here. I don't *know* what I'm doing here. I just knew that I had to do it. I'd never done one-night stands. I'm doing it because I want to experience it—for no other reason. It's crazy. I'm really putting myself out. I'm killing myself, in a way.

"I'm taking days off the end of my life, putting them in front—because *I'm alive when I'm walking that wire.*

"That is why I'm an actor.

"Not standing in front of a camera knowing that I'm going to be good, knowing that if the role is good, it will carry, knowing that I can do these things and do them well and do them because I like doing them.

"Last night, taming the animal, the other night when I opened the show—I was *alive*.

"I was walking that wire."

'It's the same reason, isn't it?' we say. 'Same reason you fly planes or go hunting? Isn't it the original, primeval, primitive man—taking on the challenges of this world—and not finding that many challenges in the Twentieth Century?'

He nods, eyes still sparkling with the look of walking the wire. "And for an actor—we have skills that —There's no point in my going out and diving off the high tower, 'cause I'll kill myself, 'cause I don't know *how* to do that. But *this* I know how to do."

'You want to test your mettle—or metal—in the old Platonian concept—'

"Right."

'You don't *have* to go out there and hunt—what is it—grizzly bears? The challenges men had in the past —take on the wilderness and the Indians and the grizzlies—which could make a man aware of that primitive self which we all have—'

"Right."

'—The Twentieth Century doesn't have those challenges so many men become something much less.'

"That's interesting," he says. "And I'll accept that explanation—because it's good and dramatic."

'And true? You don't *have* to do the things you do. Doesn't it amount to trying to expand the potential of what a man could be, but most men aren't? *Why* do you drive yourself, risk yourself?'

"That's such a marvelous concept that I hesitate to accept it, because it makes me feel good and makes me feel worthwhile. I suppose it makes me feel— 'Hey, yeah, that's *me,* man.'"

The eyes try to put it off a little with humor, rejecting the concept which makes him feel good. Then some other level of honesty cuts in. "But—" he shakes his head. "And—it sounds right. It *feels* right. And perhaps—my brother-in-law during the period when I was flying planes and scuba diving and carrying on like some idiot, said, 'What are you trying to do, commit suicide?' This was after the painful period in my life—and I thought, 'No, I'm not trying to commit suicide. I don't want to die,'—although there were times—there were nights when I wished that I could. . .

"But the thrill—the thrill—the closeness to danger. Many men feel that. That's why people go to bars and get into fights. It's because their lives have become so dulled that they do it just to get somewhere close to what they are primitively. Maybe I'm doing it in a more artistic fashion. That's quite an interesting analysis."

He wears the look of pursuing the thought which ties in with that five hour conversation in Kansas City on the biological research which is part of the "revolution." 'We *do* have the primitive within: everything we talked about which is coming out in the studies of sexuality, instinct, the primitive self—needs, instincts, sex roles, domination, yielding—what we think of as the two halves of ourselves. All that is from the animal world. Aggression—from football to fighting to wars. *Why?* Because we come by it honestly? But then how do we stop? Maybe there's a way to call in the other half?

'And maybe what you—and the man who walks the wire—are doing is realizing that a man has to actualize his potential, or become something much less than he could be. If you have unactualized potential, sexually or any other way, you're running downhill. It's like putting a racehorse to pull a milk cart.

'And that's essentially what happens to many men today. They're dulled. They're bored. They're boring. They're not *men*.

'It's only the ones who go out and find the challenges who are *not* dulled. But what makes *them* tick? An actor who keeps a man-killing schedule could easily get by with saying, "I don't have time." But somehow, all your life, you've *made* time to master all these other things. What's the list? Add swimming, canoeing, skiing, karate—half a dozen other things.

'*Why* are you doing these things?'

The question interests him. It's perhaps these kinds of questions he's wanted to get at in writing the book. Not so much "Where are you from?" He's answered the standard questions a thousand times too often. But how about, "Where are you coming from?"— intellectually, emotionally, on a gut level?

You in the blue jeans and body shirt, wearing the face of a starship captain: Where from? Where to?

Where no man?

We wanted to get at the truth of that, too, as honestly as we could, with, as he would doubtless put it, "a minimum of crap." A man is always more complex than a legend, and less clearcut. This one has grown up, man and boy, in what is possibly the second oldest profession—and certainly one of the toughest. Few men have their egos and their souls on the line virtually every day, their talents, wares, and physical assets inspected by cold-eyed buyers who hold the power of professional life, death, paycheck, and artistic integrity over them. Few, if bought, then have to perform before the eyes of the immediate galaxy—with talents and sometimes assets laid bare. Few become objects of fantasy beyond their own bedroom doors. Few cannot walk down a street alone without risking their anatomy—or at least embarrassment and often unwelcome attention.

If a man becomes the shellmouth of the galaxy, it is not without reason.

This one is wary of the standard answers, and of explanations which make him feel good. But he's searching, examining, clearly enjoying any exchange that can make him dig deeper.

In a moment he's talking about the still more primitive satisfactions of the sports, "Maybe it's all sexual—" He's still half-trying to escape the explanation which makes him feel good—talking it away with a catalog of the sexual satisfactions of the sports. ". . .you have this stick between your legs. . ."

Teasing, a little. But from there it's a swift leap of thought to "Anything done supremely well is an act of sex"—and to the dream of making love to an audience.

And we know by then that the shellmouth game isn't going to be what it used to be.

But what will emerge we do not yet know. The world has seen him wear a thousand faces. Is any one of them his own? Is Kirk's? The resemblance is striking. Is it purely coincidental?

There is a certain duality in the man even about that resemblance, a certain toughness in himself and with himself. And at some level a genuine self doubt:

Here is a man whose physical assets have always been on display, who has been regarded as handsome —which is certainly the least of adjectives applied to him in thousands of letters that we alone get about him.

But we quote a typical one which uses the word "beauty"—and start to ask him the problems, if any, of growing up with that—

"Beauty?" For a moment he looks startled. Then he tries to put it off lightly, a kind of denial. He never saw it that way. He always thought he should have looked more like Gregory Peck.

"I've never really had to deal with that—I'm working at two levels. I don't quite accept that definition —of 'beauty' and all that. I never went through puberty, for example. That off-putness—I went through puberty, but—"

That draws a chuckle: 'I'm glad you said *that*.'

"I never went through that off-putness, that adolescent, awkward puberty. I never had pimples on my face. But I never really went out with the girls I wanted to go out with. I never fulfilled that adolescent dream. I never had a childhood sweetheart. I never had an adolescence. I never had a real girlfriend. And—I don't *know* why ... I think there must be inside me a sense of unworthiness—that brings me up short, many times—so that whatever physical attributes people think I have, I don't see."

For a long moment his look is distant, as if he is trying to place why that should be:

"I always had the best. I never wanted for anything. My parents were not particularly well-off. My father owned a clothing manufacturing business in Montreal—a middle-class family—but he provided us with everything that we needed, including the bikes that I wanted to have, summer camps, on a farm usually—French-Canadian farms where I spent many summers—sometimes working in the fields, but many times just living in their farmhouses with half a dozen other kids and it was called a camp. Sometimes it expanded to thirty, forty, even one hundred kids, but it was still on a working farm. It wasn't any camp that other kids went to—organized, where a whistle blew and you went swimming and you got good desserts even though the meals were bad.

"I remember an evening's entertainment was watching a farmer slaughter a pig—I mean we all *sat around* on chairs and benches and watched the pig being bled to death—because at that time the delicacy of the French Canadian farmer was blood pudding. . .

"We'd milk cows—the feeling of warm milk being squirted into my face—postdated my mother's."

He chuckles faintly. Then the mobile face changes expression again, caught by a memory.

"I got my ass, literally, kicked—*hard*—for pulling up carrots out of a farmer's field. I couldn't make it to the fence like the other kids did and dive over the top. The farmer caught *me* with a good kick. That was his way of teaching children not to steal. So—the phrase, "I got my ass kicked for doing something,"—I remember getting caught. And getting your ass kicked—properly—is like—somewhat short of getting kicked in the balls. It's *painful* and it lasts a long time. Very few people have actually gotten their ass

kicked with a hard, hobnailed boot by a strong, angry
man. That *hurts*.

"So, growing up for me was fights ... two or three
people on one. It was losing my place on the football
team, because a religious holiday required me to stay
away from school and that was the day they made the
selection for who would be on the 1st and 2nd team.
Growing up was great summers in the Laurentian
Mountains, skiing and swimming and playing in the
woods. When I got older I became a counselor at a
camp, and—paddled from Montreal to New York
when I was nineteen with eight other counselors. We
were on television here. That was a marvelous
adventure.

"I never had a real love that I can remember as a
child, as a youngster. There *was* love at home, but there
was still a loneliness. And so, I think the first time I was
away from home after I was 21, I was even more lonely
and bereft—so that I got married very young, almost in
an attempt to assuage that."

'Were there no—no romantic relationships up until
then?'

"There was one girl that I really was crazy about in
college who was much more practical than I. And when
I expressed to her in our later years of college that what
I really would like to do was to be an actor, she chose a
businessman and got married the year she was supposed
to come back, and we were going to flower. She got married and lives in New York.

"But I don't recall any great dates to the proms or the
girls running after me, and I was a little too shy to run
after them. So—I never really had much of that when I
was younger.

'Did you miss it?—Did you feel as if you were being
deprived?'

"I was—I've always been lonely. I know what the feelings of loneliness are, very much. I've always been—I've
always had to deal with loneliness and how to overcome

it. And now being popular and recognizable, it is even more difficult. Now, because of my distaste of being recognized and being observed—how I put the spaghetti in my mouth or pick my nose, I retreat even further and find myself spending weeks sometimes in a hotel room without going out, just getting room service and talking to Marcy. Very few—very few people are in my life. As a result of that background and as a result of time spent on the road."

We are caught by it.

Here is a man who is living many a man's dream and yet there is that loneliness.

It has to be a very special loneliness which makes a man keep to a hotel room for weeks at a time.

And does it really argue emotional openness?

There is an effort in talking about it. His voice has had a tone of openness, of searching candor, sometimes of pain, often a touch of humor, usually a kind of constant undertone of enjoyment, as if the search were pleasure.

Now the voice flattens with effort:

"I have a great deal of difficulty about talking about myself. Now that's really hysterical, isn't it?—as I talk into this tape machine and to you about my background. But what I'm telling you is so locked in there that—sometimes I tell a little of it for publicity purposes in a kind of nicely baroque tale, without any of the itinerant emotions that are attached to it. I still feel these things so deeply—I'm so moved by what I really feel that—it's right on the surface here. It could just come out at any moment, if I just let it. I'm controlling it right now. But I'm letting it happen, because it's part of what I want you to write about if we're going to write about this. And that's why I'm letting it happen. But only Marcy knows what's going on inside me. Nobody else does—and *never has*. Including my family. Including people I've known for years."

And if we had never known it we would know that

here is a man who learned the lesson that men don't cry better than anyone.

What is more remarkable, however, is that he somehow also learned the opposite lesson.

We had wondered how he had learned both—and what kind of war had been waged between the forces of the two lessons within the battlefield of this man.

As it turned out, the very first question we had asked brought a part of the answer—instantly—as if it had been sitting there waiting to be called out.

But it was to take us much longer to pursue the question of which side had won.

We asked, in the context of "Where are you coming from?": 'If you had to recall the most significant event of your childhood what would it be?'

Without a pause he answered:

"There *is* a significant incident. I was at a camp at the age of six. And the camp in microcosm represented, I suppose, the way my life seems to have evolved since then and even now. That is, I was very active athletically at the camp as a kid. Swimming and boxing. I remember, I was the best kid boxer. Got strokes for that. Swimming in a marvelous river in the Laurentian Mountains. My aunt owned the camp. My parents would come up every weekend from Montreal, about 90 miles away, to visit me on Sunday. And I was very homesick most of the time. My older sister was there and that helped. But I remember deep feelings of being alone.

"I got into a camp play. It was at the time of the Second World War and everybody knew that the Jews were being massacred. And I don't know whether the knowledge of the ships that contained the children that were being turned away had yet permeated everybody's consciousness. But certainly the people at the camp, the parents, were very much aware of the situation, and that a massacre was going on.

"I was on stage apparently portraying a Jewish kid of about six who had to leave because the Nazis were coming. And the boy was talking to his dog, also played by a camper. I was saying goodbye to the dog.

"And whether it was because I had always wanted a dog and never had been able to have one, because—the excuse then was that a dog would dirty the house. Which, by the way, the first thing I did when I got married was I bought a dog. I *did* have dogs as I got older but never for any length of time and not the *kind* of dog and the *way* I wanted a dog in some inchoate way—

"So there I was talking to this camper that I now imagined to be the dog I had always wanted. And the audience was seeing a Jewish child being pulled away from his home. So that the environment was right from the audience's point of view, the situation with a dog and a child was right from my point of view, so that in some manner—or in *that* manner in which an actor touches an audience, I touched that audience.

"And it was more than just—apparently—it was more than just a nice little moment. It was such a summation of how that audience felt because of the Nazi situation, and how I felt, that I cried on stage—and the people in the audience cried.

"When the performance was over it was kind of—a little awesome in the approach that people had toward me as a six-year-old. So obviously what happened was that in giving this performance I felt good in pretending about leaving my dog, I felt good about getting the kudos and the approval and the affection from the audience, including my parents, as a result of having performed well. At the same time I was very popular in camp in all these athletics.

"So, that moment I kind of look back on as a conjoining of the desire to act, because of the approval and because of the feeling of well-being that I had acting, as well as being able to continue my activities as an athlete without having to choose one or the other.

"So, I look back on that as a moment which must have stirred the seeds into growth of wanting to be an actor.

"I also remember moments in high school when I was playing for the football team, where I had to go to rehearsals for a play—which is tantamount to carrying your violin case while passing the school—the classical 'carrying your violin case.' Because the jocks at high school would say: 'Whaddya mean going to a play? What are you, weird or something?'

"But I continued to act in high school as well as play football.

"When it came to McGill University I didn't have much time and I slowly phased out the scholastic part of my athletic endeavors and made it more of an avocation and made theater my vocation in school.

"I did very badly at the university. I never attended classes, I took notes from other people's notes, went to exams and barely passed exams. What I was *doing* was spending 18 hours a day producing, directing, writing college musicals. I was president of a radio club—television hadn't come in then—and I was acting outside the university in plays.

"So, my whole aim and focus was towards the theater. And yet, it never occurred to me—so inculcated was I with middle class values which my parents had—never *occurred* to me that I would become a professional actor.

"I knew that this was what I loved to do, but it was not—it was beyond *concept* to even think about that. I don't remember even thinking that I could possibly become an actor. I put myself through school, in a manner of speaking—I can really say I did—although I lived at home, I paid my dues and bought my books and had my spending money by acting on radio in Montreal."

It could almost be a textbook statement on the divi-

sions taught in the hard school of men-don't-cry: men
don't give up sober economics for blinding passions, nor
carry the violin case while playing football.

But this man did span those divisions—long before
liberation or revolution. For the first time we see an an-
chor in his life for that image of a masculine man who
has remained in touch with his emotions which people
saw in Kirk.

We've spoken to him of the effect we know that had,
but we haven't known the cause. How did he find that
within himself?

'Here's a possibility where that *did* come from. Can
you see that six-year-old on stage in a deep emotional
experience—showing emotion and seeing that it's good
and that people are responding to it? Not only are they
responding to your showing emotion, but they're showing it. *They* are crying.'

"That's much more—" he stops, following out the
thought. "Yes. That's true. I never thought of that. I
never thought of it in those terms, and never even really
approached what you've said in conscious terms.

"I just know now, at my age, that all people feel the
way I feel—that the universality of emotion is the same
as the universality of the sky. And that for one reason or
another, people either hide it or disguise it."

It is more of a statement of where he is from and
where he is coming from than he quite expected to
make, or we to hear, at that stage.

The universality of emotion. . .

It is a long voyage from "men don't cry"—and yet
this is still the man who for decades has revealed himself
to no one. He has learned the same lessons every other
man of his time learned, and better than anyone.

Yet there is also that other side which could move an
audience to tears at the age of six, could project Kirk's
openness out of Shatner's private silence.

It is a kind of mystery which we are to pursue finally

through his life and to a house on a hill in California.

The working session continues into the night, revealing deeper layers of the man, continues the next day on the move—we go with him while he narrates a movie, continue work on a two hour limousine ride to his one-man show in New Jersey—then on the way back and on other projects until one-thirty in the morning, when he has to catch a plane at eight.

On that ride out we have asked him: "Was the emotional openness part of your life—or of your life as you wished it could be? Was Kirk your reality—or your dream? And if it was your dream—have your years brought you closer to it?"

He gave an answer, but it is not a question a man can entirely answer in words, or for himself.

There was still another question, which a man can answer for himself still less:

If Kirk was the projection of Shatner's best dream then—were there ways in which he has grown even beyond that now?

For us, part of the answer came that night on a bare stage in New Jersey:

He stands on the stage, alone. The welcoming burst of applause for his past triumphs dies slowly as the spotlight picks out the slim, youthful figure in blue jeans and body shirt. The man's face almost glows from within.

He gentles the applause with his hands, and a hush finally falls.

The audience doesn't know what to expect from the one-man show. "An Evening with William Shatner," it was billed. A lecture on STAR TREK? A question and answer session with the man who was Captain Kirk? They would be happy enough with that. It is as much as they would expect from a STAR TREK star on tour. They are content with his presence.

They cannot know that Shatner is about to embark on

a far more dangerous journey, a walk on a high wire, a balancing act along the fine line between entertaining and being laughed at, "between the ludicrous and the lucid."

They cannot know that only yesterday he spoke to us of the first time he had given this performance, ten days before: "I was alone, and I was terrified. I did not know whether the material would work. I was terrified as I have not been terrified since I was a kid on opening night somewhere in Montreal. That's how terrified I was—to the point of suppression of panic, fear, mouth-drying fear. And I was alone."

He is alone now. At this moment he is always alone.

There is not a scrap of indication in the taut face or slim body that he has ever been afraid.

Somehow it is clear that there would not have been, even on that first night when he was terrified.

Without preamble, he speaks: "They are Bradbury's kind of people. . ."

It takes the audience a moment to realize that the man has come to act.

The opening is a poem, telling a story, setting a science-fiction theme. Perhaps some of the six-year-old fans can't quite follow the thought. It doesn't matter. Their eyes are rapt and never leave his face. The face is mobile, alive, glowing, allowing itself an intensity and range of expression which the children can never have seen on a man's face before.

Nor can the adults.

In a moment he begins to talk softly. If they will let him, he will take them flying with him. . .

The familiar voice catches them with words, images. If they will close their eyes . . . let themselves see it . . . fly with him . . .

For a long moment it is an open question whether they would rather go along for the voyage—or just watch his face.

But the voice is commanding, compelling, coaxing—

catching them suddenly in a net of magic woven of the actor's art, a gossamer web of the suspension of disbelief.

Eyes close all over the house.

They are with him.

Flying.

Where no man has gone before.

He goes on never stopping, never letting them down, releasing them, finally from the illusion of flying but not from the flying. It is a brilliant tour-de-force, woven out of the themes of science and science fiction, especially in great drama. There is Shakespeare. There is Cyrano de Bergerac—Cyrano's brilliant, funny fable about having fallen out of the moon—with seven improbable ways to get back. There is Galileo, imprisoned for his truth, on the need for the freedom of man's mind. There is the poem "Flight"—"Oh I have slipped the surly bonds of earth, and danced the sky on laughter-silvered wings. Sunward I've climbed. . ."

It is the record of man's dream of flying, of reaching for the moon, the stars. It is the dream, and the reality of what makes the dream possible. It is more.

It is Shatner.

In some manner he has been transformed, almost transfigured.

He looks like a legend, not of man's past, but of his future.

He is Icarus who did not fall back to Earth but kept on rising.

He is the dream of flying, and the flying itself, and the force of his will, the intensity of his passion, the courage with which he lets his soul be seen in his face and his whole body, lift the audience on his wings as well.

This is the promise which millions saw in a starship captain. It is more; it is the fulfillment of that promise.

A decade ago, this man created a role which became legend, shattering the brutal, hard-taught rule that men must suppress, repress, control, not only do not cry, but worse, do not express the fullness of their joy, still worse, cut off the range of what they can *feel.*

In the decade since, uncounted men and women have fought to free themselves to feel what they feel and to show it. Other roles and other actors have followed that lead. But many people have thought that Kirk could hardly be surpassed in that capacity.

They were mistaken.

The man who created Kirk has a range of passionate intensity and of total expressiveness beyond even what he showed in Kirk. It is beyond anything which even this decade's culture permits to a man.

This man asks no permission. He has the courage to present this aspect of himself as he had the courage to create Kirk. It is the same kind of thing, but raised to a higher power. Then and now he was beyond the boundaries of what is permitted or even tolerated. It would be painfully easy to be laughed at, not to be seen, but to show your soul and see it scorned by people who cannot or will not see.

But the audience did see it, on the first night of that one-man show, when William Shatner walked out, terrified—and finished to a standing ovation . . .

What they saw, that night and this night, was a man who looks so totally alive walking that wire that an audience begins to wonder whether it has ever seen a man look alive before.

People know suddenly that nothing has yet tapped this man's potential—nor the potential of most men if they could free themselves to feel this.

And they realize even more devastatingly how most men, and even many women, have cut themselves off from the whole range of the human potential, not daring to express or even to feel the range of emotions possible to a human being—as if the songs of their souls were picked out haltingly within a single octave. They realize only as they see this that at best they have heard a sonata. This is the symphony.

We turned to each other as this audience, too, was on its

feet and said with one mind, "Beyond Kirk."

It was not something we had expected to say. We had come at the question more from a philosophical angle than a personal one—the impact of the role, more than the man. It was always possible, before we knew the man, that he bore no deep resemblance to the role. He is, after all, an actor.

If Shatner had never been able to go beyond Kirk, if he had done nothing of importance before or since, it would still have been a unique achievement.

But if he had never been able to go beyond Kirk, one would have had to say that there was a capacity in Kirk which was not in Shatner—an enormous capacity for growth, for pushing back limits—the where-no-man capacity.

But Kirk comes by it honestly, from Shatner, with love.

Shatner can do it alone, on a bare stage in blue jeans and body shirt, without benefit of anything but his naked talent and the elemental courage of walking that wire.

Whatever else he is or does or has ever done, that is the fact which is central to his existence. It is a quality which we respect.

At some level, he even knows what he has done. He has a tough cautiousness against overestimating his achievement in anything, particularly in the role of Kirk. But at one point the day before when we spoke of the emotional openness, he cut in:

"If I can do this show—if the audience lets me do my material—I go even further than *that*. I take them on a trip. I do an extraordinary thing, if they'll let me do it. They didn't last night—that mob which came out in the rain. 'Wa—ah, we want to ask questions.'

"Okay. But if I can take them—and I did in the afternoon—I took them flying. I actually took them up into the air and went flying with them. And when I came down—they applauded. But I was . . . you know. . ."

The voice drops to softness. "I hope it works tomorrow. . ."

He knows.

He even knows that it is beyond Kirk. Riding back in the limousine, from a performance in which he has worked with an effort that would make a stevedore drop —and made it look effortless—he is not so much tired as coming down from an emotional high wire. He tries to answer the question of why people respond to him as they just have:

"I don't know. I've grown from a boy on television to the man I am now, and I don't know. I may be becoming an institution, without my even knowing it. People come up to me and name something they saw me in that was fifteen years ago. They followed me *then*. They've seen me in live television. I'm totally amazed. I just shake my head in bewilderment and go on. To think that people think of me in that way is just such an overwhelming thought that I can't deal with it. So I put it aside, shrug my shoulders and go on."

But in a moment he adds:

"The people who seem to like me are such a vast range, from the six-year-old child to the seventy-year old grandmother—the whole range mentally in between, from the man who wrote his Ph.D. thesis on the effect of STAR TREK on American society—who came up to shake my hand, to the kids who want to touch my hand. They follow no demographic pattern—age, sex, or whatever. But there is certainly in most cases a universality of love. They're not the screamers and the tearers of clothes. They're the people who say 'Thank you.' There's a touching quality—there's something touching about the way people look to me. I've never seen it as much as on this tour—and of course at the STAR TREK conventions, but that isn't quite the same. It's a fandom that I don't know who else has.

"It's just—it's just impossible." Shatner's voice drops. "And I am—moved to tears—many times."

"Are you?"

"Oh, yes. When those thousands of people came out in the rain night before last—I couldn't believe it. I mean, we're talking about a driving, torrential rain. And people came out and just sat there, laughed, wanted to ask questions."

His voice softens to a tone of wonder. He knows what he is doing—perhaps as much as any man can. But he is still stunned by the response.

The gossamer wings of the actor's magic remain magic, even to the actor. Somewhere there are the anomalies and tensions out of which he projects that magic, still not fully knowing how. This is the man who hunts bear with a bow—and does not go out of his hotel room. He projects the openness of Kirk—and is the shellmouth whom no one has known until the last few years of a second marriage. He has fought his own battle for emotional openness—but there are few people in his life. He set out to be a classical actor—and became legend in what is possibly a classic of the future.

Perhaps the hardest thing of all is for a man to get perspective on his own anomalies—his life, career, achievement. Let alone in the glaring light of an encounter with legend. It can be blinding, more than a little unnerving.

Perhaps that, in fact, was his deepest reason for wanting to write this book.

As with the one-man-tour, he had no need to do it. Not for money, or love. But we saw him thinking aloud, writing, analyzing his life, arguing an idea.

And the look on his face sometimes had a haunting quality which we finally identified.

It must have been there, too, when the young Shatner took up the dream which had been "beyond concept"—

of being a working actor—and set right out to try his wings. . .

It was the look of walking the wire.

And of flying. . .

Working Actor

"Golden Boy . . ." *"Wunderkind . . ."* *"The* Light Comedian on Canadian TV . . ." "Not only one of the most promising young actors around but a writer . . ." "Winner of Broadway Theater Guild Award as Best Actor of the Year . . ." "Brilliant . . ." ". . . critics liked this vital Shatner kid . . ." "Superlative performance . . ." "Superb . . ." "Unforgettable . . ."

Critics loved him. So did the audiences.

The clipping file in the Theater Collection at New York's Lincoln Center library is thick, dating from the days when Shatner took Broadway and New York, then America, by storm.

What is remarkable is that in the whole stack of clippings from 1956 when he blew into town in a prestigious Stratford production of *Tamburlaine* up to and through STAR TREK years, there is *one,* count it, *one* bad review of a Shatner performance. There's *one* bad review of his TV series "For the People," focusing on the series' scripts and direction rather than his performance, although another reporter says that critics like the series, but it was "bludgeoned off the air" by "Bonanza."

But of Shatner himself, there is not even damning with faint praise, or praising with faint damns.

There are wall-to-wall raves.

About the most—and only—lukewarm review he ever got in all the years of Broadway and live television was actually rather charming. Brooks Atkinson, reviewing "The World of Suzie Wong" for the *New York Times* (October, 1968), said: "William Shatner gives a modest performance that is also attractive—a little wooden, perhaps, which is one way of avoiding maudlin scenes."

(*That*, incidentally, of a play which, at that point, Shatner regarded as an unqualified, unmitigated disaster and the worst experience of his acting life. If Shatner's performance at that opening was "wooden," what is remarkable is that he had not turned to stone.)

The one bad review was also of the opening performance of *Suzie Wong,* and even that review had its compensations: (Walter Kerr, October 6, 1958): "Its manly hero, played with an oddly melodramatic gloss and many a deep-seated sigh by the normally interesting Canadian actor, William Shatner."

If that's a bad review, one could do worse. All the others down through the years were outright raves—their only problem, that they ran out of superlatives, including the word "superlative," which was used almost as often as "superb."

As early as December 23, 1957, when Shatner had been in America just about a year, Sidney Fields wrote for the *New York Mirror,* "He's been on most of the big TV shows, has written some himself, and if you haven't seen his recent brilliant effort on 'Medic' you can get a notion of his talents on the Kraft Theater on January 8. He's *good.*"

Having run out of superlatives, that reviewer fell back on the restraint of using "good" as a superlative. Shatner was indeed "good." There was some electric, vital quality which caught attention when another actor would have been part of the scenery—and Shatner was not bad scenery himself. But also, there was the depth of talent and training to back the vitality and other assets.

When Shatner opened in *Tamburlaine*, an unknown young actor on Broadway, with a relatively small part in a classical Marlowe play—which would get marvelous notices and fold in twenty performances—he hit the big town in a big way and the shock registered three thousand miles across the continent in Hollywood.

Major studio executives came to see the play, to see him.

Twentieth Century Fox offered him a seven-year contract which would make him a star, rich beyond his dreams. The day after *Tamburlaine* folded, he turned them down, flat. Thanks, but no thanks.

Within three weeks after refusing to sign the contract, Sidney Fields wrote a year later, "He was all over our TV screens, and MGM signed him for *Karamazov*, and after seeing him act gave him a fat two-year picture deal. He's now making more per week, than he made each year during four years in repertory."

And, incidentally, he was making something like four times as much in a year as he would have made from the 20th Century Fox contract. But there was an unwritten sequel to Sidney Fields' story. After dazzling MGM in *The Brothers Karamazov*—moving up from "featured" billing to "star" billing during the filming—Shatner got a hundred-thousand-dollar, nonexclusive contract with MGM for two pictures that year. He gave *that* contract up for sake of his art. He wanted to do what he believed would be a fine, poetic play, directed by Josh Logan. The poetic play? *The World of Suzie Wong.*

If anyone cares to ask whether the man took his art seriously . . .

Some years later, was it only Kirk who said: "The striving for greatness continues"?

Shatner was striving—and he was not immune to the more mundane temptations of stardom, money, glitter, popularity. But at bottom, the dream was of being a fine actor, a great actor—a dream of greatness.

Moreover, there was general agreement that he was reaching it. The *Wunderkind*, fairhaired, Golden Boy aura about him was no accident and not lightly won. He'd been in training in some sense since he was six years old.

He studied sober economics at McGill University for the right to steep himself eighteen hours a day in the forbidden joy of the theater, where his real life was lived.

Graduating from McGill, he parlayed the economics degree into a job as business manager for an acting company. ("I was a terrible business manager.") Presently they solved that problem—by hiring him as an actor. Then he won his spurs with the invitation to join in forming the prestigious Stratford, Ontario repertory company with great talent imported from England or recruited from Canada. Shatner's talent won him the special attention of the great English director Tyrone Guthrie. The young Shatner played Shakespeare and other classics for three years with actors like James Mason, Sir Alec Guinness, and Anthony Quayle.

Later in a house on a hill in California we were to see the clippings on those performances—and, in fact on performances stretching back to a time when Shatner was 12 or 13. Even then, there were the superlatives.

At 25 Shatner came to take New York by siege. He had won the Tyrone Guthrie Stratford Festival Scholarship, and had decided to use it to grubstake himself to a try at New York theater and television. But there was shockingly little resistance to his assault on the big town. Other actors pounded on doors for years to get a part once in a blue moon, if ever. Shatner got one part after another—movies, plays, live television—the great days of "Playhouse 90," "Studio One," etc.

And in all of them he got rave reviews:

Arthur Hailey's "No Deadly Medicine" with Lee J. Cobb as a once-great aging doctor grown careless, and Shatner as his young successor, both of them "superlative" (*Variety*) and "Magnificent" (*N.Y. Daily News.*)

"U.S. Steel Hour," "moving performance by William Shatner as the young priest" *(Variety.)* "Shatner unforgettable as the priest . . ."

"Playhouse 90," "touching and powerful performance by William Shatner" *(N.Y. Times.)* "Magnificent" *(N.Y. News.)*

Possibly one of the best ever, and evidently a brilliant demonstration of the actor's ability to play a role far from himself: "A Town Has Turned to Dust" by Rod Serling. Jack Gould reviewed it for the *New York Times* (June 20, 1958):

"Mr. Shatner gave one of the best performances of his career. As the town bully and ringleader of the lynching party, he was the embodiment of hate and blind physical passion. Mr. Shatner's attention to detail in putting together the picture of an ignorant and evil social force was remarkable . . . Two of the season's superlative performances by Rod Steiger and William Shatner."

Variety called his performance, "superb", *New York Journal American*, "compelling." Others: "superb, brilliant."

At the same time he played to fine reviews as Alexei in *The Brothers Karamazov. Variety* commented (February 19, 1958): "William Shatner has the difficult task of portraying youthful male goodness, and he does it with such gentle candor it is effective."

The World of Suzie Wong opened to less than ecstatic reviews—and ultimately was transformed into a long-running two-year hit for which Shatner won a Theater Guild Award as Best Actor of the Year.

Another long-run (one-year) hit on Broadway was *A Shot in the Dark* in which Shatner co-starred with Walter Matthau, also to excellent reviews.

There was more television—live, later taped and filmed—including many performances which people remember to this day—"The Twilight Zone," "The Defenders," and many others.

It began to look as if the Golden Boy could do no wrong and was destined to go onward and upward without limit.

Within five years of invading America, the Canadian *Wunderkind* had played three solid years on Broadway, wall-to-wall prestige television performances, and four major feature films, for one of which, *The Intruder,* he later won an International Peace Film Festival award for Best Actor.

In *The Brothers Karamazov* Shatner had starred with Yul Brynner, Lee J. Cobb, Richard Basehart, Claire Bloom, and Maria Schell. In *Judgement at Nuremburg* it was Spencer Tracy, Richard Widmark, Judy Garland, Maximillian Schell and a galaxy of international stars like a roll call of honor. A few years later in *The Outrage,* an adaptation of the Japanese classic *Rashomon,* it was Paul Newman, Laurence Harvey, Claire Bloom and Edward G. Robinson, with Shatner giving a startling portrayal of innocence as a clergyman, and looking rather more like an untouched angel.

The Intruder was filmed on a shoestring and at white heat by a group of very young men, including Shatner, who did it for and on almost no money and achieved a highly esteemed film, the first on school integration—shot at some risk in a small Southern town. Shatner played the rabble-rouser of the title, based on a real-life self-styled Fuehrer named John Kasper, who came on the scene in Clinton, Tennessee.

Shatner said at the time that he had "cleared no more than two hundred dollars on *The Intruder,*" but loved it. "People with something to say put it into a

film without being fey or pretentious about it . . ."
(New York Herald Tribune, May 13, 1962).

The film was produced by Roger and Gene Corman, written by Charles Beaumont. "What excites me so much about *The Intruder,*" Shatner said, "is the youth of the men who made it . . . all of us young men who were able to get out and make the kind of picture we wanted to make. Who knows what could come next?"

The producers and writers of *The Intruder* were in their early thirties; Shatner was not quite into his.

Just coming off the success in *Nuremberg* and *The Intruder,* and a third film also seriously intended but not as distinguished *(The Explosive Generation),* Shatner was saying, "This is it. This is the very thing I wanted to do. It's as if my whole career has been a preparation for it. I've turned down just about every TV series there is at one time or another. What I wanted to do was exciting feature films that had something to say." *(New York World Telegram & Sun,* September 23, 1961.)

He was, in fact, willing to put money, time, if necessary even his life on the line for what he wanted to do. Of *The Intruder* he said in the same interview, "We made it in and around Charleston, Missouri, and I mean we were in fear for our safety. We were chased out of five locations. We shot scenes with Klu Klux Klan uniforms, burning crosses, and the blowing up of a Negro church. Roger had to sneak back with a hand-held camera in his own car to take an establishing shot of one church. But we needed the southern small town atmosphere."

Those were the days when the word *was* Negro, the churches *were* blown up with little girls inside, and "intruders" *were* murdered in the South, when a film company and a leading actor intruding to make a statement against that kind of world had every reason to fear for their safety.

But it is out of such statements presented as drama, art, fiction, that the change has come. Less than a decade later (1969) the same actor kissed a black woman in the first interracial kiss on television, (on STAR TREK) while his alter ego, Kirk, commanded a bridge crew where the black, the Oriental, the Scot, the Russian, the Vulcan, and the Captain, had forgotten the name of the problem.

A decade later, the bombing and burning has ceased.

Some part of that victory has been won by the kind of artist and the kind of man who is willing to put himself on the line for the kind of art he believes in and the kinds of things he wants to say.

Shatner has done that, and it has cost him. And he has done also the hard-boiled, feed-the-family choices.

And they have cost him. Sometimes it's very hard to count the costs, weigh the returns.

In some sense, no one can ever look into the alternate universe of "if." And everyone tries.

There are major "ifs" in Shatner's life, and even some of the minor ones are staggering to contemplate. If he had signed the 20th Century Fox contract . . . if he hadn't given up the MGM contract . . . if he hadn't taken a long-shot chance on a losing, already rejected series called STAR TREK . . . But also: he did reject roles on almost every TV series going. One of them was the lead in "Dr. Kildare." The rest was history—for Richard Chamberlain.

His Best Actor award-winning performance in *Suzie Wong* did not land him the movie role, which went to William Holden.

Shatner played the young lawyer to Ralph Bellamy as his lawyer father in the live TV production which, several years later, became "The Defenders"—biggest series hit of the time—with the son played by Robert Reed.

Frank Farrel reported in the *New York World Tele-gram (December 12, 1959)*, "Bill Shatner, the young Canadian who played the kid brother in *MGM's Karamazov* is top choice for the lead opposite Liz Taylor in *"Cat on a Hot Tin Roof."* It didn't happen. What did happen in the Tennessee Williams hit was a triumph for Paul Newman.

The "ifs" in Shatner's professional life were partly a matter of his choice, partly a matter of choices offered to him, or not offered.

There was luck, chance, irony and the hard-rock reality of show business.

And there was his judgement.

Where the choice was his, as if very often was because of the opportunities his talent drew to him, the choice was always tough as hell.

When it was not his—that was tougher.

And when the choice was his, there was no one to guide him, only the solitary decision over his own career.

It was as uncharted a sea as any trackless depth of stars. There were no guidelines, no safe courses, even if he had wanted to play it safe. There were few landmarks —and sometimes they were not recognizable until they were years behind. There was only his own judgement, not infallible: when it was good, it was very, very good, and when it was bad . . .

Shatner was still following the dream. And it was still the dream of greatness.

But the price of the dream could be highest of all. And it was beginning to be apparent in the years just before STAR TREK that he was paying a price.

There was a point at which the Golden Boy legend and reality imperceptibly began to lose some of its glitter. At some point, somehow almost overnight, he was no longer a boy. He hadn't changed perceptibly. He still looked boyish. But the calendar inexorably said that he was no longer quite so swiftly rising, and had not reached quite the height which the promise of his youth argued so eloquently.

He had, indeed, achieved the critical esteem. It never left him. Given any kind of role with potential—and some which he had to turn inside out to find the potential—he could do a brilliant job. Even some fairly ordinary television role he could take apart to add depth, making memorable roles out of workaday television.

And it was not that he was not getting roles. He was. But where were the great roles?

There seemed to be an increasing scarcity of really great parts—not only for him. The years just before STAR TREK were rough.

Live television died from under him, and taped or filmed performances were no longer taken quite so seriously as drama. Broadway virtually died, too. The great movie parts did not come. He took some roles to feed the family. He gambled on dreams he believed in, but which did not work out. His pilot for *Alexander the Great,* made for $750,000, for which he had prepared for a year, died unsold. His television series, "For the People," died. And the articles written during STAR TREK began to have a brutal tone. The brutality was coming from a surprising source—William Shatner.

Said Shatner to the *TV Guide* interviewer who dubbed him "The Intergalactic Golden Boy": "The dream was hollow, all the things I thought went along with it,— good parts, money, and acclaim—weren't happening. As a star I was one step down from Paul Newman—a good actor, but not popular enough to bring in big audiences."

Interviewer Robert Higgins described STAR TREK-vintage Shatner (October 15, 1966) as: "Cradling a phone between a ham-sized shoulder and his handsome head . . . whizzing through an ankle-deep pile of phone messages ... Shatner doesn't look very different from the way he did in the early 1950's. . . .

But, Higgins continues, pursuing Shatner's ruthless self-examination: It is not the 1950's, Shatner *is* older. ("It's a good age this year, but what about next?") And Higgins says he has "not achieved what seemed so close at hand as a kid of 25." And:

About the time his first series, "For the People," was axed, Shatner: "started losing parts—something that never happened to me before." He made the STAR TREK pilot and vowed to quit if it didn't sell. Shatner, who had brought an audience to its feet as a 22-year-old Henry V, seriously considered, as he puts it, "selling ties at Macy's."

In point of fact he would not have gone that far, nor needed to, but he and his first wife, Gloria, did seriously discuss the idea that if STAR TREK did not sell, he would go into writing and directing.

He had been a wonder-child writer, too, selling his dramatic script, "Dreams" to Canadian television in his early twenties, and starring in it with a blonde actress, Gloria Rand, who became his wife and the mother of his three daughters, Leslie, Liz and Melanie. Shatner had sold other scripts over the years to Canadian and American television, among them a "Checkmate" episode. He'd studied directing and directed himself when directors failed him.

It would have been a plausible second career. But it was not his dream.

Then STAR TREK did hit, and, as writer Higgins said, "now Shatner can pretty much write his own ticket."

Suddenly he *did* have the enormous popularity to be a big draw. In fact, hardly anyone realized just how enormous that drawing power was, or how it would continue to grow over the years.

Kirk became, among other things, Shatner's show-case. People got a chance to see the range of his talent—doing things no actor had been called on to do before—dual roles, woman in a man's body, etc.

And they got to see Shatner playing a *hero*.

That was such a rare event—the role of an authentic hero such a rare phenomenon, the combination of that with Shatner's talents and his capacity to express emotion was such a potent mixture that many people have not quite recovered yet.

The role of the authentic hero is something which Shatner has found hard to get into perspective. Kirk is, among other things, one of many roles for him. It's far from being his whole career. It was a popular success, and he loved it, perhaps more than he quite wanted to. But the groundswell of response which said that it was one of the great roles of all time, an immortality in itself, whatever else he did, came as a surprise, and an idea which he has resisted.

Throughout the STAR TREK years, although he was delighted with STAR TREK, he continued the theme of brutal self-examination, even asking: Had he betrayed the dream he started out with?

He continues with something of that theme to this day.

He became the golden boy again with STAR TREK, riding high, writing his own ticket. Then STAR TREK was cancelled. But he has kept and increased that popularity. There was a tough period for him after STAR TREK, but he slugged it out and worked all the time—fifty-two weeks a year. He still does.

He has the house on the hill now, the money, the fame.

But there still is one problem. Where are the great roles? The heroes? Even the great villains? The dramas with themes that are both important and gripping?

It is not merely that *he* is not getting them. Essentially, *nobody* is—at least not more than once in a blue moon. Popular roles, perhaps, as he does, too. Great roles in the old classics, which he could do anytime, he chose. Money-making roles. Plenty of roles. He is one of the very top-rated guest stars on television. Even apart from his drawing power from years back and before STAR TREK, he now has a massive following of STAR TREK and Shatner fans who scan *TV Guides* and newspapers and keep each other posted on any new Shatner performance—even on game shows. Many will drive hundreds of miles—sometimes fly thousands—to see him in a play or a personal appearance.

Speak to almost anyone about William Shatner, and a face lights up and usually names or describes one or more of his performances in a role which had genuine substance. Many of the early roles are favorites remembered to this day. More recently "The Andersonville Trials"—is a popular favorite, considered a classic of Public Television and a triumph for Shatner—still more recently "The Tenth Level," for which there was talk of an Emmy nomination.

STAR TREK itself was nominated for 15 Emmys including twice for Best Dramatic Series, and ultimately won an Emmy in its revival in animation—also starring Shatner: (1973).

And yet there has still been the scarcity of new acting challenges he could really get his teeth into. Sometimes there has been the choice of sitting on his anatomy, or doing roles that are less than he wants to do. He's not built for sitting.

But there has been a cost to that, too.

Once we asked him: 'What was your dream?'

"The dream was—I was in Ottawa, shortly after graduating from McGill. I was walking across the capital grounds on a crystal-clear, snowy night. I could see the stars. And from the Peace Tower, which is part of the capital building, carols were playing. I was on my way to the theater. I even remember the crunch of the snow. Snow has a different crunch at different temperatures. I remember the thought that was in my head: 'I want to be a great actor. That's really what I want to do—more than anything. More than money. I want to be an actor.' "

The hazel eyes look distant. "I was asked to Stratford to play the youthful Shakespearean roles. Tyrone Guthrie was there—a great director. He took me under his wing as his protégé those three years. And he told me that he thought I would be great—it's difficult to use these words—"

For an instant he breaks off, then makes himself say it, "—that I would be a great actor in the tradition of Olivier. And that I shouldn't worry if I had to serve tea to leading ladies until I was 45—because that's what Olivier had to do. The great roles lie beyond that period. Guthrie's phrase for it was 'serving tea to the ladies.' "

Shatner looks a little grim, shifts forward with that energy which cannot be still for long—the last man in the world to serve tea to the ladies until he was 45.

"I feel—that I've let that ideal go in some ways by opting for the fame and fortune of Hollywood life.

"But the circumstances have changed and I'm not entirely dissatisfied. Broadway is no longer the Broadway it was when I was there—although it's coming back. The Stratfords require you to stay for six months—awful long period of time.

"Which is not to say that I'm not hungry for the good roles and the challenges as an actor. But I'm not overwhelmed with the need to play Hamlet at Stratford—if it means physically spending six months at Stratford, Connecticut or Stratford, Ontario. And—England hasn't beckoned yet. I can't leave my family for that long.

"I want to play the challenging roles, extend my

range as an actor. And I know that I *have,* these past years. But what remains is a desire to raise the level of what I do—in any moment. You can always improve the moment. . ."

The eyes seem to be weighing the dream. "There was a time, before STAR TREK, when I wouldn't accept a role that I didn't think worthwhile enough to play. Then, because things are so cyclical in show business, I needed to take those roles."

He does not mention the birth of three children as he still struggled—even in the golden days of being offered all the roles . . .

"There even came a point when I thought—I don't know whether I'm ever going to break through—to get those roles that I think I should be playing. That was just before STAR TREK. STAR TREK hit. And after STAR TREK I've had the opportunity to play a few of those things that I thought should be coming my way.

"But—I was in a financial bind and had to accept a lot of things that I wouldn't have done in an earlier day. Now I'm in a different part of the cycle. I can afford to turn down work, and have.

"On the other hand, there are certain jobs that are offered that pay so extremely well that it raises a whole question as to whether to turn down that kind of money and be noble—and still not really get the role I want, or to take the jobs and the money—and as a result of *that* maybe not get the roles I want. So it raises a very complex question."

The question becomes even more complex when we learn the real nature of the "financial bind" he mentions after STAR TREK. But also there is simply a restless energy here which, money aside, would have a hard time sitting it out between jobs—or perhaps even on a Shakespearean stage.

We question him on that: is that *really* his dream?

Our impression would be that he's really more interested in exploring new roles, new ideas.

"Well, the Shakespearean roles are invested with a new life by each actor of any importance. What it amounts to is: how good are you? Can you make that role different and more interesting than has ever been done before?

"An interesting part of my training has come from television—having played in so much doggerel—and in the effort to make that stuff livable, one is required to search and grope for ways of investing it with some kind of life.

"I went back one year to play Antony in *Julius Caesar* and took the same approach—took it apart like workaday television. And, interestingly enough, I got mixed notices—some really great, some really poor—which is terrific, the way it should be—because I was not trying to do a classical performance, *per se,* but to do Antony as if I approached it with the same intensity and curiosity and desire for change as I approach television."

But—isn't he much more inclined to take on challenges nobody has done?

His voice is suddenly terse, flat, a kind of protest. "Well—they're not *writing* those. They're not *writing* roles like that."

There's an undertone which says that he's accustomed to it—and will never get used to it.

We are brought up short for a long moment.

Here is a man who, child and man, could move an audience to tears. His dream was of greatness.

Now when he questions whether he has betrayed the dream—is it possible that the dream has, in some sense, betrayed him?

The great roles are not, for the most part, being written. The great roles of the past, while still a challenge for an actor, do no strike most people as either sufficiently entertaining or sufficiently relevant to their lives.

The level of starvation for the heroic is attested by the long lines outside the box offices of anything which manages to capture some element which is heroic.

There is another kind of starvation—for the powerful, the hard-hitting, the new—what amounts to the new mother-lode which must be mined for the drama of tomorrow, incorporating the knowledge revolutions of today. In effect—a drama revolution.

And the box office lines or Nielsen ratings of the rare pieces of writing which tackle some of those themes are mute testimony that greatness is good box office.

The man who set out to be a classical actor is probably best known these last years for reports from the revolution:

He won high critical acclaim and excellent ratings for "The Tenth Level"—possibly the only piece of recent television drama to deal directly with a piece of the new research on human nature. (The research, chilling. Well over 90% of subjects would obey a researcher to the point of inflicting "the tenth level" of pain on another subject.)

"The Andersonville Trial" dealt with his struggle as prosecutor with another aspect of that problem—compliance with authority to the point of atrocity, as revealed by Nazis at Nuremberg, and reflected back to illuminate the civil war case. It won the Peabody Award and three Emmys. Both "Tenth Level" and "Andersonville" were serious, hard-hitting drama on important questions about human nature. Both were critical successes and drew strong popular responses.

STAR TREK was the critical and popular triumph of the decade—and a preview of those revolutions which have arrived in our laps, not in the 23rd Century, but within the decade.

Recently the Photoplay Awards focused on Shatner's face as STAR TREK was voted the second most popular television show of *all time.* (It was edged out of first narrowly by the 20-year hit, "I Love Lucy").

Now STAR TREK has become the only hit to be revived by popular demand, after a lapse of more than a decade, and with its original cast.

There's gold in them thar themes. And it's not only money. It's the kind of satisfaction which the golden boy set out to reach one night walking alone in the crunch of the snow. . .

He is riding high again as the star of the reborn legend in one of the most expensive productions of all time.

And he is there on soundstage and starship solely because the way he played Kirk in the context of STAR TREK so moved people that they demanded for ten years and in a deluge of mail to Paramount that he return to the role.

It's true that there can be a conflict between greatness and popular success if greatness is thought of as arty and ingrown, and success is presumed to be mindless.

But what is forgotten is that when the great classic roles of the past were written—they were also the great *popular* hits.

Shakespeare was the STAR TREK of Elizabethan England. It was a hit long before it was a classic. And *it* was exploring ideas.

The great roles of today are or could be in things like STAR TREK, science fiction, "Andersonville," "Tenth Level"—which aim to reach a mass audience with the seriously intended.

When the quality parts are being written Shatner is getting some of the best of them.

And he got one of the best parts of this or any other century, one which will not be recreated by any other actor—for the plain reason that he put his stamp on it as actor and as man so completely that to tens of millions of people, Shatner *is* Kirk.

To many of them, he has been a source of change in their own lives—a part of their changing image of what a man could and should be.

They may also argue with the image—and even chide it somewhat gently for male chauvinism or womanizing. But many also recognize it as a trailbreaking lead toward emotional openness.

William Shatner did not set out to be a revolutionary. He would smile at you in some bemusement —or devilment—if you called him one.

Nevertheless, at the root of the impact of Kirk is a singular fact which STAR TREK permitted and encouraged: Much of the character was shaped and reshaped by Shatner in a way that is really a writing function. Others in the cast have told us how heavily he was always involved in the day-by-day reshaping of scripts, character. As it turns out, it was *he* who did shape both the humor and the openness which became the bombshell effect of Kirk.

If STAR TREK is Shakespeare to the stars, Shatner not only has a patent on playing its Hamlet. He owns a piece of the writing.

Which is not bad for a golden boy who set out to become an actor and a writer on the side. It's not bad for a man who is barely at the beginning of what should be the greatest period in his acting life.

And it beats the hell out of serving tea to the ladies.

Landmarks

[It was by no accident that William Shatner was, and is, also a writer. Gene Roddenberry has said of Shatner's writing, "It was so damned poetic that I caught myself wishing that *I* could write that well." A Shatner script would have been produced as the next episode of STAR TREK if the network had picked up its option for three more episodes. We expected Shatner to do his writing for this book by talking, which we would then incorporate for his feedback, etc., as we've done. We didn't fully expect what happened. What he said frequently had the quality of writing. At times he would almost talk a whole chapter. And once he did it so well, with plot, pace, theme, scenes, language—and with barely another word spoken—that we felt compelled to transcribe it verbatim in that form. As an autobiographical document composed virtually without pause, aloud, from one end to the other, it is perhaps the best testimony to his own view of the landmarks of his life, and to what turning his life might have taken if he had turned chiefly to writing. . .]

'If you had to look back over your life and pick out certain moments, events, times, roles, people, ideas

which affected you most deeply, where would you begin?'

"What affected me most deeply. . .

"There was an evening at my parents' home in my third year of college, when I told my father that I wanted to be an actor. He was very upset, totally against it. He argued with me for days. And I had to keep saying, "I want to try it."

"Up to then, I had remained the dutiful son, locked into a prescribed course of life. It was the same course which all my friends had followed and all the people I knew at college. Practicality. Good, solid success. Education. Hard work. Money. I had to tell my father, and I had to be consistent, even insistent, that I wanted a period of time in which to follow these desires. But he was afraid, with some reason, knowing the dog-eat-dog world which professional acting would have to be, that I would become merely a 'hanger-on.'

"I remember him sitting on the side of the bed in my bedroom and my walking back and forth, pacing, trying to explain to him what I wanted. And he—finally agreed.

"It must have been a terrible disappointment, a bitter blow for him, because he had the small business and with the influx of my youth it might have been built up, father and son working together to make something more of it, to make it my inheritance from him, and give him my youth. But I chose not to, and he had to give up his son.

"In fact, some years later my father brought in some young man who took the place which would have been mine. My father entrusted the young man with the successful clothing manufacturing business.

"There's a sequel to that. When my father died, the man, in effect, got the business for a steal. But I re-

member best that night—those days and nights of
coming to that decision with my father. That was one
moment that was critical, a landmark and turning
point.

"Another was a thunderstorm night here in New
York when I asked that girl I loved to wait for me
until I graduated from college. It was on Fifth Ave-
nue—around here somewhere. And she then told me
—this was the college cutie I was crazy about—that
she had met somebody that summer, that she was
very serious about him and that she wasn't coming
back to McGill. Who knows what would have happened if she *had*—for me, I mean. But my decision to
be an actor wasn't 'practical.' She married the businessman.

"I remember meeting Tyrone Guthrie at Stratford.
I was down on the stage. The stage was below earth
level. It was a huge pit in the ground, then paved over
so it looked like a cup. Over the top of the cup was a
tent. The sides of the cup were lined with seats and
the bottom was a thrust stage. I was there on the
thrust stage on the first day of this prestigious company—this legendary Canadian theater company
about to be formed, ready to begin. Suddenly a flap
in the tent flew open. There was a terrible steep de-
scent—50 or 60 feet in length. Down it came this
massive giant of a figure, this huge guy. He stopped
three or four steps above me, bent down and shook
my hand. It was like Zeus coming down from Mount
Olympus. He was there for us all, that first meeting,
to see us work. And when I came out and did my
scene, he bounced out of his chair, clapped, and came
down. He came onto the stage and looked at me very
carefully. I realize when I look back now, that of all
the thirty or forty people in the company, or, indeed,
around the world, here and there, Tyrone Guthrie
must have found scattered nuggets of talent. And

there were others than myself, of course, but I can imagine what he must have felt in that moment—that here he was in Canada trying to start a company of classical players, suddenly he found somebody that might have some promise. It must have been a good thing for him, too, as it was for me, that he had found me and suddenly was paying me attention. He became my mentor and I his protégé at Stratford for the next three years, and he, who was a great director, told me that I had the capacity to achieve greatness.

"I remember a stormy night in Stratford—about two months before I was going to get married. Stormy night, and I was in such a turmoil wondering whether I should get married or not—and I walked out into the storm. It was like something out of Shakespeare—which I was playing at the time. I was drenched, wet, storm crackling around me and I was walking in the park at Stratford alongside the stream wondering what was to become of me—the actor, the man . . . Finally, I did marry my first wife and I had thought that the storm was over, but perhaps the storm within was an omen.

"I remember the loneliness of walking the streets in New York as a young man, an actor, wondering whether I would ever get enough money ahead to do anything. I always had just enough to pay the rent. That, in itself, was more than most actors had. Five years in New York. I was one of the most popular actors on live television, getting roles after roles after roles. But they only paid six hundred dollars and it took about two or three weeks to do a live TV-play. The rent was one hundred dollars. So by the time you got through with all your expenses—you could never get ahead—for years. And I was a *successful* actor. I was always working. And I had chosen to be where I was—twice.

"I had the experience of being asked by 20th Century Fox, after I opened in a play here with Stratford, to sign a contract. I went to see some guy I'd never seen, in an office—seven people from the studio sat down in chairs all around me and cross-examined me. They had seen the play, *Tamburlaine*. And then they offered me a salary. Now, I was making—at Stratford at that point, I was making $80 a week, with income tax—it was like $60 a week, and I was living in New York on $60 a week. And they said we'll start you off with a salary of $500 a week in Hollywood, and you'll have a contract with 20th Century Fox. God, I was so *overwhelmed*—it was the gold at the end of the rainbow. Then a guy came up to me, and I never knew who he was. I really *don't* know who he was. I don't know *who* he was—whether he was some weird guy at some party or another actor—I have no recollection as to who he was. But—he had nothing to do with 20th Century Fox. He said, 'Look, you don't know me—I'm going to give you a piece of advice. Trust me—don't sign that contract.' It was like being visited, you know.

"I said—'Don't *sign?!*—$500 a *week*—I'm making $60 a week here. That's *everything!* I want to go to Hollywood. I can be an *actor*. I'll have a studio. I'll be a *star*."

He said, *'Don't sign the contract.'* And—he left.

"The next morning I went up to 20th Century Fox. Some man came out of the door—it was a huge office —three times the size of these two rooms, with a little desk at the end. He said, *"Well!"* My cousin, whose mother was secretary to the head of 20th Century Fox, was representing me. He had just graduated from law school. I was his first case. He was going to get me this contract and he was going to make some money out of it.

"And they both said, *'Well!* Okay, Bill, here we are.' 'All right, Bill.' and 'Here we are.'

"And I said, 'I don't want to sign the contract.'

"And I was, God, I was a *child*—really—not so much chronologically, but I'd been protected from the rest of the world for so long.

"They said, 'Well, why not?'

"And I said, 'I don't *know*. I'm out of my mind. I don't know why. I really don't know. I *want* to sign, but I can't.'

"They said, 'Don't be foolish. *Here, sign the contract.'*

"I said, 'I don't want to sign.' I didn't know what I was doing. I was following my instincts.

"They said, 'Well, I mean, Geez, we're wasting our time, I mean, two meetings. I mean, we're—' You know.

"The contract had clauses for seven years—it was a seven year contract, which went up to thousands of dollars a week. In the seventh year, I mean, I was going to be—incredible.

"And I said, 'No.' And I left.

"And what would I have done if I had signed it? Hollywood was still Hollywood in those years.

"Sometime later I went to MGM. I had a different agent who got me a contract for two pictures a year —and it was non-exclusive—I could do anything else I wanted to. Two pictures a year for something like $50,000 a picture. You're talking to a guy who was making sixty, seventy dollars a week. Also, it was what is called 'pay or play.' If they didn't give you a movie, they gave you $50,000. I was rich beyond my wildest dreams.

"Then somebody in New York said, 'Come to New York, Josh Logan wants to see you.' So they flew me to New York—this was before any movie was made.

"And Josh Logan says, 'Here's "The World of Suzie Wong." Read it.'

"I read it. It's a beautiful, poetic play. And Josh

Logan had just come off of *South Pacific*. It was the *theater*.

"So I said, 'Mr. Logan, I'd like to do the play, it's a beautiful play, I'd love to play the lead.'

"He said, 'Well, I want you to read for me. I want you to audition for me somehow.' He said, 'Bill, throw the play away, just play the scene the way you want.'

"I said, 'All right, Mr. Logan.' I threw it away, I ad-libbed a scene, and I left his house in the country. By the time I got back to the city, I had the job.

"*But* it required my getting out of my contract. I went back to the coast and I said to my agent, who had just made the deal for what was going to be a $100,000 of which he was going to get $10,000 I said, 'Phil, I want to go to New York and do this play and I don't care about the money.'

"He said, 'We can't do it.'

"I said, 'But you can get me out of the contract.'

"He said, 'I can't.'

"By that time, I found another agent, some young kid. I said 'I want to go to New York and do this play.'

"He said, 'I'll get you out of the contract." He went to the head of the studio and he told the head of the studio something about, you know, getting out of the contract. I forget what the reason was, but it didn't have anything to do with doing a hit play.

"And the head of the studio, by this time realized that they didn't have any movies and they were going to owe me $100,000—cause MGM was dying at this time—and not put me in a movie. At least, that was the supposition.

"So, whereas under ordinary circumstances a clever agent might have gotten me twenty or thirty thousand dollars, because they wanted out of it, too, they said, 'Okay, we won't give you any money, and you can go.'

"So I gave up $100,000 that year and went in to do a play which was cut to shreds and became a ghastly apparition of what it was.

"It opened as a turkey—got seven bad notices. It was directed as a turgid drama. People walked out in the middle of it—you could hear whole rows of people getting up and walking out. There were other problems.

"But we had a million dollars advance before the show came to New York, so it had to run three months. Everybody kept hands-off when they saw they had a turkey. But during that three months I began to pick up the pace, and instead of playing it as thick drama, I began to play it as a comedy. I took twenty minutes out of the running time and *forced* people to stay in their seats. I felt that I was doing battle alone. But by the end of three months people were coming to buy tickets because by word of mouth they heard about it and it became a hit—ran two years, won Drama Circle acting awards. [For Shatner and his co-star.]

"So you see—the conflict of idealism and commercialism—it's hard to make up my mind. Those sums of money which are large today—twenty years ago—*whew*!"

'There was no support? You were all on your own?'

"I had no agent. And a mysterious voice came one time and said, 'Don't sign.' I thought, 'God, somebody *knows* something.' Nobody else seemed to know anything."

'Did you feel in any of this—"What's the use? Is it worth it? What am I doing?"'

"Oh, yeah, I must have felt that. But I wouldn't quit. For example—I went on stage with my voice going, my throat so swollen I could hardly talk, but I was talking. I got hit on the head one time when some stage scenery came down. I went on. I never missed a performance. Two years. Actually not in *anything,* all these years. But—I guess those things kind of leave a mark on your soul. And—it becomes part of your life."

'Maybe it could have been a little less painful if there were somebody that you felt close to.'

"If I had some strong representation, or something. . ."

'Well, not even so much strong representation, just someone who would have—'

"Well, I was married then. I was married to my first wife. But that wasn't—wasn't a help in that instance. Eventually, that also was a kind of landmark, the breaking up of that marriage after thirteen years. It just didn't work out. And it broke me financially. Absolutely stone broke."

'Absolutely what? Stone broke?'

"Stone broke.

"About eight years ago, I went to cash a fifteen dollar check—and I couldn't. And that was the year after STAR TREK.

"It was a three-year series and they didn't pay me anywhere near the terms that they're paying people now or even that they were paying people then, but it certainly was not anything to complain about. I'm not complaining. All that money which was to have been saved so that I would have the leisure of being able to select roles and do productions of my own— capitalize on that—was all gone. And I was right back to where I started.

"It was shattering. Shattering.

"That was a tough—the toughest thing. That was the crucible of my life. I look back on it like that.

"And then—my luck came back in the shape of Marcy.

"A guy came up to me and he said: 'You helped me

once, and I'd like to help you. I'm a producer now, I'm
going to do a show on educational television and it
doesn't pay any money, and it's going to take a month
of your time. But it's a terrific part and I'd like
you to do it. And the reason I want *you* to do it is
because I want to repay you for a kindness you've
done me.'

"And I read the part—"The Andersonville Trial."
Jesus, a marvelous part. And I said, 'Yeah.' And I spent
a month working.

"And there was some pretty young thing there. I was
going out with a girl then. I felt no real need—besides
which I was in no way shape or form available for any
sort of emotional contact.

"And I did that play and I got marvelous notices. It's
considered a landmark in television.

"And I met Marcy.

"And that relationship with Marcy has changed my
life. So—the vagaries of life.

"Those are the landmarks."

The Crucible: a Love Story

I was insane. I was insane the way an animal is insane, because I'd lost my family, I'd lost everything, and I was scrambling, clawing to get everything back and put it together again.

W.S.

My whole life has changed, from that of an anxious guilt-ridden, loveless person to the exact opposite.

W.S.

Marcy hung in there. . .   W.S.

The clipping is brief, brutal, with that factual casualness which dismisses 13 years of a man's life, and a woman's: WILLIAM SHATNER DIVORCED.

It doesn't say much more. ". . .She charges. . ." that he "keeps irregular hours. . .is often away from home." She gets their home, alimony, child support, etc., and "Half of community property estimated at half a million dollars." (In fact, the newspaper story is in error. It is less than half of that, less than a quarter million, including the house—perhaps $125,000-$150,000.)

Actually the process of divorce and its aftermath consumes the whole of the property.

He's alone.

Maybe he's always been alone.

He is to realize fully only years later the extent to which nobody has ever known him—what is going on inside him. Nobody.

But he has intimations of that. When his father dies while the marriage is breaking up and he looks down at Montreal from the plane bearing his father's body: "But I was really looking into myself. I saw—an empty pit—and it terrified me."

Love dead, dying, his whole life threatened, finally crashing in ruins, even the dream, perhaps, dying. . .

When he says, "It was—shattering," you can hear the crash of the pieces.

But what is perhaps most interesting is that he should *see* it as the "crucible" of his life. The very concept implies going through the fire, being seared in the flame, heated to white-heat, to emerge transmuted, transformed—something new, burned clean, stronger.

What certain sense of life does it take to think of being burned clean by what amounted to a years-long walk through a personal hell? Whatever it takes, we hear it in the voice of William Shatner—soft, willing to reveal the pain, flat at times with effort, quiet, with a certain bleak pride.

There is almost an unbelief in the voice, as if it is beyond concept that this should have happened to him.

The kinds of hell it was to come out first of all in a word, a phrase, a quick reference in another context: ". . .This was during the painful period in my life. . . 'No, I don't want to die, although there were . . . nights when I wished I could.' " ". . .Things weren't going too well at home . . . going home would be of no value . . . (the day his father died.)" This was from a man for whom home and family had been a major part of his life, the three girls, adored, the marriage, if not perfect, one he had expected to last.

Articles just before and during the early part of STAR TREK depict a strong commitment to family life. But there were the stresses of his career—once the strain of filming his series "For The People" in New York, coming home when he could, while the children were in school in Los Angeles. In earlier years his first wife, Gloria, had usually been with him wherever he was. Then STAR TREK became physically and emotionally consuming—10, 12, 14 or more hours a day, plus an hour or so driving each way, plus a run on the beach with his dog to keep in shape—and on weekends perhaps an explosive unwinding on a motorcycle.

He had married young—still in the days when he was acting Shakespeare and writing "Dreams," which he played with Gloria, and perhaps he had married partly, as he says, in an effort to assuage his own loneliness. But the loneliness was of a stubborn variety. It is difficult to say what makes or breaks a marriage, but it could not have been much help that he became a world-name in his career, while whatever her acting career might have been, Gloria remained largely undiscovered.

Nor has Shatner ever claimed to be a plaster saint. There was, doubtless, the emotional remoteness, the fact that he had never fully revealed himself to anyone, which he was to realize fully only much later. The search for something to fill that empty pit which he was beginning to see in himself with his father's death could not have been easy—on him, or on a wife.

Nevertheless, the breaking came as a hammerblow.

During the last two years of STAR TREK this man's life was coming apart, and that vision which people saw on the screen of a man's confident, unclouded strength came out of a private agony.

Speaking of the universality of emotion and everyone's disguising it to one degree or another, he says:

"And I, having grown up in the ivory tower of being an actor have never really felt the need to do that, even in my personal life. Well, that's not entirely true. I've had to steel myself.

"The one thing that I have acquired the ability to do, now that I'm older, is to focus on the task at hand, to keep my personal emotions out of my performance. I now know that I can be half-dead from fatigue or from some personal emotional upheaval and still bring my focus to bear on what is needed to entertain that audience, that night, make that piece of film. . ."

STAR TREK owes its unclouded sense of life to that ability to focus.

Perhaps it owes more.

He starts to speak of his personal life during STAR TREK. The voice goes flat with effort:

"Well, just essentially I was getting a divorce. My wife was divorcing me during the last two years of STAR TREK—with all its itinerant hurts—and breaks."

'Do you think that affected the show in any way? For better or for—'

"I hope not, because I tried not to let any of it—anything that was happening to me personally—affect my performance. It may have not helped the social climate on the set—although I don't recall its being bad—I mean, I think it was very *good*.

'Could it have helped to the show's advantage?'

He looks as if it's the first time that question has been raised, but he's very quick.

"Living on the force of that emotion, do you mean?"

'Yes.'

"It's possible."

'You suffering the way you were. . .'

"Yes. It certainly is possible."

'Even greater empathy than perhaps you already had with some of the character's—'

"In fact, it may have been too much. I mean, there are times when I look at that film and I think, "I should not have played that as broadly as I did.""

It's hard to avoid the doubts of a performance as outside-the-square as that. And, indeed, there may have been moments. But some of the moments when the force of that emotion came through are the very ones which have moved people most deeply.

What is remarkable is that he could do it at all. Consider the effort—and the restraint—of playing a scene like the loss of Kirk's great love Edith Keeler in "City on the Edge of Forever" under the force of his own loss. Or—the loss of Miramanee, Kirk's only wife, and of his unborn child. Or—think of the sunlit lightness of "The Trouble With Tribbles."

Whatever that took or cost, he did it.

But by the third year of STAR TREK, he was alone, and with the ending of the show, more utterly alone.

And broke.

Back at his beginnings. Except that now he had tasted the heights of success, fame, critical esteem. And now in the minds of producers, as well as the world, he *was* Kirk. And he was a series lead, just coming off a successful—but finally cancelled—series. There were roles they would not offer as being beneath him, or because the identification was still too strong in everyone's minds. You don't turn around and put Ben Cartwright or Matt Dillon or Captain Kirk in another series. Certainly not right away.

But payments to his wife, child support, etc., were

set at the level of a high-paid series lead.

Shatner went out and dug in to make a comeback from immortality.

Except that nobody knew that it was immortality.

He reached the day when he couldn't cash the check for fifteen dollars. And he was homeless, but still with family responsibilities.

It's one thing for a man to be broke or poor at his beginnings, or even to have a modest success or a continuing struggle.

It's something else when you have made it to the top in what is perhaps the toughest, chanciest profession in the world.

He speaks of it with a kind of stunned surprise:

"I furnished—I was able to put together enough money to make the down payment to buy a little house. And I furnished it with used furniture and damaged furniture from downtown Los Angeles. I furnished the house I bought for *three hundred dollars*. With a sofa and a bed that had a torn mattress—that had come from a damaged crate. And the whole—I did the whole number. I did the whole number that hippies must do or kids out of high school, out of college, must have done. For three hundred dollars I furnished a house, including room for my children."

But it was not only the money. He'd lost his children. But he was still responsible for them. The girls speak of his love for them, and of him, with a kind of awe to this day.

"So I took jobs—unbelievable jobs. I took jobs for two hundred fifty dollars that took me out someplace to—I did everything. I did some game shows that were demeaning. I went places, did things, night after night—I'd travel—two or three jobs in one day, if I could—just to make some money to get this thing together again. I became frantic, obsessed. And I've only begun to come out of that—that I then fell into a pattern of that kind of obsession. It's been Marcy who has pointed it out. My agencies—they're only too happy. She says, 'What are you *doing*?' Well, what *am* I doing? I don't need to do this anymore. Suddenly, through her, that whole pattern—curtained."

And in fact, it is in the context of Marcy that he speaks of all of this, as a pain so deep that it is almost beyond remembering, except that it has ended, through her.

In point of fact, their love was forged out of the crucible of his disaster. And by his own account the first three years even of their love story were a walk through fire. The realization of what she was, and what she could be to him came slowly.

Speaking of what she is to him now, "a spirit, a saint," he can barely believe that he didn't know it always, but he admits with unsparing honesty that he didn't.

'You didn't see this the first three years?'

"No. I was in a terrible state all those years. I don't know *where* I was—I've heard things that have happened to me from 1968 to 1973-4. I have no recollection. People come up to me—I see people I met then and knew, in fact I had a whole relationship with them, with a beginning, a middle and an end, and those relationships, those people—I see them now and *I don't remember them.* I don't remember what I did. I don't remember what I felt. Some people say, 'you were awful then.' There was one girl who was a very lovely girl, and extremely intelligent—she was so intelligent that she was a member of the Mensa Organization for people with extremely high I.Q.'s, geniuses. We were going out together and she was—taking care of me in some way.

"And I met her about two months ago. She had

married a very famous person and she was fine, and we talked. I said, 'What was I like?'

"She said, 'You were terrible. You were really a bad person then. I didn't like you at all after a while.'

"So obviously—I was *insane*. I was insane the way an animal is insane, because I'd lost my kids, I'd lost everything. And I was scrambling, clawing to get everything back and put it together again."

The tone of unbelief is in his voice again, a certain wry, bleak astonishment. He cannot recognize himself in those years, can barely believe that even the memories are gone. It is almost as if the momentary amnesia which he has told us came to him in the grief at his father's death had returned to him again in his own grief and animal frenzy—to encapsulate, perhaps to heal, some of the worst agony of the crucible years.

Yet most men would try to cover even the existence of those years and that animal fury—perhaps even hide it from themselves. He seeks out the knowledge. He speaks of it without sparing himself. And it is plain that he has been back over the years since Marcy with her.

It is always only in context of Marcy that he speaks. He has told us from the beginning, from our earliest phone conversation how much she has taught him about people, how much she has changed him and his life:

"I got so that when I would leave for anything, whether it was a day, a week, or—I was going out those summers, two of them, for fourteen weeks living in a cabover camper over a truck, playing summer stock, because I wanted to save money on motels. Drove a truck across the country."

Clippings from that second summer after STAR TREK reported nationwide on his driving the truck. "Bill Shatner is parked in my driveway. . .Captain

Kirk...in his camper...sort of all closed in like a spaceship." One reporter blandly wonders whether he "pines for" the STAR TREK days. Others try to probe his father's death, the divorce.

His personal popularity is greater than ever: "...people are wild about him...he's mobbed...doesn't matter *what* our show is. They just come to see 'Shatner's show,' as they call it. You should see how the rest of the cast sulks over this."

Which is all very well, but he cannot bank immortality. Nor does it assuage the loneliness, the rejection of his work implied in the cancellation of STAR TREK—and of his very self implied in the divorce.

He gives solid, positive interviews on the working level, without complaints, says that he "loves a live audience...," the camper gives him "room for all my sporting gear, creature comforts..."

But it's doubtful how much of the joy of walking the wire he can feel while touring the country in light comedy and a heavy truck, parking in somebody's driveway in some town in New Jersey to save money to furnish a house for three hundred dollars...

None of the reporters of those days reached what was below the surface of the smooth, white-hot mass glowing in the crucible. He didn't speak of it, then or since, never has until now.

If he could not steer the interviewer away, so smoothly that the interviewer never knew where he or she had been steered, or away from what—he would finally say, if necessary, "I don't want to talk about that." One interviewer pressed on things he'd already said he didn't want to talk about—his father's death, the divorce—and wound up calling him in print "tight-lipped." It was the only complaint. Most went away charmed—with quotable quotes and no word of the inferno within.

He's very aware of that. Speaking of how he is letting the barriers down this one time for this book, of how no one has ever known him except, finally, Marcy, he says:

"Whenever I get with people, I never talk about myself. I try *not* to talk about myself. For two reasons: one is that I talk about myself on a superficial level with reporters all the time. So when I say, 'talk about myself,' I mean really basic things—things that I wouldn't want—that I know would be mis-written and mis-interpreted in print anyway. So it's of no value. What they want to hear is not that, anyway. They want to hear an interesting anecdote about a particular show so that they can get a column out of it. So I'm talking about myself in that manner all the time. And I have no wish to talk to some stranger about, 'How does it feel to be an actor?' If I hear that question one more time—I mean—you know—and then you hear it tomorrow night. So I try to give the earnest answer that I've given so many times, and try to embellish it a little bit more. Maybe today I can find some other things to give in that answer.

"But—it's a bore. Or maybe—it's worse than that. So I find I have evolved over the years a whole technique of avoiding talking about myself. Not only with reporters, with anybody—acquaintances, friends, anybody. And I would leave a conversation and I knew that they were going away saying, "Gee whiz, he's nothing like I thought. He's not egotistical at all." Meanwhile, I'm going, "God, that's an interesting person—but I don't want to spend time like *that* again."

'And you had no one who really could see you all those years—not anyone, not even your first wife, who knew what was going on inside you. Now, there is Marcy—but meanwhile there were close to forty years before Marcy, and hard years before you un-

bent even to her. There's the problem of what you
were doing all those years. . .?'

He says, rather tightly, "Well, I suppose that those
feelings were being put into my acting. That's where
the artist, I suppose, comes in."

That artist projected unclouded openness out of his
solitary crucible, forged a legend out of his private
fire, while the man who was that artist did what he
had to do, and went quietly—and very sanely—mad.

"I got so that whenever I left, I'd get frantic. Everything had to be right—are my kids okay?—'cause my
kids were going through a lot of problems. There was a
whole area of my life that had to do with my children
which was so macabre and bizarre that it would drive—
it *has* driven men to insanity.

"Then there was my whole life as an actor, a busy
actor, who had to make travel arrangements and deal
with weird people who were always there with their fingers out—you know—seeking some kind of essence
from you.

"And I had to juggle both elements of my life. I got so
that whenever it came to traveling, the first thing, my
first reaction was, when they'd say, 'All right, Bill, you
have to go to New York for a day,'—I'd get depressed.
If it was on location for three weeks, I mean—for the
following four or five days, I was a basket case.

"Then I'd have to get myself together and start packing. Then I had to start making arrangements. Including
family arrangements. Making sure the kids knew how to
call me every day on the phone. Having to deal with my
former wife.

"Then, when I was away, I knew that I was going to
get besieged by phone calls to ameliorate fights and difficulties, and deal with homework—then be faced with
the possibility of being besieged by lawyers—

"Then I would come back, I would have to wonder,

what was the situation now? What was I going to have to do—?

"Well, what you had on your hands was a crazed human being. You had a man who left the city and came back to the city crazed and depressed. And that became a pattern for five years.

"So, I'd be shaking—I'd shake. I would literally *shake* as I got on the plane, out of the anxieties I was leaving behind and was going to come back to."

He stops and his voice, his manner, his whole face change, as if the Marcy theme comes in to clear away the discordant music. He doesn't smile. The transformation goes deeper than that.

"That's all gone. That's all—all *right* now."

He goes on with the Marcy theme.

But he backs up here and there to let the crucible years show through. He would perhaps like to make it a love-at-first-sight, happily-ever-aftering story.

But he's trying not to rewrite history. There was the first spark. But there was not the instant ever-after effect. At least, he was trying to resist it.

'What were you attracted to in the beginning? Did you know then—?'

"Her legs."

'Her what?'

"Legs."

'Her *legs*?'

"She was wearing jeans for about three weeks. And then one day she came in a skirt. All the guys in the cast —they were *all* guys—and they said, "Hey look at that —it's a *girl*!" They hadn't noticed her before."

'You called her out on the basis of her *legs*—and asked her out—?'

He looks a little sheepish for a moment, and there's the look of an internal debate. Then he decides, comes out with it.

"Well the truth of the matter is—Marcy'll kill me if I tell this story—but it's really a funny story. Her job was as the production assistant, and it was her job to help anybody with his lines who needed help. And I had this enormous number of lines. I was on the job lunch hour. So every lunch hour Marcy and I would meet in the board room or somewhere. We'd get hamburgers and then I'd run lines.

"And then one day I looked at her. I gave her my 'look,' (He laughs.) And I reached out and kissed her.

"And she—*fell to the ground.*

"It's the truth.

"Her knees *buckled.*" He laughs. "And I was about to follow her down to the ground, when the door opened and the cleaning guy came in.

"And that was the beginning of our relationship. It was really hysterical. We laugh about it."

'One kiss. Bill, if we print that we're going to have millions of women who want to know, "Hey, does it work? Or—" '

"Either that or she has trick knees. One or the other."

'What does she say about that?'

He chuckles and shakes his head, remembering the moment. Then for a moment a shadow seems to cloud his face.

'Well, we'll ask her about that.'

"She'll tell you about that."

'When did you start to realize that there was something more than the pretty legs and the devastating effect of you on her?'

"Well, she'll tell you more about that, too. Because— it took about three years."

The effort comes into his voice again and the shadow deepens.

"We knew each other a long time, we were together more and more for a long time, for three years—and I couldn't have cared less. I'd stay away for days. She was just somebody to be there—pretty girl who cared for me.

"And she *cared*.

"For three years she hung in there. And even to this day she says, '*I hung in there,* you bastard, you didn't give a damn.' "

You can hear the overtones of her voice in his, laughing over an agony past—and you can hear the love, speaking volumes. Then he goes on in his own voice, and it also speaks volumes.

"And then one day I realized that this person with an incredible brain—she's an incredible person, she's a—spirit. And I—we've known each other for seven years, and for three of those years, if it hadn't been for her. . . ."

He shakes his head, as if he looks into the blinding heat of the crucible again, contemplating what it would have been like for him if Marcy had not come to him or had not hung in there.

Finally he smiles:

"So you see, there's an angel on my shoulder. I know that I am—blessed. I really am blessed."

We probably look a little startled, knowing something about the nearly ten years of the crucible. Marcy, yes. But it would not have occurred to us to think of him as blessed.

His eyes laugh:

"I'm just lucky. I'm *lucky*. People pull out of parking spaces when I come to a theater, and I find them. I mean, it's just incredible. I miss airplane connections. There's always another airplane. Rarely, rarely has it really turned out badly. I mean, things just work out. I don't know. I don't know what the secret is. But I just —I'm a—

'Do you try to help them happen? Mentally? Do you focus on these things happening?'

"Not consciously, but I just, I just—No. Marcy refers to me as a blessed person."

He smiles and it's plain enough where the concept has come from. He expands on it fondly.

"Because things just—I mean, I just had the flu. I really *did* have the flu. I had a high temperature. And I went to bed one night after the performance and I was shaking. I was really sick, and recovered—it couldn't have been better that I'd gotten sick on Monday, because I didn't have a performance the next day and so I was able to recover. And in New York in a hotel, instead of traveling every day. I mean, it was unfortunate that I got sick, but it couldn't have happened at a better time. That *kind* of thing—that, in a minor way—seems to be happening to me all the time."

Or then again, maybe the concept isn't just from Marcy. This is the man who sees the bad years as the crucible. Why *shouldn't* he see a bout of flu in the midst of a man-killing schedule as a piece of luck and an example of blessedness?

But still again, he regards himself as blessed in one way which perhaps colors everything else.

'What happened with Marcy that got to be so fantastic, after three years? What did you find out that you didn't know?'

"What happened with Marcy was that I learned to trust her. And for the first time with any human being, I began to reveal myself. I mean: reveal what I am and what I think, what I feel, times when I was hurt, things which gave me pain. And—they welled up, and they were there for a while. And then—they went away. Or at least I was able to deal with them. And I was able to talk about myself. I was able to listen to *her*—feel her pain, because I really wanted things to be good for her. I opened up as a human being to Marcy. She's been my conduit to the world."

So there it is, very simply: what might just as well be taken as a textbook statement of the need for, and value of, emotional openness—from the actor who staked a claim to the territory before it existed, and from the man who—later—explored it as *terra incognita,* where no man had gone before, in his own life.

It is not something which we have asked for or prompted, but it is not only an eloquent statement of love, it is also an eloquent confirmation of the question which could not be answered in words: how much of the emotional openness in Kirk was Shatner's dream, and how much was, or became, his reality?

It is one thing to project the ideal of openness, and another to pursue the reality. This man has done both. Reality is tougher. There are no guarantees. There were not even any guidelines, for him—it was long before openness in men became the talk of the revolution—nor any image for him to follow—except the one he had projected. And he had done that, never knowing the kind of openness he was to find only by going through the crucible, and only, perhaps, by testing his love—and *her* love in the flame.

She was not found wanting.

She hung in there.

What it took for *this* man to learn to trust a woman, and a person, after those years of flame is the kind of thing to which monuments are built. Taj Mahals.

He would build one. And he has. But you can see it first of all mainly in his eyes, in the relaxed stretch of his body as he speaks now of her, of home.

Being a practical sort of dreamer he has built his monument as a home, or home as a tribute.

"Home. . .Marcy came into my life. She helped me redo the house as I got a little more money, but, eventually, there were, with my three kids and the two of us, five people in what was essentially a two-bedroom house, and one bedroom was very—both bedrooms were very small, but the one containing the three children was, you know, a closet. The house wasn't big enough.

"Every day—well, when I *did*—I would jog on a mile-and-a-half route. It was a lovely area of Los Angeles. Sometimes Marcy would jog with me, and we'd see a Spanish house on the hill. We'd say, "God—*love* to own that."

"Finally got to the point where we had to move. And a friend of ours who had come into our lives said one day, 'Did you know that Spanish house is for sale?'—'cause we had mentioned it to him.

"*Ran*. Looked at the house. Bought it, within a day of having seen it. There wasn't even a 'for sale' sign on it. It had just gone on the market.

"The house has turned out to be the essence of both of us.

"It's—peace. It's—gardens. It's room for the breeding of dogs. It's—it's *private*. It's protected.

"There's a maid's room if there's a need for it, room for the children. I've built a whole area with a gymnasium and a pool and things, so I don't have to go anywhere and be gaped at, looked at. We've planted fruit trees all around that in a few years will begin to bear fruit.

"The house has become an entity in itself. It's a haven." He pauses, still on the catalogue of what Marcy has done to transform his life—and realizing that he has been talking on that subject for a long time.

He smiles, unabashed, then continues gravely:

"I mean, I could go on and on. My whole life has changed from that of an anxious, guilt-ridden, loveless person to the exact opposite."

It's a look which says a great deal about the woman who evokes it. We have not yet been to the house on the hill to meet her.

'How would you describe Marcy if you had to? What would you say if you were giving someone the essence of what Marcy is?'

He looks as if he's been asked to describe the universe in ten words or less.

"Have you ever seen her?"

'On television. "Tattletales".'

"Marcy is one of the most beautiful girls, physically, that you will ever see. She is a very beautiful woman. Extraordinary. I mean, extraordinarily beautiful. And— the beauty that she has physically doesn't come anywhere near matching the beauty of her soul. And—she's a *cum laude* graduate from the University of Southern California. Her intelligence is extraordinary. In fact, some people say, the one thing about Marcy is her intelligence. So—here is a beautiful—a physically beautiful girl who has the soul of an *angel*.

"And I mean, I really mean: the *goodness*. She is essentially good, whereas I am *not*. Her essence is good, but I can be evil. She can't be. She can't because she's psychologically—unfortunately—she's having to *learn* to be evil. She's having to learn to express anger and resentment and negative emotions because she just doesn't *do* that. And then combined with that there's the high degree of intelligence—"

He pauses a moment, more out of superlatives than out of virtues. It is the one subject on which he does not mind being carried away.

'I've talked to her a few times, as you know. I know she's a remarkable person, just from those phone conversations. There's a kindness about her—'

"And you can see how protective she is of me. That first time, if you hadn't convinced *her* that you were worthwhile and I should talk to you—well, *you* might have gotten through, eventually. But she keeps so many

of the problems away from me, and puts through the
real things. And she *knows*. I mean she's—sometimes
I've heard her on the phone—you know, she's—she's
really an extraordinary individual. I don't know what I
would do—I really *don't* know what I would—I'll put
freshness into that tired cliche! *I don't know what I would
do without her.*

We talk for a moment of the kindness she has shown
us, sight unseen, in the last two years—from the first
moment when we called—strangers out of the night—
before *Star Trek Lives!* was published, and reached her.
After a conversation explaining our purpose, she
vouched for us, and shellmouth Shatner took her word
for it—deliberately saying that that was what he was
doing—and gave us an unprecedented phone interview
for more than an hour. That was, in fact, the beginning
of the events which led to this book.

But that was only the first of the reasons why the
book would doubtlessly not have been written, certainly
not now or in this form if William Shatner's blessed
"luck"—and a forgotten kindness he did long before—
had not brought him "Andersonville" and Marcy, and
his own love story.

A man, at least this man, does not write a book about
his life from out of the crucible. He writes it when he has
come out of the fire, stronger.

This man would have done that, sooner or later, in
our judgement, even alone. But it would not have been
the same, and he might well still be alone now if it were
not for the woman who hung in there.

We realize that we have one half of an extraordinary
love story, and an invitation to get the other half.

But when we ask, 'What attracted her to *you*, do you
know?' Especially when you were talking about the state
you were in then—'

Words fail him. Or—he won't say *her* words:

"I don't know. She says all kinds of things. I don't know. She says she—she says she—ah—you'll have to ask her."

It's possibly the first time the shellmouth has ever just been speechless. And as to whether actor or captain was blushing, shellmouths have nothing on us.

There's some other level on which we are speechless with still another emotion. He *has* come through the crucible. Whatever it cost or took, out of him or anyone else, he paid the price—and he doesn't deny that sometimes so did they. But he paid, not sparing himself, and finding somewhere the strength even to accept the help he needed.

From some depth he found even the strength to reach for that emotional openness which he had projected as an ideal, and which became, at least so far as he has been able to reach it now, his reality.

And—he is still reaching.

"I Am Kirk"

I am Kirk.   W.S.

I never said of Kirk, "he" would do such and such, because it was me, I gave myself guidelines, as I would have wanted to be. I acted Captain Kirk in the manner that I wished that I could behave—as the way that it really would be. That's the definition of Captain Kirk in my mind.   W.S.

We always tried to follow the dictum: "If there's a message, send it by Western Union." No one ever attempted to sell a message. And yet the shows composed themselves into areas of optimism and hope—that something better lay ahead. There was always a cameraderie between the members of the crew, each trying to help the other out. And there was a feeling that man could master his fate—aboard the Enterprise. That was the essence of STAR TREK, I believe.   W.S.

"Man could master his fate—aboard the Enterprise. . . ."

". . .in the manner that I wished that I could behave—as the way that it really would be. . . ."

"I am Kirk."

* * *

Those three statements are the key to the lasting legend of STAR TREK—and of Kirk.

However hard-boiled the effort to say, "Send it by Western Union," there was an even harder effort by the working actors and creators of STAR TREK to project that vision of man's future as if it were *real,* as it really would *be.*

Whatever faults, flaws, foibles any of the creators of STAR TREK may have had, whatever pressures or agonies in their own lives—and however much they may have tried to be hard-nosed about not preaching the message, they *had* one: man *could* master his fate. There *was* cameraderie aboard the *Enterprise.* There *was* hope.

The shows were not, in fact, "composing themselves"—exactly.

And one hard-boiled working actor was busily composing the message of a man who was master of his fate, captain of his soul—and of the *Enterprise.* That man cared enough to put himself into it, still cares enough to acknowledge that he did.

Nothing he could say about STAR TREK or Kirk could be more eloquent than "I *am* Kirk."

An actor plays many roles. Shatner has played more, perhaps, than almost anyone. As a young man he was already master of a hundred roles in sixty classical plays. Few men have had the lead in one television series. He has had three—one before STAR TREK, and since with "Barbary Coast." He's played Broadway hits and every conceivable television guest role, including modern classics. In "The Tenth Level" he tackled a role and a topic so sensitive and so important that for a time it was kept off of television. It was one in which he, in fact, did cry.

Shatner has played heroes, villains, and men who were neither: saints, sinners, characters, sophisticates, virginal innocents. It's an actor's pride to be able to do that.

He's played Alexander the Great, one of his own great heroes.

Of no other role has he said, "I *am* the character—I *am* Kirk."

It's a daring statement, requiring courage. He knows very well that many people would dismiss Kirk as merely a television role—even as space opera —although that is getting harder to do as it becomes increasingly plain that STAR TREK is such a phenomenon and classic. But he was making that statement years before the rebirth of STAR TREK lent it respectability.

The statement is particularly touching coming from William Shatner. There is that hard-boiled streak in him which doesn't want to overestimate the importance of what he's done, which doesn't want to get hooked on the legend. "Maybe I *should* acknowledge that it *is* the phenomenon it is. I mean—I *do,* but in order to retain some sanity I pull back further than perhaps I will in a year or two or ten."

But there is also another side.

He will say, very simply, "I love STAR TREK." The love comes through even in the words he does not say, even in moments of trying to be hardboiled.

He'll joke about Kirk. ("Well, you know Kirk beds 'em and leaves 'em, as people are always saying. But bedding and leaving are a two way street. Who's to know, except myself, that they aren't better off when they left than when they arrived?" 'Where are all those arguments where the woman was saying—"No, no," and Kirk was saying "Yes, yes"?' "Maybe *I* was saying, 'No, no.' ")

He slips over very easily into the first person of Kirk.

There's an interesting contrast involved. Leonard

Nimoy titled a book "*I Am Not Spock.*" (Although as he also points out, "If I am not Spock, who is?") In nine hours of interviews with Sondra and several more when we interviewed him with Shatner for this book, Leonard Nimoy nearly always referred to Spock in the third person—("Well, if you ask *Spock* . . .")—and made a clear distinction between the actor, Nimoy, and the Vulcan, Spock.

Leonard Nimoy: ". . .if you were talking to Spock, he would say that you were insulting him (saying that he felt emotion, love). . .there's no point at which you and Spock are going to arrive at an agreement on what is happening."

In point of fact, both attitudes worked extremely well for the actors and roles involved. Nimoy *was* playing a Vulcan, and required a certain detachment, a certain careful distinction between himself and Spock to create that alienness.

Shatner was playing a human being, and playing him as the man Shatner wanted to be, as himself and the best of himself. Speaking to us about not wanting something to be made too easy for Kirk (having Spock take care of him too thoroughly), Shatner said, "That is not the lot of mankind. And—Kirk represents mankind."

But Kirk represented mankind and man in a way which was only then struggling to be born—man free to be himself, to feel and reveal his deepest emotions.

Spock represents something which also goes deep in mankind and especially in men—the idea that emotions are dangerous and to be denied.

The two characters became the ultimate embodiment of the two sides of that coin.

Spock was the archetype and definitive example of the traditional idea of the stiff-upper-lip carried to its —you should pardon the expression—"logical" conclusion. As such, he was more familiar to us than a brother.

It was Kirk who was the alien. He was what, perhaps, we had never seen before: a man as man was intended to be. Or the closest to it, in drama, that we had seen. He was the projection of the man of the future.

STAR TREK eventually amounted, among other things, to a kind of living essay on the subject of emotions—not only in men, but in humans, in intelligent beings. The effects of that essay in seventy-nine episodes repeated for nearly fifteen years now can hardly be calculated—but one look at the top hits of television these last years will show a whole crop of men much freer to show emotion than anyone in pre-STAR TREK days. Yet it is still tough to surpass the prototype for a combination of clear-cut masculine strength with openness.

How did Shatner arrive at that dramatic projection?

Curiously enough, he does not consider it particularly remarkable:

'The pattern of emotional openness in Kirk was very clear. Almost every scene showed Kirk's willingness to express emotions, even those which a man is allegedly not supposed to express: fear, uncertainty, love, tenderness, grief, joy. At the same time, it's clear that Kirk is profoundly masculine and very much in control. How do you think you were projecting that?'

"I was really being myself. That's in essence what it is. I really do think that a man should have no problem in expressing an emotion to another man or a woman. Emotions are what we live by. There's nothing to denigrate in feeling emotion. And yet at the same time you can express an emotion and be in control of yourself. A policeman solving a crime can be moved by the crime and still solve the crime—like a soldier in war. And a man in love—a man in love *should* tell the object of his love that he loves her.

Otherwise it's not half as much fun, if you leave the other person in doubt. And that's what human beings *are.*"

But a good many of them—not only, but especially, men—have fought against recognizing it. They may have broken down emotionally under stress, but they did not regard the full expression of emotion as *right.* Their dramatic ideal was Clark Gable and Gary Cooper and Gregory Peck. Strong, silent, stiff in the saddle. Tarzan, stoic and impassive lord of the jungle. Heroes of every size and stature, whose heroism consisted, at least in part, of emotional control to the point of suppression.

The dream-image which towered largest in men's minds was Rhett Butler.

And, in fact, most women agreed—and most still find Rhett Butler sexy, not to mention Spock—even if they now also have an alternate image in Kirk of what man could be, and many find *that,* in the last analysis, most attractive of all.

What is striking is the power of the dramatic image of Kirk.

It is, for once, a *new* archtype of what man could be.

In some sense Spock is the distilled essence of a long line of impassive heroes—the legitimate heir of Tarzan and all his stoic breed.

People had words for Spock—two of them: Logical. Unemotional. It was a brilliant stroke to establish Spock's character on that premise—essentially a philosophical premise: that emotions and logic conflict. The argument of the Spock premise is that emotion must be sacrificed to logic.

The argument of the Kirk archetype, as conceived and played by Shatner, is that no irreconcilable conflict exists, and that the reality of emotion is not only inescapable but is the essence of what man *is.*

Spock's character was, in the first instance, a creation of the writing. In the first pilot of STAR TREK Spock did not have the logic/emotion premise, nor a character like Shatner's Kirk to play to. In the second, he had both, and it was then that the character of Spock caught fire.

Nimoy elaborated the alien perspective and philosophical premise of Spock brilliantly, precisely by keeping Spock separate from himself. Spock acquired a life of his own. After a time, it was true: Nimoy was not Spock. Spock was not Nimoy. Both were fascinating men, indissolubly linked—but not the *same* man.

What happened with Shatner and Kirk, however, was still more remarkable.

Kirk was *not*, primarily, a writing creation.

What we saw in the pre-Shatner first pilot of STAR TREK, "The Cage," (later incorporated in the two part STAR TREK episode, "The Menagerie") was the original writing creation: the character of Captain Christopher Pike, as played by Jeffrey Hunter. Captain Pike was sober to the point of grimness—even to the point of contemplating leaving his job and responsibilities for a simpler life. At best he was cut in the mold of a rather ordinary hero, from time immemorial. At worst, he was not merely controlled but vacillating. The character had no essential key or core. It remained opaque.

The stiffness and humorlessness of the first Captain of the Enterprise were partly in the way Jeffrey Hunter played the role, partly in the writing. Just about the only emotion Pike expressed was a certain glumness.

Contrast that with Kirk and you will know what a difference Shatner made. Here was no stereotype and no passive plaything of forces beyond his control, but a man who *was* captain of his ship and of his soul, and yet recognized his vulnerability as a living being.

Kirk was the new archtype: the essence of controlled, disciplined, open passion.

Did Shatner know what he was doing?

Was he Kirk, in some important sense?

Is he?

And what, in truth, was the impact of the new image of man which he projected?

We have pursued those questions throughout the book. But we were to find out: He knew.

And doubtless that is why the impact was off the scale.

"I may be wrong, and I may be talking from an actor's egotistical point of view—but if you look at some of those scenes, they could go any way. You could play them cool and unemotional, so that talking to the crew is just a boring exercise—like some commander on some ship might do. I *chose* not to do that. And I was on some occasions told 'Man, you're going a little far on it. You're playing it too broadly.' And maybe I did. But I chose to play the scenes emotionally, where on the black and white page, it didn't necessarily indicate that it should be played that way."

He's absolutely right, of course. Our collection of the early and final drafts of all the scripts shows that the scripts gave no indication of many of the most telling things Shatner did on the screen.

Further, he was acutely aware of the risks involved —even of the actor's nightmare of being laughable.

As for the question of whether he *is* Kirk, in fact— it is clear that that is another question which he cannot fully answer for himself.

It is always possible for a man to put his best face forward—over a brief period of time. It is tough over a period of over three years of in-depth working sessions on a book. It is impossible with someone you live with. And it is impossible with people you live and work with ten, twelve, or more hours a day for three years.

We went, therefore, first, to the professional colleagues who did work with him on STAR TREK.

And we found a useful kind of touchstone.

You can ask exactly that. *Is* he Kirk?

Especially of people who know, best of all, what that means.

Or, as we usually phrased it: "How much of Kirk is in Shatner?"

And: "How much of Shatner is in Kirk?"

Curiously enough, we got a single answer.

What is remarkable is that everyone we spoke with agreed: the qualities which they saw in Kirk, including the heroic qualities, they saw also in Shatner. He was the source.

Leonard Nimoy:

"How much of Kirk is in Shatner? I would say: *All* of Kirk is in Shatner. *It's all there."*

'How about the other way—? How much of Shatner is in Kirk?'

Nimoy (laughing):

"That's interesting, *interesting*. How much of Shatner is in Kirk? I think, a lot. You know, I really have to think very hard, because I was going to say that there's more humanity in Shatner than there was in Kirk.

"But that's probably not true, either, because there was a lot of use of that facet of the person in the character.

Gene Roddenberry (creator and producer of STAR TREK):

"How much of Bill in Kirk? Oh—an enormous amount. I think—it was more than *he* realizes. You can fool a motion picture camera for a film, but you can't fool anybody day in and day out under the driv-

ing pressure of being a lead in a television series. Just
—the camera is going to get to you, and what the
camera reveals—is *you*. If Bill had gone another way
in his life, he'd have been a naval officer or an airline
pilot or something like that. He'd have made a good
leader, with the ability to bring warmth and humor to
his role as leader."

Or, as DeForest Kelley put it, almost in the crusty
manner of Dr. Leonard McCoy:

"I think that he really *is*—Bill may fall down on the
floor and roll and laugh when I say this, but I really
think that all of Kirk's qualities are in Bill—plus a
couple more, like I was telling you. The even greater
concern and caring—*that's* Bill.

"But I have to say, I think he *is* Kirk."

Nichelle Nichols (who played Communications
Officer Uhura):

"*All* of Kirk is in Bill. But all of Bill is not in Kirk."

Interestingly, asked to specify *what* of Bill is not in
Kirk, both De and Nichelle tell stories of Bill's sensitivity and caring and concern. (Which probably tells
you something right there. Kirk was not exactly lack-
ing in those departments.)

De tells of Bill's instant, unqualified backing of
De's fight for better billing in the second year when
Bill immediately went to bat for De, saying that De
had built the role of Dr. McCoy far beyond what had
been the role of the doctor, to the point where he was
the third lead. De got the billing, with Shatner's help
—and it is only one of the stories De tells of Shatner's
concern for him and others.

Nichelle:

"Right in the middle of filming I fainted one day.
I had the flu. Bill noticed first thing in the morning in
makeup. He was the only one who saw it.

"Then—it was take number 699,000 under hot
lights.

"I fainted—in slow motion.

"Bill was across the set. And before I hit the floor he was across the set and caught me. I never hit the floor.

"And that's how sensitive he was.

"He carried me to my dressing room and took care of me and did the whole number. And he was trying to make a joke so I wouldn't see he was that concerned about me. But Najinsky never made a leap like that."

It's one of those little stories from the set which shellmouth Shatner would not tell. We heard them constantly. His concern over every area of the show, the people, the scripts, the ideas, the series. His performance. Everybody's performance.

Grace Lee Whitney (Yeoman Rand):

"He *wanted* me to be good. He helped me. He's good at what he does. The best. Tops. I respected him and I loved working with him. He *made* me a good actress. His reactions were *there*. They were on the double. When you read a line to him, man, you got it right back. You felt like *you* were the one he was really saying that line to, and did he really mean that, or was that a line he was reading? That's how good Bill was.

And she tells one small, telling example which we hadn't heard before, from "The Enemy Within." (A dual-role episode for Shatner.)

Grace Lee:

"There's a scene where the "enemy" half of Kirk is fighting with the other half of Bill and he has to take on both parts and do the fight scene—and I tell you, when he got through, *the whole crew gave him an applause*. That's a *pro*."

Jimmy Doohan (who plays Chief Engineer Montgomery Scott):

"He's a damn good choice. We've started watching

STAR TREK again, and he's *still* a damn good
choice. Great insight into the character. He put it *all*
into that character. Somebody could be as good an
actor and not put into Captain Kirk what Bill did. It
would have lost so much. A great sense of humor. A
terrific sense of command. There's a hell of a lot of
Bill in Kirk, and Kirk in Bill. I think Kirk is the complete Bill Shatner.

"But it all came out of Bill. The emotion—a beautiful thing.

"Kirk showed to me a leading man the way he
should be shown.

"Somebody at a convention asked me, 'Who do
you think is the best actor on STAR TREK?' I said,
'Eight or nine years ago, I may have given you a different answer, but I have to come right out and say,
it's Bill Shatner.' "

What James Doohan is saying is no small
statement—from a cast where every one of the professionals there is remembered to this day particularly for *those* roles. Nimoy's Spock was a classic and
startling creation in its own right. DeForest Kelley
transformed the role of the doctor from invisible
background to the third lead—with Dr. McCoy's
crackling, electric three-way interaction with Kirk
and Spock. James Doohan himself has scenes as
Chief Engineer Montgomery Scott which cause
whole audiences viewing the episodes at conventions
to break out in spontaneous cheering. George Takei
and Walter Koenig are still known worldwide for
Sulu and Chekov.

Nichelle Nichols is greeted at conventions as the
living embodiment of a strong, confident, respected
woman professional, as Nichelle and as Uhura. Majel
Barrett Roddenberry, although she appeared in only
some of the episodes as Nurse Christine Chapel (and
in the first pilot as the female second-in-command

"Number One") has captured imaginations to make Chapel a regular figure in STAR TREK fan and professional fiction. Grace Lee Whitney, although she appeared as Yeoman Janice Rand in only some of the first 13 episodes of STAR TREK, has been remembered by the millions of fans all these years with startling vividness. (The perennial question is: "Whatever happened to Yeoman Rand?" Answer: *very* alive and well and living in Southern California —and now coming out again to be a favorite guest at STAR TREK conventions.)

It is that cast, and the whole creative production crew of STAR TREK, which applauded Shatner on the set for the dual-role scene in "The Enemy Within." It is clear from the way Grace Lee tells that story that *that* is unheard of, in her experience (more than 80 roles—often lead roles opposite the top actors in Hollywood). The cast, the crew—these hard-boiled pros to stop and applaud a fellow-pro's performance in the middle of a working day?

It is a spontaneous tribute.

The respect of your fellow professionals is the toughest of all to come by, and always the most valued. The working actor William Shatner *has* that, universally and without qualification, in public and in private, from all of his fellow professionals—many of whom we have known long before starting this book, and well enough to hear their straight opinion. He has that respect from everyone we spoke to— before and after starting this book, and we spoke to practically everyone. Not only Gene, Leonard, and the STAR TREK cast, but other professionals who have worked with him over the years, on and off STAR TREK—the old and the new—directors, writers, technical people.

The respect is unanimous and profound—from pros who have worked with the best and *are* the best:

DeForest Kelley (Dr. McCoy):

"I don't think I've ever *seen* an actor with that kind of discipline. And I've worked with a *lot* of actors. I've seen him on rare occasions get into trouble in a scene—under really terrible circumstances—late at night, time pressures; he had *mounds* of dialogue, and such *difficult* dialogue. *Rarely* did he get in trouble, but when he did —I've seen him stand there and laugh at himself—really get hysterical, but keep going and keep going and coming back to it until he would finally get it. Great discipline. Phenomenal. I admire him because he could laugh at himself. There is a lot of Kirk in Bill. Bill is a man of tremendous energy, intellect. He's a *very* bright guy. He would have been a leader in *anything*. He has a *great* sense of character interpretation, script interpretation. And he has that deep concern about the people on his ship, and a *great deal* of deep concern about the show and the people on the show.

"When I look back, I think that his role was *such* a difficult role, not only from a mental output, but from a *physical* output. He had very tough physical things to do. He enjoyed working directly with the stunt men, doing his own stunts—you don't *have* to, you know. You have that option. But he was very adept at it. He expends just as much energy physically as he does mentally—and not only on a soundstage.

"He is so *integral* to that show.

"Bill is the driving force, the energy that is so necessary to STAR TREK. No one could ever take his place."

And from the new revival on the movie set, speaking of today's Shatner, Robert Wise (director of *STAR TREK: THE MOTION PICTURE, THE SOUND OF MUSIC, WEST SIDE STORY)* told us that Shatner was perfect for the role and:

"Very professional, a highly professional actor—he's always extremely disciplined—a pleasure to work with. If there are ever any problems, it's never with him. One of the most thorough-going professionals I've ever worked with."

Shatner himself always simply talks and thinks in terms of doing a job—and he approaches it in much the same workaday fashion as he would expect Kirk to use in commanding a starship.

The two jobs have more in common than would off-hand meet the eye.

And the hazards for the actor are, in a way, as great. Possibly in some ways they are tougher. It is one thing, and a heroic thing, to risk your life against a tough universe, knowing that you will be respected and honored.

But it is still another level to put your soul at hazard.

Perhaps an actor will not—as quickly—be buried for or with his mistakes. But he will see them immortalized in celluloid. He will know that they can be seen by tens or hundreds of millions of people, possibly for decades, conceivably for centuries.

If he is laughable, as actor and as man, there is no hiding place. And he has to *know* that before every scene.

Particularly in something like the role of Kirk in STAR TREK, that threat becomes gut-wrenchingly acute.

Even Nimoy's role had always the advantage of distance. Nimoy could always feel: that's not *me;* that's Spock, that's the Vulcan.

Shatner had no such refuge.

And some of the scripts were bone-crushers, particularly for him.

If he had to play a dual role or a Kirk under the influence of some strange effect—virus, spores, possession by another consciousness—it had to be done yesterday. If he had to play a woman in his body—it had to be right, or Kirk, and Shatner, would look the fool, or worse, in front of the galaxy.

We spoke to him, and later to Leonard, of "Plato's Stepchildren"—possibly one of the most powerful episodes in STAR TREK. It is hated, and loved. Sometimes by the same people. The theme is the corruption of absolute power—the underlying menace of the Platonian idea of philosopher kings of unrestrained power. The Platonians use their psychokinetic power to torture and humiliate Kirk and Spock. Kirk and Spock's feeling for each other is used against them as they witness each other's humiliation and danger. Spock is almost forced to smash Kirk's face with his boot. Later they are forced against their will to kiss Uhura and Chapel, and it is clear that there is more to come, with heavy sexual overtones and implied threats in the torture.

It is a scene which could have taken place nowhere else on film, much less on television at that time—and with difficulty even now.

Shatner's discussion of that episode reveals the risks which were inherent in all the most demanding roles for him in STAR TREK. He knew the cost.

That first scene in "Plato's Stepchildren" of the humiliation of Kirk and Spock—with the dancing and chanting, the unemotional Vulcan forced to laugh and cry, and Kirk being ridden like a horse by the dwarf Alexander—is so strong that some people literally cannot bear to watch it. The impulse at the beginning, when Kirk and Spock are moved in a dance and made to chant "I'm Tweedledum, he's Tweedledee," is almost to laughter—the kind that is a substitute for hysteria. It is so simply and eloquently horrible that the viewer cannot quite take it in. By the end of the scene, when Spock collapses in a heap, the audience is in approximately the same condition.

But it would have taken only a gnat's fraction of being off in the acting to make it merely grotesque, laughable, absurd—horrible in *that* way.

'The themes of that show were so powerful—you could hardly believe that *that* got on television in the 1960's. How did it feel, doing that humiliation scene? crawling on your stomach, saying that quote to the philosopher king—"Being your slave. . .to wait upon the hours and times of your desire. . ." Spock almost killed you. The dwarf—riding you. What'd it *feel* like to do that?'

"Well, you know, doing these kinds of things—that and the girl occupying the body and all the double-character shows—required such quick—such quick decisions about what to do—that it required courage to go out and do something like that and not look like a complete idiot. I remember thinking I want to play the horse—I thought, I hope what I'm doing, trying to appear a horse, and not like some idiot, is going to really appear like a horse—and not like a horse's ass. It required courage to go out and do that and to let yourself be free enough to travel that narrow edge between laughter and lucidity."

Shatner had that courage, and it was one of the components of Kirk shock. People could sense behind the Captain a man who had an equivalent kind of courage in his own field.

It was one of the things which made Kirk's emotional openness acceptable, and effective. A man who was less a man would have slipped over that line into being laughable. There *were* people who told him he was playing it too broadly. There were people who have since been deeply moved by the character of Kirk who did not quite know what to make of him—or even were quite critical of him at the time. There are some—although the questionnaire indicates a vanishingly small number now—who still are critical.

In the end, people could accept Kirk because there was a reality to him.

Shatner *was* master of difficult and dangerous physical skills, *was* adventurous, exploratory, constantly testing himself.

He was, like Kirk, a rising star and "Intergalactic Golden Boy," as that *TV Guide* article called Shatner. As Kirk was the youngest starship captain, so Shatner had been the rising most promising young actor. But, as for Kirk, not everything had been roses—a somewhat different crop of thorns perhaps, but not fundamentally so different. A certain loneliness, a quest for love and friendship—a rejection here, a decision there. A loss of love. A need to keep on keeping on. Kirk did it. So did Shatner.

In all of those ways, and more, Shatner was, in fact, very much like Kirk. If he had not been, it would not have worked.

The questionnaire shows that of all the characters in STAR TREK, Kirk's was the one which more people understood better and valued more as time went on. That in itself is perhaps the greatest tribute to Shatner's skill, and to what people believed they saw in the man behind the role.

Some other actor could doubtless have walked through the part of some kind of starship captain—a much more conventional one. But it could not have come off with the reality factor of Kirk if there had not been an authentic raw courage in the man behind him—and a formidable man on many levels.

But there was a further level at which Shatner was operating and which was responsible for much of the character of Kirk.

It was the level at which Shatner assumed responsibility for everything which went on on that show.

No actor is expected to do that, of course.

It can be dangerous. It is much safer merely to read the line as written, to do as you are told. Then if something goes wrong, it isn't your fault.

The only trouble with that is that there isn't a bone in Shatner which is built that way. We heard the stories about it—not from him.

It would slip out without prompting.

We'd be asking Nichelle about anything on the set Bill was involved with that was funny, as in the infamous STAR TREK "blooper" reel.

Nichelle Nichols:

"Everything that happened on the set Bill was involved with——that was funny or not funny. If it wasn't
right, or if he wasn't bringing Captain Kirk to that
scene, he would stop the scene so it couldn't be a take.
I used to get mad at him, until I really realized what he
was doing. Or, if it could almost be a take and we were
under heavy time pressure, he would go ahead. Time
constraint, he'd do it. But he would say, 'I want to do
that scene again.'

"And most of the times he had complete cooperation
with the directors, because they totally trusted him and
respected him artistically.

"And so did I. We all did.

"And if he had to, he'd argue, fight, whatever. If he
didn't think something was *right*—script, acting, his performance, anybody's, he just didn't want to let it go
down. And most of the time he would find a way."

We heard from several people how much Shatner was
involved in what was essentially a writing function or a
directing function——the script, the scene, how it should
be set up:

De Kelley:

"If he disagreed with how a director was setting up a
scene, Bill would say how he felt it should be done. Usually it resolved itself. And as the star and as Bill, he often
got his way. We all wound up doing things I don't think
happened on any other show. We'd stand up to anybody
for what we thought was right for the characters, right
for the show. Bill would say, 'I think we ought to do so
and so, I think this ought to be your line, De, and not
mine.' And Leonard or I would do the same. We'd *give*
each other lines. Actors don't *like* to give lines away. But
we *did.* We did it for the show. But that's what *made* the
show."

It was, and they were, in fact, all involved in that kind
of thing at one time or another. We heard a number of
stories of major changes Bill had made in scripts—in-

cluding some of the classic ones.

James Doohan:

"In the third year Gene had backed his word not to produce actively unless STAR TREK was given a decent time slot. It was given the destruct-slot "10:00 P.M." which was a major factor in the show's demise.

"In the third year, Bill held the show together.

"The kinds of statements STAR TREK was making, the effect it had on the world—I think Bill was *very* important to that, especially in the third year when Gene let the third year go.

"By that time Bill had the power to change things in the scripts. Some of the scripts were really not that good, and when a script wasn't up to snuff, Bill said, 'Come on, we have to do so and so, and so and so.' He did have the power. Leonard, too. But Leonard was more interested in the character of Spock. I think Bill was more interested in the *series*.

"Bill was fighting for the whole thing, his ability to fight fought for the *show*. None of the rest of us, because we didn't have the power, could possibly have done what Bill did for STAR TREK."

It is probably not so much that Bill is being shellmouth Shatner about that, as that he just regarded that as *normal*.

It is not, however, normal.

There is another aspect to the kind of thing which Shatner does as the "normal"—which everyone notices from the beginning—and which sneaks up on 'em as a kind of double-whammy.

The humor.

Everybody who has gone to STAR TREK conventions has seen it in the "blooper" reels—out-takes and put-ons from the filming of the series. The humor spins off the top of Bill's head with apparent effortlessness. It is there almost all of the time when he is "on"—and he is "on" almost all of the time, while he's working, even when he is allegedly "off." The camera may not be rolling, but if he is working, he is probably keeping up a steady stream of one-liners, puns, put-ons, stories, whatever.

Yet all of that can drop away to quietness with one or two people and to only the faintest glint of humor in his eyes.

He is doing it partly because he enjoys it. But he's doing it partly for a purpose. If you look at the process closely, you can see that he's carrying people along, keeping them loose, drawing the best out of them.

And occasionally driving them up the wall.

De Kelley:

"Bill has a knack. He'll do these quiet, silly things. Say something the director doesn't hear. And then Bill knows he's *got* me. I'm broken up, already. And then he looks at you with that funny face, like 'What's wrong with *you?*' *He's* the guy who created—The director says, 'Come on, De, let's go. Can't stand here laughing all day,' and Bill's saying, 'That's right, for God's sakes, De.' One day I remember *vividly*—it got so bad, he was going to feed me lines from off-camera for my closeup. I said,"Don't let him do it." The director said, "Okay, Bill why don't you just go wait in your dressing room—" I was laughing so hard. They had to *drag* him—he was making a big thing of it—they're shoving him off and he's saying 'What did I *do?* What did I *do?'* "

What he did was to keep people laughing so hard that they barely noticed that a lot of good work was getting done, with a minimum of friction. It looks effortless. Who, me? What did I *do?*

De Kelley:

"He's never been used properly in *comedy*. A tiny bit, in STAR TREK. But he would have been and would be a tremendous *comedian*. Things like Jack Lemmon did, 'cause Bill has a tremendous sense of humor and a wit which translates beautifully onto the screen.

But there are times when it is not all that simple, and perhaps it was the bad times also, which allowed

Shatner to give Kirk the qualities which touched everyone.

There are the times when you make a joke, and nobody laughs.

You reach out, and nobody reaches back.

The two key words which, after these years of sorting out their responses, everybody *does* use about Kirk are: strength and vulnerability.

Nichelle said it—in a statement which could be the summation of almost every letter and questionnaire in our files.

Nichelle Nichols:

"What turns people on about Bill? I think, his vulnerability. And the opposite turns them on to Leonard. Leonard has no sense of vulnerability, but every woman wants to get through to him.

"On the other hand, with Bill there's that duality of no-nonsense strength and vulnerability to the human side.

"It's really not even just women. That's an intellectual turn-on for men, too."

We asked: 'Kirk was played as emotionally open long before we ever heard about emotional openness in men. Does that turn you on?'

Nichelle:

"Yes. That's what I was talking about—his vulnerability in alliance with his strength. He had an enormous impact. A shock that the world was ready for. It was okay to cry. You don't have to lose masculinity to be real and open. Bill showed that."

It was part of the impact of Shatner's Kirk that he did not project an unbroken image of perfection and invulnerability.

There *have* been heroes of such stainless-steel virtue that they provide not so much models as monuments to frustration. They never fail, never do anything awkward or wrong or mistaken or dumb or heart-stopping and irretrievable. They have no "enemy within"—no "wolf," no darker side, no passion, no impulse to the forbidden, no fault, no flaw, no temper.

We all know, however, that we are subject to moments of error, dumbness, acute terrors and fears of being laughable, wrong, naked, alone. We know that we do have the enemy within abiding with us always.

And if people see that in Kirk, and yet know that he achieves an authentic greatness, that knowledge can be an enormous liberation. Yes, it is possible, in spite of fault, flaw, or bad moment—even bad year or bad decade.

And if people can see something of the same in the real man, William Shatner, that may possibly be even more important and more liberating.

That is at the root of what people mean when they ask themselves the question: *Is* he Kirk?

They are asking whether there is a reality behind the legend—not a plaster saint, but an authentic man, regardless of fault or flaw, and including any fault or flaw, who has some quality of the heroic and some sense of striving for the best that is in him.

In the end, that question can only be answered by each person who asks it.

What we are doing here is to give some of the raw material from the life of the living man, from which you are free to draw your own conclusions.

It is a part of that raw material that he would give us also the stories of the bad moments—or bad years. And from that, too, you may also draw your conclusions.

There is a story which the man told us which we found perhaps most touching of all—the story of the day when his father died. Later, we were to hear that story also from Leonard—and hear the bottom line on the first time the two men had discussed it since STAR TREK.

And we found that story perhaps the most eloquent comment on what the two diverse men were and are—and how they were together in a real universe, where things are not always perfect, but the striving continues. . .

Bill told it without interruption, in the soft, flat voice of the crucible years.

"I got the news about noon, and I fought back my grief. There was a late flight—he died in Miami—which I was going to take. It left me from noon to nine to fill. And things weren't going too well at home. I realized that driving home wasn't going to be of any value. As I went back to the makeup room to take my makeup off, 'cause they were going to stop shooting, I suddenly realized that the best thing I could do was to keep on working. So I stopped and yelled to the production man, 'Wait a minute, don't cut it. I think I want to go on.' And there was a brief moment of, 'You don't have to.' And I said, 'No, I just want to go on.'

"We had been preparing a long scene, a three or four page scene in which I was addressing the troops about something. (The script was "Devil in the Dark"—the scene where Kirk sends men to search for the monstrous Horta.) And I knew it, cold. I had everything down that I wanted to do with it, and we were ready to shoot it when I'd gotten the phone call. We went back and I started to remember the scene—and I couldn't *remember* anything. So I started from scratch again, learning the lines, the script girl feeding me the lines—learning where I had gone. I totally now had blocked out everything that had taken place that morning. It was as if I had amnesia. I had to relearn it. By three or four in the afternoon I was getting it and had gotten back to where I had been in the morning. Meantime, in my peripheral kind of vision, I could see people coming in through the stage door, whispering to each other, and then dashing out, until everybody was on the set.

"The cameraman, Jerry Finnerman—his father had been a great cameraman too, a cinematographer. And during one of the breaks when I was—crying or something—he said, "You know my father died on the set. He was the cinematographer and I was the camera operator. He died in my arms." And *he* was crying. And

Leonard came beside me during this period of time and stood very close to me, very much like—I've seen pictures of musk oxen standing in a circle facing outward to protect the young, or elephants will stand shoulder to shoulder, or whales that will try to protect another sick member by lifting him up. It was as if he was trying to help me with his very physical presence.

"We quit around five or six o'clock and I went home. And *everybody* was crying when we made that scene."

Shatner's voice drops low, and it is plain how deeply he was moved. He could leave it at that, a touching picture, complete in itself, moving, showing a moment of emotional communication which was silent but eloquent.

Most men would stop there, remembering the good moment and leaving themselves looking good. He goes on:

"I left. That was Thursday. Friday I picked up my mother and my—my father's body, and flew to Montreal. We had the funeral that weekend and I came back for Monday morning shooting. And I—tried to overcome what everyone must have been feeling by being—by thinking of being funny, amusing, trying to crack jokes. And in some manner I was not only not funny—I think I hurt Leonard's feelings. He was acting off-screen—it was the story about the Horta—and he was saying something like, "Pain, pain." And I said something like, "Get that man an aspirin." And—nobody laughed. I heard later that Leonard was very hurt by the fact he was trying his best to help, and I was trying to be amusing. Well, of course, later on this was all explained. But at the time I was—crazy."

We might have left out that part of the story, too. But we found that perhaps most important.

Nobody ever said that it had to be easy.

And the response to STAR TREK, Kirk, Shatner shows plainly enough that anyone who has ever had to struggle with the problem of emotional openness and human closeness—if there is anyone who *hasn't*—needs to know that he or she is not alone.

It's worthwhile to know in real life, too, that even if there are moments when the best you can manage is a silent closeness of physical presence, or a leaden moment when nobody laughs, the effort is still worthwhile.

Victory is not easy, but it is possible.

That was the "message" which registered as Kirk shock. And Shatner Shock. Off the scale.

It is one thing to project the dream, and another to try to learn to live the reality.

Shatner has done both—even more in the years since STAR TREK. It has never been easy. Money, fame, the esteem of colleagues, even the self-confidence which can undertake the kinds of risks involved in Kirk do not insulate a man against the hazards of his own mistakes, bad moments, lessons learned too well—nor against the special hazards of a close brush with destiny.

He knows also the hazards of returning to recreate the legendary role. But he has long been prepared to face those hazards.

While **STAR TREK: THE MOTION PICTURE** was still proceeding at warp factor zero, he was saying:

"I tried always to play Kirk close to myself—in the way that I would have wanted to behave if I were in that situation, as if it were real. I played Kirk as I was, and as I would have hoped to be.

"I will play Kirk again as I always have, close to myself. I have grown and he will have grown.

"I'll strive for even more emotional openness, more depth, more subtlety, more communication, more love.

"I've learned—that's really what life is all about."

What the millions who have wished for the re-creation of STAR TREK have learned is that it was *that* which people saw in Kirk and in Shatner.

And, they have been concluding over the years, it was *there*.

Actor's Eye View: One Man's Star Trek

The joyful moments of hysterical fun—the gob-bledegook that was given us to say and the fact that we could barely get our tongues around it, and the fact that it broke us up falling down laughing—all that goes unsaid—and I guess the blooper reel gives everybody some idea of that... What got cut out? Well... W. S.

I felt a tremendous sense of responsibility about the whole show... W. S.

STAR TREK as entertainment, as a show, had a very high standard. It was put there by the management. W. S.

As for the role, the role was perhaps the most challenging leading role on television. I don't think anything had come along or has come since, in terms of what it required the leading actor to do every week, as an actor, which was as demanding as STAR TREK. W. S.

Shatner speaks of STAR TREK as of a first love: a dream, a joy, a delight, a challenge, a memory—an angel, a wench, a witch.

STAR TREK was all of that. An absolute man-killer of a show, magnificent and terrible, demanding a schedule which any of the most responsible people were lucky to survive. Most episodes were shot, start to finish, in six very long days—in which Shatner was the only actor who had to be there all the time. Scripts were often being rewritten and re-directed down to the last second—fairly often by the actors, especially Shatner. The show took its toll of producer, creative people, actors. For the leading actor, particularly one of Shatner's talent and his perfectionism, his inclination to take responsibility for everything he does—and for everything around him—it could easily have been a killer, even literally and physically.

Even physically it was one of the most demanding shows on television for a leading actor, and Shatner played it as a very physical actor. When Kirk "rolled backward over a table like a hero"—it was Shatner. He coped with routine Klingons, gladiator ladies, and demented Vulcans unleashed by a virus or some Vulcanism mostly on his own—and frequently on his knees, his back, and assorted other anatomy.

Psychologically, the demands were worse. They went where no actor has gone before. Lorne Greene and James Arness *knew,* within reason, what kinds of problems Ben Cartwright or Matt Dillon would have to face. And they would plow stoically through it. A stiff upper lip, a touch of compassion, and the smell of gunsmoke would get them through.

They were heroic and effective—some of the best of their breed—in a mold which had been cast long ago.

Shatner's Kirk broke the mold. But even apart from the uniqueness he put into the character—even Kirk's *problems* fit no mold—they didn't *have* to be within reason. There *were no* set patterns for responding to the unknowns he would encounter in where-no-man country. And such patterns as there *were* were probably wrong: gunsmoke. It may be necessary in Dodge City—and sometimes even out on the final frontier of space, but it doesn't work exceedingly well against a Melkotian illusion of the O.K. Corral, and it's irrelevant against a space-going giant amoeba, irreverent and not recommended in the face of gods, goddesses, immortals, androids, Romulan commanders, and T'Pau of Vulcan.

Some other character may have friend, son, brother, or sidekick.

Kirk has a Vulcan.

Somebody may fall in love or out of love.

Kirk may get kidnapped by an alien female who can wrap him around her finger—by main force.

Somebody may develop an inner conflict.

Kirk may be split in two. Duplicated. Taken over by an alien intelligence. Voluntarily. (Sargon.) Involuntarily. (Janice Lester.)

This leading male actor may have to figure out how to play a woman who takes possession of his body and his ship. ("Turnabout Intruder"—which *TV Guide* bills as "a showcase of William Shatner's talents.")

For an actor even to find *some* halfway plausible way to respond to each of these challenges on the shooting schedule of *STAR TREK* would have been more than anyone could expect. To find ways which have withstood the test of time to become a key part of a modern classic—to say nothing of the particular impact of Kirk—was little short of impossible.

Shatner would regard it simply as a job. But he knows what kind of job it was:

'Tell us about how you saw and now see Kirk as a role, STAR TREK as drama. As an actor would you say that the role of Kirk presented unique acting

challenges—a role like Kirk in a setting like STAR
TREK where you might be called upon to play two
halves of yourself, woman in your body, savage
double from the mirror universe, or yourself in all
kinds of strange states and situations?

"That high standard which STAR TREK set as entertainment, as a unique show, was built in by the
management—the studio heads, Herb Solow, Gene
Roddenberry certainly, Gene Coon by leaps and
bounds—far above anybody else, and the story editors, John D.F. Black, D.C.—Dorothy—Fontana.
They were people responsible for the telling of the
story, and in many instances they were able to insert
underlying themes which gave the stories more impact than they would have had if they'd been told
more simply or strictly as entertainment. It was *intended as drama.*

"But we also set ourselves the standard of *being*
entertaining. We couldn't go off and preach a
message to an audience of three people.

"Still the shows did have a kind of message.

"We may not all have been aware of it all of the
time. We were working actors, writers, producers, directors, doing a job. We didn't have twenty-twenty
foresight, although it's a temptation to say that we
did. And sometimes probably we succumb. You
know—we knew all about it since 1966—how important it was—all of that. No. I don't remember it that
way.

"I don't think we spent much time thinking that we
were doing anything spectacularly unusual—but just
once in a while, then and now, you think of some
aspect and it strikes you—Jesus, who ever had to do
that?

"I do think that the role of Kirk has to have been
the most challenging, demanding leading role in
weekly television, hourly television, to have come

along before or since, in terms of what it did require
the leading actor to do every week.

"You've described and I've described the various
and sundry roles that came up, the various and sundry things I had to do. But not only *that*. There were
other problems to be solved. Interrelationship problems—how to deal with one person and another
within the same context and yet to try to differentiate
how you feel about one person as against another.
Moreover, the relationships change, grow like real relationships over the years. They have a past, and a
future.

"Then there is how the actor must deal with the
overwhelming responsibility to convey to the audience that this wasn't a fly-by-night person; this was
a heavyweight man. I've talked to nuclear submarine
commanders, for example, and they are very serious
men who are highly educated and highly trained.
How to do that aboard a spaceship, and yet not appear deadly dull, was another problem, probably
equally as important as the ones to be solved like
"Turnabout Intruder."

"And then to invest all of that with an energy and
a life and a humor—each day—was a difficult problem.

"The problems of the more difficult shows had to
be solved immediately. Television moves so quickly.
We were shooting the episodes in *six days*. And these
are not relatively routine police or western shows. It's
not really "wagon train to the stars." We're dealing
with whole new worlds—new life, new civilizations—
I mean, that prologue wasn't kidding. Some of those
shows also dealt with very basic problems, themes,
ideas. Some were unique problems for an actor. Some
could have easily been total catastrophes.

"And all I had to rely on were my instincts, which
had been honed over the years of a lot of playing in

theaters—audience reactions—and also whatever talents I may have had that were there naturally. That's really all I had to rely on. In some instances some directors helped. The producer helped at times. Gene Coon was an enormous help. But the total effect is one of being alone—and *responsible* for what you are doing—and of committing yourself to a course of action which threads that fine line between buffoonery and entertainment.

"So—those problems did keep me awake at night. And those solutions did require as much thought as I could possibly give them in the limited period of time available. And there comes a time when you go out and do it, right or wrong."

Shatner pauses. It is a theme he has touched before and will again. There is always the walking of that fine line—that, essentially, *is* the wire he walks. It is perhaps, both the attraction and the terror of being an actor. And the slightest hesitation, the slightest error or misstep can turn the look of controlled power and daring into the ludicrous and terrifying look of a drunk act on a high wire—losing the kind of horrified laughter which that always evokes.

And when he says that he felt "a total responsibility for every aspect of *Star Trek*. . ."—he's not just whistling Dixie. He's been there before and since, and he's been there when it was a crusher. He adds, ". . .more so than maybe I needed to. I did that about "Barbary Coast" and practically killed myself. Took me months to recover from "Barbary Coast." I mean physically, literally physically. [Apart from anything else, he broke an ankle on "Barbary Coast"—again doing his own stunts. A horse stepped on it. He was back filming within weeks.] I had to stop working. I'd get out of bed tired. I'd have nine hours sleep and I'd get up—I couldn't *move*. Took me three months. 'Course you've got to listen to your body. One gets older."

Maybe. Doubtless by the calendar. This one doesn't seem to listen too well. More likely one gets the difference between when that kind of total effort and courage pays off, and when it does not. One suspects that he would have been in much the same shape in his mid-twenties if he had failed to pull "Suzie Wong" out of the fire, or later if STAR TREK had turned into "Lost in Space."

In point of fact, it *could* have—for all he could know at the beginning without benefit of 20-20 foresight. And he could not have been in much better shape, at least psychologically, at the beginning of STAR TREK. Little more than a year before his pilot for *Alexander the Great* had failed to sell as a series. His series "For the People", produced by Herb Brodkin, who produced the long-run hit series "The Defenders", [recently Brodkin produced *Holocaust*] was not renewed after 13 weeks opposite "Bonanza". By the television industry, that counts as two failures.

Television doesn't care whether you were opposite "Bonanza" or your producer had last decade's blockbuster hit. The word is: three strikes, you're out.

The next curve anybody threw Bill Shatner was a busted series which already *had* an unsold pilot—and an unprecedented second turn at bat: a chance to make a second pilot.

Was it opportunity knocking? Or—the risk of striking out?, spectacularly, with all the fanfare which greets Casey at the bat—until that moment when there is no joy in Mudville?

It was, in fact, both. And it was Gene Roddenberry calling.

We asked Shatner about his worries about making his third pilot which might not sell. He has said that he could have made as much money in guest shots and films. Why did he go with STAR TREK? Why did STAR TREK go with *him?* What did he think of the first pilot?

"Gene called me in New York. I had just been finishing up 'For the People'. I remember it was sometime in April (1965) 'cause we had just finished the last segment. Gene introduced himself as the producer of 'The Lieutenant', the writer. I had seen a couple of 'Lieutenants' and thought they were quite good. He said that he had made a pilot which hadn't sold, but NBC wanted to go again, and that they, NBC and he, wanted me, and would I be interested, and when would I be back in Los Angeles? I had intended to fly back to L.A. because I had finished shooting, and so I got a plane. Met Gene. And they took me to a screening room and I saw that first pilot.

"And my impression was that the essential thrust of the series was fascinating—that it was badly done in that everybody took themselves too seriously, that they were playing, 'I am the captain of the ship,' and 'I am the communications officer,' and 'I am the second officer,' and all that stuff, instead of being workaday people who were familiar with each other.

"Real people on a team, even a common project, even just a job, have relationships going on—little bits of by-play, in-jokes, memories. They're comfortable with each other, they know each other. The captain wears his authority like a comfortable, well-worn jacket.

"This was: 'look at me—I'm on a starship.' And I think that was—that ponderousness was the thing that mitigated against its selling.

"So I agreed to be in it.

"They started working on the script. And I made some very definite contributions to the script. We tried to get as much lightness into it as possible. Gene and the writer, Sam Peeples ("Where No Man Has Gone Before"), were writing all the time, and the new drafts were coming in and they were giving me the pages to read—which was good of them to do.

"And *everybody* was making contributions—including the head of the studio, Herb Solow. There was a great deal of excitement. It seemed to catch people's imaginations. I mean, creative people often try to contribute to something new, even if it's not their job. Actors write, and so forth. But this was almost as if people were designing the real future. I felt it myself.

"I got involved in the writing, then and later, not in terms of 'I want more for *me*' but in terms of 'I think the script has a problem here. Here's an idea how we could solve it.' Or, 'I don't think this is right. This dialogue isn't right. Could we do this?' Sometimes it worked, sometimes not. Sometimes it sparked somebody to have a better idea.

"I tried to get lines and scenes I could play for lightness, humor—for the heavyweight, wearing-authority-like-an-old-jacket aspect of the character, the down-to-earthness, the relationships with the other people on the ship.

"Spock. By this time, he was my second-in-command, gradually the concept was that he was unemotionally developed. Kirk teases Spock in a way that only the closest kind of friend would be allowed to tease. 'Terrible having bad blood like that.' I mean—they can *tease*—even Spock is teasing back—about the Vulcan-Human difference.

"You had something to *work with* in STAR TREK."

What you had to work with, including the somewhat infamous Shatner sense of humor, sometimes comes out in answer to a straight question.

'STAR TREK tried daring, startling, often sexy themes that would have been possible nowhere else in television—or even films, probably—at the time. Look at the season opener of the second season, "Amok Time" by Theodore Sturgeon—a science fiction classic with a theme that jolted everybody: an intelligent being—Spock, for God's sake—having a letal mating cycle, having to go back home to spawn.'

"Yeah, right. A salmon. My phrase at the time was, 'What makes salmon run?'"

It's a groaner.

Shatner laughs, rather fondly:

"You know, he *was* a Vulcan. I found it an increasing problem from Leonard's point of view—and somewhat to my advantage, that everything Leonard thought of—the neck pinch and so forth—kept giving more invincibility to the character of Spock. Thus the more of a corner he was painting himself into. The less and less jeopardy he could get into.

"And drama *is* jeopardy.

"If there were two men to fight him, he said, in effect, there should be six. Now I don't remember whether Leonard said that exactly or whether a director said that or whether Roddenberry said that. Maybe all three. But you rarely saw Spock fight two men. I mean—there were always a *lot* of men.

"And if he didn't fight them he pinched their nerve and they dropped, like, dead and there was no fight at all.

"And then there was one show where he smashed his hand through the wall, and another where he could put his hands to the building material of a prison and project his mind-touch, get a guard to come where we could grab him.

"Well, if Spock could do that in one show, then in order to keep the continuity—you had to get rid of him to have any jeopardy.

"Like you had to get rid of the ship. The ship was always being immobilized so that we could get into jeopardy. Otherwise the ship could beam us up, fire its cannon, send down a platoon, or whatever—so the whole guise of telling the stories became: get rid of

the ship. I think they even locked it in plastic one time
—you remember, it was a magic show, a nice witch.
I was told, 'The ship can't move.' 'Oh? The ship can't
move?' 'I guess we're stuck.' And then you fight it out
for fifty-three minutes and in the fifty-fourth minute
the plastic "melts" and the ship beams you up.

"Well, Spock got so powerful that to have him
along was like having the ship along. You had to get
rid of Spock.

"So you'll find many shows where Spock gets (he
makes a 'thwonk' sound, with illustrations) on the
head. Okay, that disposes of that. And now we can
get some threat into it. You see?

"And I kept saying—at least, I think I kept saying,
'What are you *doing?*' Why is Spock made so invincible? It's detrimental to everybody. Except *me*—
'cause I have to fight everybody and rescue people."

'Spock the starship—What did they say to that?'

He shakes his head. "I don't remember. But he just
kept on being invincible."

"Leonard's famous comment—if we use this in the
book we've got to characterize it—I say with great
fondness, his classic line to a director when he was
told to do something was: 'A Vulcan wouldn't *do*
that!' That's a classic actor's line. I mean—where else
but STAR TREK?"

We had touched on something of the same thing
with Shatner: Not every captain can have a Vulcan
along to protect him from aliens and androids and
things that go "boomp" in the night.

'Did you miss him when they had to keep writing
him out to get him out of the action? Did you prefer
the interaction? Or did you like it just as well—?'

Shatner laughs. "Does a captain miss his starship?
But—no. You know, along would come a pretty girl
and off I'd go. Sure. It was a nice change. Although
—the captain always comes back to his ship."

'Those girls. Do you think Kirk was promiscuous?'

"Oh, *sure*. I certainly hope so. All those lonely days on the ship."

'Well, he wasn't promiscuous on the *ship*.'

"Oh, no. Those Yeomen weren't yes women," Shatner laughs. "Of course they kept saying he was married to the *ship*—"

'Speaking of not being promiscuous on the ship— what was your feeling about what was between Kirk and Uhura? Say, when you were playing that kiss with her in "Plato's Stepchildren?"'

"Well, I thought that it would be a good idea that Kirk, who was—who liked a lot of women—would be attracted to an obviously attractive woman, but also would hide it under the professional exterior of doing his job. And I think that came out occasionally —a glimpse, a smile, but it had to be—underlying."

'What were you thinking just then?'

"I just smiled." (And on the manuscript in his own handwriting Shatner adds: "—underlying—lying under. Lying under duress." You figure it.)

'We haven't asked your first impression of Nichelle. . .

"Oh, well, Nichelle is delightful. Nichelle is really a great talent—not only what she did in STAR TREK, the acting, but the singing and dancing. She's a professional from way back. And of course she's a gorgeous woman. I was always tantalized by Nichelle."

'It's hard to believe now that the kiss between you and Nichelle on STAR TREK was the *first* interracial kiss on television. But it *was*. And it was a risk for a television show to take. Even for an actor, an actress. This was not today. There *were* the riots and the bombings and the burnings. This was when there had been serious objections to even having Nichelle on the *show*—let alone Spock or the interracial, interstellar crew. Gene fought that battle. But what about that kiss? Were you aware that it was the first interracial kiss?'

"Yeah, they mentioned that. I remember now that they had mentioned that earlier and said, 'Would you mind?' and I said, 'Mind? No, I don't mind.' And then they kind of backed off on it, in that I was being forced to do it. It wasn't Kirk actually kissing Uhura. It was Kirk being forced by some power beyond there —to kiss her.

"So the edge was taken off the first interracial kiss on television by the fact that this guy was going, '. . .uh, argh, not me—*no*'—kiss."

Shatner laughs wryly, shakes his head, as if the thought that he, let alone Kirk, would resist kissing that tantalizing female is an absurdity needing no explanation. And in fact what registered with most people was what amounted to a tender love scene between a man and a woman who loved each other, who could have been and might have been in love, on some level, but who were totally in the power of an evil force.

Still, there was the white male Southerner who wrote in saying *he* damn sure wouldn't have protested that much.

'Did you want to play it that way, or did you want Kirk not to be protesting quite so much?'

"Oh, well—but it was part of the whole story. The story involved Kirk's having to do things against his will. And, of course, Spock, as well. Spock was being forced to kiss Christine Chapel, who was in love with him, and *they* were protesting too. There's a very basic thing going on there, if you think of the reality of what is happening—not only the plain knowledge of what the next step can be—but the bottom line is probably that you can't protect that woman. That's basic. It's biological. If you can't do that, what good are you? And yet, and yet, we all know that we can get into situations where we are powerless even to protect a person we love. That is the essence of terror. And *then* what do you do? Well, Kirk was saying things like, 'Don't let it bother you, it's going to be okay, just go with it, it'll be all right.' And Uhura, knowing what it was doing to him was trying to protect him, too—saying that it *was* going to be all right, no matter what, and she was not afraid. Well, they both were afraid, and had every right to be. But they did what they could—for each other.

"No. I'm well aware that there could have been different ways to write the scene or play it. We did try some variations. There could have been a whole different story, if anybody had wanted to emphasize an interracial love story. But in fact, that wouldn't have made the point as effectively. Kirk and Uhura wouldn't even think of a kiss or a love story as interracial. That would be the *last* thing they would think about. If we did any good with that kiss or anything we did on STAR TREK, it was to push in the direction of not having to think about that. No, I liked that scene. . ."

It was one of those first steps which was taken on the STAR TREK set.

It has become part of the legend of STAR TREK that it was a great set, a happy set, with a magic of its own. *Was* it?

The hard-boiled actor smiles.

"Well, I think it *was* a great set. We were working people, functioning, producing something we liked, which had quality as entertainment. We couldn't anticipate the kind of response it actually got. It would have been crazy to expect that. It had never happened.

"I love STAR TREK as I have loved almost nothing else in my professional life, perhaps nothing else so well and so long. The best way I've found to put it—and I've said it in front of conventions—is that *every day* driving to work, with such rare exceptions that I can't even remember them, I was *happy*. And *you* know that that was in spite of what was going on in my personal life. So you know the enormity of that statement."

'Yes.'

"And of course the people I worked with had a great deal to do with that. There was a great deal of affection and respect. More between some of us than others, of course. Leonard and myself. DeForest. Nichelle. Jimmy. We weren't all there all the time, of course. I was the only one who was there all day every day. Leonard, close to that, then De and so on, until George and Walter and Majel weren't there a great deal of the time.

"I've always felt that the cast had a typical actor's sense of competition. We weren't saints, and we had actor's needs. But it was a good, healthy sense of competition, mostly focused on doing a good job, mostly good for the show.

"I know I felt *great* respect for anyone who was doing an exceptionally good job. I fought for DeForest's billing in the second year, urged them to give him the billing he got, because I felt that he had carved out that spot, was playing essentially the third part, with a special relationship to Spock and to me which he picked up on and amplified—and then the writers picked up on *that* and wrote it into the role. You can see the difference between the first two doctors and him. There was a lot of creative feedback like that. Jimmy Doohan—I believe I was instrumental in getting him his job. I can't remember exactly whether I first suggested his name or they mentioned it to me and asked me if I knew him. But I knew him as a fine actor from Toronto and I had worked with him. I recommended him. Nichelle of course, I've talked about. A great talent and a delight. There was more talent on that set than we could use properly."

'Let's talk about some of the hard times and bad moments on the set.'

"Oddly enough there really weren't that many. There

was the day my father died. That was quite a trauma for everybody.

"But other than that, the stint of hours spent on a television series set is such that your nerves get frayed and your temper is short.

"One day Roddenberry came to me and said, "You know, I've got a complaint from the production manager that you have spent x amount of minutes before you appear on the set when you're called."

"I said, 'What does that come out to, Gene?' 'Something like half an hour.' I said, 'You mean to say over the period of a day I've kept them waiting a half hour?'

"He said, 'Yes, you know, five days a week, that's 2-1/2 hours a week. It mounts up.'

"I said, 'But I'm here *all day,* and nobody else is here all day. I'm the only one that's here all day and there'll be an occasional telephone call. They're going to say, 'You're wanted on the set,' and I'm going to have to say 'Wait a minute.' Or I may have to go to the bathroom.

"And Gene looked at his list and he said, 'You know, you're right.'

"I mean a half an hour a day of the leading actor being delayed in one form or another—on paper it looks —2-1/2 hours a week—we're losing—at $10,000 an hour, we're wasting $25,000 while he goes, you know— But I said, 'I'm only a human being.' I remember that incident and that kind of—that stopped me—that moment.

"The mornings getting ready to go to work were sometimes difficult. Leonard had to have those ears put on and over a period of time it became very painful.

The glue irritated the back of his ears because his ears had to be pinned to the back of his head and glued. So there were times when there was irritability there from everybody concerned. There was one day on that show where I aged, where everybody aged—we were all 90 or something. It took 3 hours to get into that makeup.

Three o'clock in the afternoon we started on the make-up, 6 o'clock I was ready. And the director said, 'Look I don't know how to tell you this, but we've got to stop shooting, the studio's ordered us to stop shooting at 6:12.' or something. So I had spent 3 hours in the makeup chair for absolutely nothing. Took me 20 minutes, you know, half an hour to get out of the makeup. That blew my top.

"But there were some beautiful people on that set. Man who's dead now, his name was George Meyerhoff, was a great gaffer. He could direct people up on catwalks to move their lights and get things organized in the lighting way by whistles. He'd do—wheet, whew, (illustrates) he had a whole set of signals. There was never any (illustrates) 'Hey, move the light and get 'em down.' There was none of that. It was all done with, like sheep-dog whistles. The guys would go '—wheet, whew—oh, yeah, means to the left and down.' And it was really wild. George was either a Ph.D or an M.A. in English. He was a great favorite. And I was at his house for dinner and he was at mine. There was this unspoken hierarchy in the studio on the stage set, you know—again, a mutuality of interest. But George cut through all the barriers. He was an electrician, in effect. But he was a friend of mine. Died"

Shatner's voice is flat. He doesn't speak easily of friends or of death.

We happen to know that there were other people on that set who said, "*He* is the reason why this is such a great set."

He doesn't speak of that. After a moment he talks about the bloopers, "The joyful moments of hysterical fun. . .the gobbledegook that. . .broke us up falling down laughing. . .all that goes unsaid."

Well, not quite.

Those are some of the favorite moments of STAR TREK and its fans, stars, creators. They talk sometimes.

Not everybody is a practicing shellmouth.

'Have you see the blooper?—The way fans see it at conventions?'

"Oh, sure. Saw it when it was supposed to be seen, at the Christmas parties. And a cutdown version at conventions."

'What are some of the parts that got cut out?'

"Well, one of the parts that got cut out was—my habit was every time I'd make a mistake I'd say 'Oh shit.' Well, they put in about, I don't know, five minutes of, 'Oh shit's' in various—"Oh, *shit*. Oh, shit! *Oh,* shit.' " He laughs.

"What else got cut out? There was some stuff with girls—long kisses—where they'd yell "break" and I'd still kiss her. And there was all kinds of fun stuff. It was amusing."

'How did you go about planning some of those? Some of those little put-on scenes for the blooper like the one where you're carried into the cave with an arrow in your groin? Did you do that deliberately to lighten—

"Absolutely. It was just part of that sense of responsibility for the whole show. Could be I took it too seriously. But I couldn't work any other way. It's maybe not too different from the problem which I had as an actor with Kirk—how to play the character without becoming so deadly serious. But still, every week here was the guy who was responsible for 400-odd men and women getting into battle with some monster of the week. And how to play that seriously and yet not deadly was a problem that I faced— You know, keeping people going. You can't just move people by the force of your will. It's been said that with humor people will follow you anywhere."

'There were subtle shapes like that in Kirk—the emotional openness, the caring, the humor, the friendship, the love, the respect for diversity. Where did those come from in *you*—the actor, the man? Such as the respect for diversity, the humor, the friendship? You didn't *have* friendship as you were growing up—and not, really, for a long time. How did you manage to put something into that role that electrifies people, as you did with the friendship of Kirk and Spock and, in a different way, with McCoy. Where did it come from inside of you?

"Well, the loneliness of command is something that is very real. Again I've just recently come back from these atomic submarines and talked to those guys about it, the skippers. As familiar as they are with their crew, I said, what about that—when you're alone? I mean, you can only be so familiar with your executive officers. There comes a point when you come back to this little cubicle — you're really alone, man. You lose your command position if it's, 'Hey Jimmy, what's new?' 'Oh, hello, Mac, what's goin' with you?'—on the bridge of a ship. You can't *have* that. People stop listening to you and in a moment of emergency, they'll question—'*Jim*, don't turn the ship left, Jim, turn it right.' *No!* There's a difference. And the commander of a ship is *alone*—as much as he yearns for touching out—to touch out to another human being—he's alone because of that position. I visualized that in playing the part. And as we've seen, loneliness is not a stranger to me, so I understand where he must have been at, where Kirk must have been at. So —the reaching out and the desire for friendship has got to come from a human emotion. He's alone for so long —every so often—'Please talk to me, let me tell you about something that hurts me'—even for a moment. Almost impossible to do on a star—on that show."

'The humor?'

"Humor—is probably more my own. Humor comes easily to me. I think things are funny. My eyes, when I'm healthy and well—see things through a more humorous light than a more serious. Humor comes easily to me, so that I tried often deliberately either to get the writers to write it that way, or maybe they wrote it that way before

I talked to them, and then to play it as a man who had a great deal of humor. Even—I liked to think that even the monsters—even the monster of the week—was kind of amusing—because it wasn't the *first* time you faced a monster. And so I tried to look at each new week's strange person—alien—through a kind of 'God damn—isn't that the most interesting thing you ever saw?'—attitude, rather than, 'Oh, shit, I hope we can—let's get our phasers out to kill the bugger.' Do you know? That came from me, I think. Because it's much more dramatic to say "Let's get our phasers out."

"So the humor aspect of it is—is, mine, I would say, although there were a lot of funny people."

'Where did the humor come from in you? How did you develop that?'

"I don't know. I don't *know*. My mother is an amusing person. (Chuckles.) My mother will be glad to read this. My mother is probably the source of the humor—she's not a clown, but she's—I think she probably provided me the impetus of trying to be amusing."

'Did your father have any humor?'

"Very little.

"What was the other attitude—? Oh, respect for diversity. Well, that, of course, was part of what I really do believe. I love to see the variations in people and things. I love the variations in skin tones and characteristics, and the slant of the eye and the color of the skin. Diversity is the magic of the world."

On occasion, Shatner will come out with those phrases. When Kirk, on rare occasions, makes one of his small speeches with a touch of philosophy or a touch of poetry, it's not necessarily just in the script.

There are many things which were never in any script —including what is doubtless the essence of why Kirk could become the main focus of the where-no-man themes in the sexual fantasies which STAR TREK sparked.

Spock might have his own "biology—as in reproduction." The others might have a love story or two. But that attitude of "Damn—isn't that the most interesting thing you ever saw?"—which Kirk came by from Shatner with love, gave Kirk no fixed program. He didn't respond only to Dragon Ladies or only to virginal innocents. Bring 'em all on:

An ultimate virgin who had seventeen advanced university degrees—and who ultimately proved to be an android—whom he still declared human, and still loved. . ? (Rayna, "Requiem for Methuselah")

Okay.

An Amazon who could kill him, and very nearly did? (Shana, "The Gamesters of Triskellion.")

Why not?

His great love, Edith Keeler, who could move a world? ("City on the Edge of Forever.")

Women who could move him—by main force—and did?

Worth a try.

Kirk was not a man who could respond only to stereotypes—or only in one way, only if he was in control—or only if he was not. It wasn't the first time he had faced a virgin, or a dragon lady—and there was that touch of slightly impish humor in him, the real appreciation of diversity—in spades—(perhaps occasionally prompted by one story-line too many.) And also there was the heavyweight understanding of a tough universe where things could get very elemental, very fast.

At various times with the actor who played that Captain, we ranged all up and down themes of the revolution—the sexual themes of STAR TREK, their connection or lack of it with some of the revolutions of the decade and with the emerging research into sex fantasies, sexuality, and the basic biological nature of man.

It is perhaps the area in which you would most expect the shellmouth routine.

That wasn't exactly what happened. We asked Shatner about the sexual themes in which Kirk has been involved in STAR TREK.

'Kirk gets into the real where-no-man fantasies. Nobody has ever run into such a nice assortment of amazons, aliens, gladiators, androids who can outthink you or toss you around, Romulan fleet commanders who have you outgunned, queens who kidnap you, ultimate virgins to awaken, women you belong to or who belong to you. Kirk is up against women in command, aliens of different physiology and customs, strong women—let alone being a woman yourself—your mind in the body of a woman. Do some of those themes turn you on, too?'

The shellmouth's eyes laugh. "Um-hmmm: Sure."

'Which?'

"I think *all* of them. (Chuckles.) I didn't find one that repelled me there, that you named."

Which also is not exactly fear of flying.

Especially when you consider that only a handful of years ago, essentially nobody admitted aloud to having fantasies—let alone sexual fantasies—let alone where-no-man fantasies.

The actor doesn't seem to mind. What would be, say, an actor's fantasy for a starship captain? We return for a moment to *Turnabout Intruder.*

'Not only did you have to play a woman in your body, but the premise was that your mind was in the body of the woman. What would have happened, say, if Kirk had not been able to get back—if he had had to *stay* in the body of a woman?'

"Well, I think Kirk is cunning enough to have used the woman's wiles to get his way—the way many women use their bodies and their sex to get their way, to do what they want. I think he would have, at some point, said, 'Okay, I'll just go with it.'"

Which is a pretty revolutionary thought for a very masculine actor, let alone captain—and yet doubtless what Kirk would have done.

STAR TREK fiction written and published since
STAR TREK has often taken such themes or implications and pushed them to their logical conclusions. (e.g.
"The Procrustean Petard" in *Star Trek: The New
Voyages II*, in which that is what Kirk does when faced
with a similar problem. It was written before Shatner
made the statement.)

Privately published STAR TREK fan fiction
circulated in 'fanzines'—fan magazines published for
and by fans—ranges from the nonsexual to the most delicate romantic fantasy to stories which are published or
circulated privately as clearly labeled "adult" material.

As Shatner, the working actor has never even seen
some STAR TREK fiction of the professionally publish-
able variety which goes even more where-no-captain.
We talked with him about one of our other fiction
projects which he saw in manuscript in which Kirk is up
against an alien woman stronger than he is, who has him
in her power:

'Did that turn you on—sexually?'

"Yeah. I thought that would be very interesting."

'What do you think will happen?'

"Well, in that particular case, he was angry. He
wasn't there out of desire. He was—paying something
off, sacrificing himself for Spock or for the world. Well,
that being the case, if he's there ennobling himself and
he's not there by force—then if I were Kirk (he laughs),
I would—relax and enjoy it."

As it turns out, studies are showing that most people
use fantasy—including but not only sexual fantasy—not
only for enjoyment but to reshape their real lives.

Art—especially fiction and drama—is a powerful
source of both sexual and nonsexual themes—of how
we see ourselves, and change ourselves. We see a powerful image of what it can be to be a man, and it is
through fantasy that we ultimately integrate it into our
lives.

Just how vivid the impact of any one dramatic creation can be on a mass society remains open to question. But we know that ideas sweep our world with a startling rapidity—for better or for worse.

One of the ways we know it is through what happened with STAR TREK.

People have wondered whether the man who played Kirk did believe in or care about the kind of things Kirk was projecting. Was it only an acting job? Only words put in his mouth? That was all the contract called for, and it would take nothing away from the character of Kirk or the meaning which people did see in him or in STAR TREK.

We put it to the actor who denies that he or anyone had 20-20 foresight about the birth of a legend—as a "Mission: Impossible" opening:

'What if somebody had put it to you on the STAR TREK set... 'Your mission, should you choose to accept it, is to bring some of the major attitudes you are projecting for some two centuries from now—into actual existence in our world, within a decade...?'

Some of that has, in fact, happened. The black woman with whom he shared the first interracial kiss on television—while there were race riots in the streets—can now go anywhere in the deep South in perfect safety—and be interviewed by Uhura's counterpart: a black woman newscaster who has her own television show in Huntsville, Alabama, the heart of the deep South.

And on seven soundstages in California, the new STAR TREK is struggling to get out in front of its own revolution again. STAR TREK broke dozens of barriers for races, minorities, women—and within five years was itself accused of being "sexist" and "male chauvinist"—an accusation from which it may never have fully recovered.

STAR TREK is certainly not the only cause of these ongoing revolutions—and yet it is almost certainly responsible for some of the changes of attitude which have, in fact, affected individuals, and, therefore, movements. Without preaching and in a form of entertainment which held people glued to their reruns for more than a decade, it presented a world of equality, diversity, logic, courage, openness, love, hope—and a sexy enjoyment of the mere process of being an intelligent being.

But would anyone of the STAR TREK set when it went on the air, September 1966, have taken that Mission Impossible seriously?

Shatner shakes his head definitively:

"Not at all. For us to have said at the beginning of STAR TREK 'that is what is going to happen,' would have been the height of arrogance, not to mention a little crazy. And we didn't feel that. You may hope that what you do will have some cumulative effect. But you cannot *expect* something like that. To say even now how much effect it has had is difficult. Some things you can see objectively—the conventions, the letter campaigns, the naming of the space shuttle ENTERPRISE, the things coming in to you by mail. But if that's the tip—it's still hard to say what kind of iceberg it represents. Other things are tougher to measure. Maybe in a few years, we'll know more. And probably it doesn't matter too much *what* the source is.

"There's something else. If you're also raising the question of how some of us would have *wanted* to change the world, or would want to *now;* how I would—"

'Yes.'

"I do have a thought in that area: Most of the human brain is unused. From that the thought could be extended: the brain is there, waiting to be used in manners that we haven't yet begun to see—toward the kinds of thinking and the kinds of actions that would stop the idiocies you see around you.

"Why is it better for a man in Lebanon to kill another man now, today, than to work out some kind of arrangement? Why is it the Irish are bombing each other with such a bloodthirst as to be bestial? Why is there so much strife when common sense can show you what's to happen? In Africa—I mean, we're about to see a bloodbath. Things are going to happen that are really going to be terrible, unless something is done—and common sense—the use of the *head*—could prevent it and do something else.

"And if I were able to do anything about people, I would point to their heads and say, "There is that large mass sitting on top of your shoulders of which 10% is being used. The rest is lying fallow, waiting for ideas and functions that have not yet been given to it. And that, maybe, is what the next three hundred years will do."

And that, maybe, says what needs to be said about one actor's STAR TREK, and whether he believed in what he was doing.

Shatner:
The Face of Where No Man . . .
The STAR TREK years

(Photo by Del Hayden)

Young actor from Montreal (*Personal*)

Man in the Making . . . (*Personal*)

One of the earliest radio plays: "Making the News."
(*Personal*)

Early Shakespeare (*Personal*)

Hitchiking around the United States (*Personal*)

Early personal publicity photo, while represented by Ashley
Famous Agency

"Youthful male goodness . . ." as Alexei in *The Brothers Karamozov (Permission of MGM)*

The three brothers Karamazov, Shatner with Richard Basehart and Yul Brynner (*Permission of MGM*)

With Brynner, Maria Schell, et. al (*Permission of MGM*)

With Claire Bloom, on screen . . .

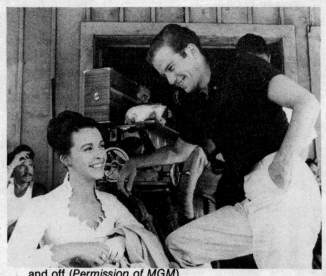

. . . and off (*Permission of MGM*)

As courageous schoolteacher in "The Explosive Generation"
(*Photo credit: "Explosive Generation"* © 1961 Vega
*Productions. Released by United Artists Corporation. All
Rights Reserved.*)

Appearing on "The Ed Sullivan Show" in *The World of Suzie Wong* role, a two-year Broadway hit for which he won the Drama Circle Award as Best Actor. He starred with Frances Nuyen. (*Permission of Sullivan Productions, Inc.*)

Broadway: *A Shot in the Dark* with Julie Harris. (*Photo by Fred Fehl*)

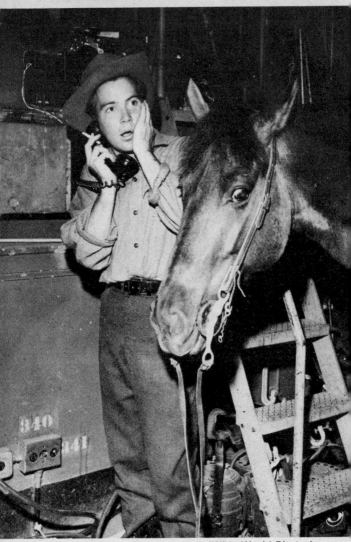

Live TV: Backstage with hayburner (*Wide World Photos*)

In a guest role on "Dr. Kildare," a title role Shatner turned down. (*Photo from the MGM-TV series, "Dr. Kildare," ©1966 Metro Goldwyn Mayer*)

Judgement at Nuremberg with international cast including Spencer Tracy, Maximilian Schell, Richard Widmark, Burt Lancaster, etc. Pictured here with Judy Garland. (*Photo credit: Judgement at Nuremberg copyright ©1961 Roxlom Films, Inc. Released by United Artists Corporation. All Rights Reserved.*)

Personal publicity photo at time of MGM contract.

With Edward G. Robinson in *The Outrage*, also starring Paul Newman and Claire Bloom.

As young clergyman in *The Outrage* (*Permission of MGM*)

"For the People," Shatner's first starring role in a TV series, as an assistant D.A.

Shivering off-camera. Cold-weather gear between takes— otherwise bare-handed in zero temperatures. (*Permission of CBS Entertainment*)

Alexander . . . "a civilizing influence"

Alexander on location, riding Greek bareback style.

Warrior King

Hug

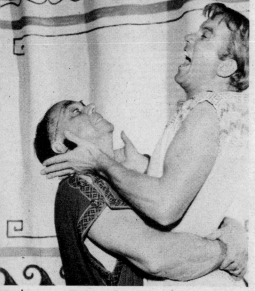

ear hug

And rather more bare . . .

(Alexander © 1964 Paramount Pictures, by permission of
Paramount Pictures)

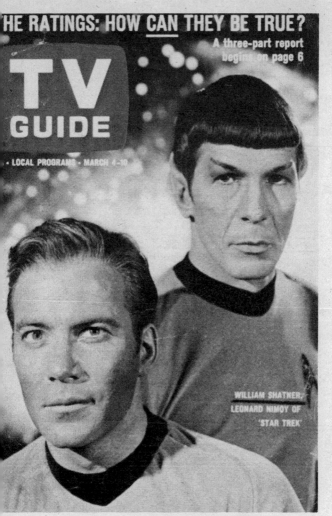

THE RATINGS: HOW CAN THEY BE TRUE?

A three-part report
begins on page 6

TV GUIDE

· LOCAL PROGRAMS · MARCH 4-10 ·

WILLIAM SHATNER,
LEONARD NIMOY OF
'STAR TREK'

ne of the *TV Guide* covers (*Credit: Reprinted with
*rmission from TV Guide® Magazine. Copyright © 1967 by
*iangle Publications, Inc., Radnor, Pennsylvania. Photo and
rmission by George Long and Jack Sheady.)

With car and dog "Morgan" the Doberman he had for 12 years. (Photo by Del Hayden)

arly STAR TREK years (*Personal*)

"Anything done supremely well is an act of sex . . ."
(*personal*)

Working out off set (*Photo by Del Hayden*)

. . . soloed after 8 hours . . . (*Personal*)

In "The Andersonville Trial," winner of the Peabody Award for drama and three Emmy's. Richard Basehart, Jack Cassidy, Cameron Mitchell, director George C. Scott, Shatner. This is also the production on which Shatner met Marcy Lafferty . . . (*Courtesy of KCET/Los Angeles, where the landmark drama was produced.*)

Love Story . . . At the wedding . . . "I looked around . . .
Who's that sobbing? It was—me."
(*Personal*)

Shatners today.

The Legend Lives—at the biggest STAR TREK conventions, Chicago & New York 1975-76. On full-size model of *Enterprise* bridge: left-to-right: James Doohan (Engineer Scott); DeForest Kelley (Dr. McCoy); George Takei (Sulu); Leonard Nimoy (Mr. Spock); William Shatner (Captain Kirk); Michelle Nichols (Uhura).

Shatner appearing at the convention (*Photos by Ann C. Teipen*)

On stage

Star brothers . . . (*Photos by Ann C. Teipen*)

"Barbary Coast" series, with Dennis Cole of pilot.
("Barbary Coast" © 1975 Paramount Pictures, by permission
of Paramount)

With Leonard Nimoy—first time together for publication since STAR TREK. (*Photos by Marshak/Culbreath*)

THE HOUSE ON THE HILL

Marcy Lafferty Shatner

With Bill

In his study overlooking grounds

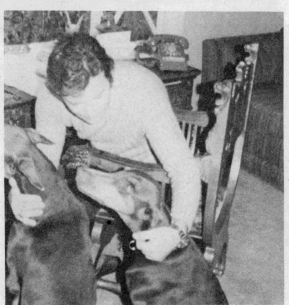

With dogs (*Photos by Marshak/Culbreath*)

House before divorce

" . . . the *way* I wanted a dog"

"Captain Perfect . . ."

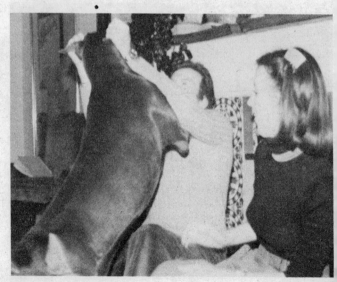

Shatners with Kirk

With Kirk and Heidi   *(Photos by Marshak/Culbreath)*

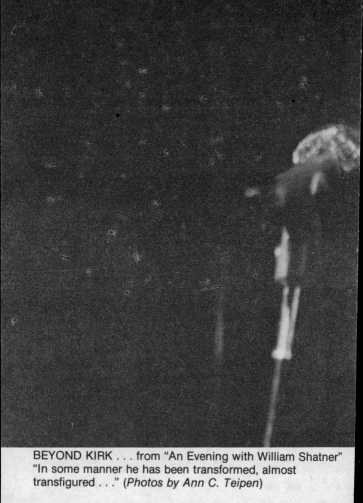

BEYOND KIRK . . . from "An Evening with William Shatner"
"In some manner he has been transformed, almost
transfigured . . ." (*Photos by Ann C. Teipen*)

". . . the face is mobile, alive, glowing . . ." (*Photos by Ann C. Teipen*)

"I was alone, and I was terrified . . ." (*Photos by Ann C. Teipen*)

"This man asks no permission . . ." (*Photos by Ann C. Teipen*)

The Man Who Invented a Universe—
Roddenberry, The Common Ground

On the trail of the man, we went to those who knew him best.

How did the legend see *him?*

There were the people who shared with him three years which were, in themselves, a pressure cooker on a soundstage.

The searing heat at which STAR TREK was produced burns away barriers, shields, reserves, defenses—and any scrap of pretense. Whatever a man *is* sooner or later stands unconcealed and undefended for all to see.

Some inner core of thought, of privacy, of solitary pain, he may, indeed, be able to keep to himself, particularly if it is his native bent to be private. But what he is in his essence will become known. Actions speak. What he is as an actor and a man will become clear in a special way to those who work most closely with him.

It was a pressure cooker. And—it was fun.

It may even have been a kind of Camelot to the stars —if you consider that things got pretty hot at Camelot, too.

Certainly it was not a stuffy Camelot. A belly laugh was part of it, and a giggle. There was a certain lustiness about it—in the stories which it was creating on the screen. Sometimes off. Bold men and fair maidens. (Or was it fair men and bold maidens? Or, as in Uhura's classic answer to ". . .fair maiden," "Sorry, neither.")

We went to those people. Roddenberry, Nimoy, the cast, others. Gene and Leonard—each of them with Bill for the first time for publication since STAR TREK.

It all started with Gene Roddenberry. He invented that universe.

In the beginning the universe, the legend, the fantastic voyages were his.

It will doubtless not remain a mystery to you, if it ever was, where some of the lustiness and sexiness of that Camelot to the stars came from—or some of the humor.

And if you consider getting William Shatner and Gene Roddenberry together in the same room. . . .

It was 1965 when the first pilot of STAR TREK was produced—created and produced by Gene Roddenberry.

Now, more than a decade later, Bill has made an appointment for the three of us to meet with Gene in his office on the Paramount lot—the same offices where STAR TREK had been created. Those offices are haunted now by very lively ghosts. In the flesh. (Bill tells a story on tour and on his one-man-show album WILLIAM SHATNER "LIVE" of taking a nostalgic walk past those offices while doing "Barbary Coast". He heard typing. Looked in. Gene Roddenberry. Typing. "Gene—the show was *cancelled!*")

It is the Tuesday after Gene's triumphant weekend announcement of the renewal of STAR TREK as a television series. (Susan Sackett, Gene's personal assistant and author of *Letters to Star Trek* tells us that the office was besieged with nine hundred phone calls Monday—from actors, agents, technical people. "Don't call us, we'll call you.")

We congratulate Gene on the fight he made. It was an

enormous risk he took to fight the proposed movie script—in fact to fight two proposed story treatments, on the ground that neither one was Star Trek. We had known that neither one was. But Gene did fight, knowing that to protest could kill the movie, which it did. And he could not know that it would lead to a television series revival.

(And, after many vicissitudes, lead back to a major movie.)

He is elated now, of course. We talk about the book, what we are doing with it, what it's about—the man, the actor, the role, the legend. That vision on the bridge of a starship where a black, an oriental, a Vulcan, could love each other—and its Captain could call the Vulcan "brother"—and have the Vulcan agree.

We tell Gene something of our recent interview with Bill and Leonard—touching on the Kirk-Spock relationship, and Nimoy's feeling that Kirk was essential to Spock's life:

'I know you've told us you designed that relationship as "two halves which come together to make a whole." Is that how you still see it?'

Gene:

"Oh, yes. As I've said, I definitely designed it as a love relationship. I think that is what we're all about—love, the effort to reach out to each other. I think that's a lovely thing. Also, dramatically, I designed Kirk and Spock to complete each other, and, in fact, the Kirk, Spock, McCoy triad to be the dramatic embodiment of the parts of one person: logic, emotion, and the balance between them. You cannot have an internal monologue on screen, so that is a way of personifying it, getting it out where it can be seen—that internal debate which we all have within. And, I designed Kirk and Spock, as I told you, as dream images of myself, the two halves. But in terms of the characters, yes. That closeness. Absolutely."

We ask him 'How much of Kirk is in Shatner?'—and he glances at Bill, saying that he thinks it is even more than Bill knew, that what the series camera reveals is *you* —and if Bill had taken another turn he would have been a naval officer, airline pilot—a natural leader with warmth and humor.

It's an interesting observation—especially in the light of the fact that Gene *was* an airline pilot, and military pilot—and a L.A. police sergeant who had gun, would travel, while he wrote scripts for HIGHWAY PATROL, etc., on the side. When he went full-time as a writer and eventually became head writer for "Have Gun, Will Travel", then a producer ("The Lieutenant"), and finally the designer of a universe, his dream-images were coming from some pretty real places.

This dreamer is no Walter Mitty. And his estimate of Shatner as a leader is intriguing.

We ask him the opposite question. 'How much of Shatner is in Kirk?'

He pauses for a long time. "Well, a great deal, obviously. I'm trying to find a way to say it. He took a skeleton and put flesh and skin and contours on it. And the more he played it, the more he became identified in my mind and the writers' minds partly for the living presence of the man who would walk on stage—who was wearing the uniform. Gene laughs. He was wearing the uniform—it *must* be the Captain."

Bill joins in. "I had a drunken interviewer one time during an interview thrust a microphone in my face and say, (he imitates a drunken tone), 'So you think you're Captain Kirk!' I said, you know 'Was there anybody *else?*' "

'Is there anything in Bill which is not in Kirk?'

Gene pauses. "Yes. I suppose so. There'd have to be." He thinks for a moment. "It's not in the area of character flaws or large, dramatic things." He chuckles. "I think Bill tires a little more easily than Captain Kirk."

Pity the poor starship crew which has to keep up with Kirk, in that case. Kirk might find it interesting trying to walk in the actor's shoes.

A dozen people in the course of the interviews—several of them hard-boiled pros—producers, directors—have told us that Bill looks fantastic, lithe, glowing—as in first season STAR TREK, or, some say, better than he ever has. The maturity is there—when it can suppress the imp and the schoolboy—but it is mainly internal.

Roddenberry, back from a short break, and now riding the crest of triumph, looks fit and rested. He looks as if a weight has lifted—after ten years. It has.

'What do you think made Bill go for the part of Kirk after he saw the first pilot?'

"What do I think? I think part of it was the romance. Here's a guy who had played Alexander the Great. To do something in Alexander's vein—I think there are a lot of things that Bill and I share, but I know that's one of the huge areas that Bill shares—the romantic vision. . . What the rest of it was, I don't know. Perhaps some of the things that made me do it." He chuckles. "Other than that, I had financial obligations."

'Are you very fond of Alexander?'

Gene's answer is immediate. "As a matter of fact, I am. I have Mary Renault's new Oxford book—in fact, I'd have everything in the bookstores a few years ago. Passionate admirer of Alexander. Passionate man. When I first heard that Bill had done Alexander, the only—the first thing in my head was—'For God's sake, who *dares* to do this thing that I was saving for myself?'"

'There's a great deal of writing in the STAR TREK movement now which compares the relationship between Alexander and Hephaistion to the relationship between Kirk and Spock—focusing on the closeness of the friendship, the feeling that they would die for one another—'

"Yes," Gene says. "There's certainly some of that with—certainly with love overtones. Deep love. The only difference being, the Greek ideal—we never suggested in the series—physical love between the two. But it's the—we certainly had the feeling the affection was sufficient for that, if that were the particular style in the 23rd Century." (He looks thoughtful.) "That's very interesting. I never thought of that before."

'There are poems, stories, articles, some of them of professional quality, along that theme. Never mind so much the idea you mentioned of physical love, some do see a possibility of that, too. But say what we said earlier about what Leonard said—that Spock would not survive long if Kirk died. Well, look at Alexander. He survived Hephaistion by what—a big three months?'

"Yeah," Gene says.

It's interesting that the legend and reality of Alexander keeps cropping up. It was Bill's model of how he would play Kirk, Leonard spontaneously remembered Bill's playing Alexander. Now Gene has himself brought it up without prompting, not only remembered the role but named the romantic vision of Alexander as the first reason Gene believes Bill wanted to play Kirk—and as a major element of the common ground which Gene and Bill share. That romantic vision of the value of passionate intensity is something few men today—let alone a decade ago—admit.

Roddenberry is one of them. Shatner is another.

We are to ask Susan Sackett later, "How much of Kirk is in Gene Roddenberry?"

Her answer is immediate, "I think that Gene is Kirk too."

Kirk came by that passionate intensity and romantic vision honestly, not only from Shatner, but from Roddenberry. And, even, from Alexander.

Alexander was an explorer to the outermost limits of his world. He marched across all of Asia minor and across almost the whole of India, where no man had gone before. He was a collector of specimens, a scientist tutored by Aristotle, who was recognized as the father of logic, science and rational ethics in the Greek world. Alexander respected and preserved the customs of the peoples he contacted.

STAR TREK has embodied that principle in the "Prime Directive" of non-interference and the philosophy of respect for diversity.

Alexander founded cities, libraries, centers of learning and civilization. He was an unequalled military leader with the fire of both courage and intellect. From his teens he commanded and won impossible campaigns, and was always the first to hurl his own body into the breach. His army worshipped him. He himself was a man of passionate intensity, enduring loyalty, undying love—an open man who stood by anyone he loved in the sight of all the world, or against all the world. His friendship with Hephaistion was lifelong and to the death. Alexander's wife and child did not long survive him.

But Alexander would no doubt find it interesting that he has descendants-in spirit-who are still finding new worlds to explore—in the Twentieth and Twenty-third centuries.

The vision of STAR TREK is also a passionate and lusty and heroic vision in another sense—in a sense of heroic laughter and sexy fantasies and fantastic voyages.

We've spoken with Gene about some of this before—for example in the interview where he first introduced the two of us to each other a few years ago.

A lot of space has gone under the warp drive since then. We return to an expanded question:

'We get tons of mail showing that people's response to the sexual themes of STAR TREK is very powerful. We think STAR TREK is an absolute gold-mine of sex material, including many of the outside-the-square things which now turn out in recent scientific studies to be the subject for sex fantasies: like role reversal for women, women stronger—all those kinds of things which you did. For instance, man in a woman's body. None of that could take place on Earth here and now—and it obviously hit people where they lived. We've been interested in how STAR TREK affected people's sex fantasies and why, or why so strongly.

'We've been following the studies lately which say that almost everybody has these reversal thoughts. Remember when we discussed for the book that the top male fantasy is to rape, and the second top is to *be* raped? With women it's the exact opposite. Top is to be raped, second top is to rape. Now what do you think is going on there? What is the source of the profound sexual impact of STAR TREK?'

Gene looks thoughtful, "That's very interesting. I suppose it would be interesting for me to go back through those STAR TREK stories and work out how many of them would be—in the initial storyline scripts, something that I could see in fantasies, in my own self. It may be that I have very healthy sexual fantasies." He chuckles, looks at Bill, deviling. "I don't remember Bill ever objecting to playing any of them, either."

Bill laughs, giving as good as he gets. "Rapee or rapor?"

"Rapier," Gene says.

'Rapier?'

Gene gives his best look of Vulcan innocence. "A long steel rod—"

'How about rapiest?'

They break up, these two having a moment of looking like schoolboys up to no good.

Gene laughs, then sobers. "No. We are all sexual creatures."

'Do you think that the roots of some of these scripts

might have been in fantasy material? Say, think about
Turnabout Intruder—where did that come from?'

Gene frowns thoughtfully. "I'm not sure. Came out of
some ideas— For myself, now, if you're asking about
my own feelings, I'm capable of an extremely wide range
of sexual fantasizing, because I have—there are no particular do's or don't's. I have no particular list of things
that are normal or abnormal, or anything like that. I
have certain guidelines which I try to guide my life by,
sometimes successfully, sometimes not. But I don't have
any forbidden ground in fantasy. No taboos. I've often
said I'd like to do an X-rated STAR TREK episode. It
would be great fun. There's everything else out there, so
why not?"

'You'd get sixteen zillion dollars.'

Gene chuckles. "I've read some interesting articles
saying that there must be some great whorehouses out in
space."

Bill chimes in instantly: "That's what the black hole
is."

Gene cracks up. Bill is unrepentant. Then Gene goes
on seriously. "And I know enough about myself to
know that these sexual fantasy themes can be very important."

'Were you aware of what a major attraction this sexuality is?'

"No, I wasn't aware. I have become aware over the
years. And I've seen these—seen certain STAR TREK
fan magazines that specialize in that. And I've also seen
the straight magazines, where they almost always destroy the woman who turns to Mr. Spock, or. . ."

'Well, it's a fantastic vehicle for that, because, 'If
women's second top sexual fantasy is to rape men or to
be in control—now how the hell are they supposed to do
that on Earth? Well, women have got a few ideas, but
they're not too practical. So science fiction and especially STAR TREK are a way to visualize it and to fantasize

about it. Never mind what you do with the fantasies.
Many of the episodes on screen deal with role-reversal in
one way or another, and you've seen, or maybe you
haven't, how some of the fans have taken off on that
from the episodes themselves. But how else is a woman
on Earth today, given the physical limitations, supposed
to actualize the *other half of herself*—the half that would
like to be strong enough to be in control? *I* would. Now
how the hell am I supposed to do it?'

They chuckle encouragingly. Some might say insufferably.

Gene says helpfully, "I have a couple of
suggestions. . ."

"A handful. . ." Bill adds sweetly.

'No. I mean, there are various ideas of course that
we've worked out in writing, or that other people have,
for Earth. But one way or another it would usually come
down to restraining the man in some way artificially,
and that's not really what a lot of women would like to
do. They'd want to be able to do it by their own power.
Carry him off to the desert. Why should the other half
have a monopoly?'

"Well," Gene says. "I've heard it said that one of the
best kept secrets of all time is the fact that most coupling
that happens on this planet is initiated by the woman
and set up by the woman. Women have been very adept
at letting men think over the centuries that it has been
their forcefulness and *their* mastery. . ."

"I have a thought," Bill adds. "It's tough to rape a
man, since a man physically is apt to get upset and nervous and not perform—you'd need a man who would
become excited by the thought of being raped—"

Gene cuts in, "Actually, if you look up the definition
of rape in the California Penal Code—you know, as a
young officer I looked up all the dirty sections first. I
still know the numbers. 288a— Then after a while you
get around to burglary, murder."

"That's called penis code," Bill says.

Gene groans. "But the definition of rape is not exclusively force. It is "force or deceit or artifice." So women are really just as guilty of rape constantly as men."

"It's a fascinating theory," Bill says. "It reverses the whole thing completely. There was the zipless —you know—from the Jong book— It's very interesting— There is the opposite existing."

Gene nods. "No, I have been chosen at bars and parties and different places by women. I'm always walking away thinking, 'Wasn't I forceful and clever in the way that I seduced her?' Looking back, I didn't seduce *her*. She picked me to say that she wanted to have love made to me—and 'embraced me by deceit and artifice.' "

'Poor thing!' we commiserate.

And Bill chips in: "That's Artifice Brown and Deceit Jones."

Sigh. 'By the way, what you were talking about— what kind of man would appeal to the other side of women in those fantasies— What the women are interested in is really an alpha male. Totally. No masochism, nothing like that—to actualize the other half of women that is dominant and powerful."

We ask Gene whether he remembers any of the themes or fantasies which didn't make it into STAR TREK.

"Not a lot that you actually went to work on. Most of us who were engaged in making television for a long time were simply not about to go and do any work on something that had no chance. We consider, you know, all of the forbidden areas—no, you can't do it. You really don't work with it and learn to your surprise that the network won't permit a nude woman on the bridge. You know basically what they're going to permit."

'But you got away with some incredible things. For

example, take "Plato's Stepchildren," that overpoweres people, practically chokes them, and it's obvious there that somebody was going to get raped, and we don't know who.'

"Well, you know we did have our disappointments, wanting to make things much more clear. Say, that Apollo had made love to Leslie Parrish and given her a child. . . (in "Who Mourns for Adonais".)"

'I saw an early draft of that script where she has morning sickness.'

"Today we could have done that."

'How about the first interracial kiss on television, between Bill and Nichelle?'

"I was very annoyed by the way it was handled. The fact that anybody had taken out an advertisement—they should have done it and not advertised in *Variety*—'see how brave we are.' "

'They did that? I didn't know that. Who took out an advertisement?'

"I forget who it was. I didn't feel it was worthy of an ad. I felt it was something that should have gone on all the time, and I felt out of camera range on the vessel, it of course *did*. I suppose maybe in this new STAR TREK we will do the first unisex kiss, or something."

That's an outside-the-square thought. It's been a long ten years.

'Many people feel that the implications of "Turnabout Intruder" (the woman in Kirk's body—a script co-written by Roddenberry) are that women do not command Federation Starships and would be regarded as unfit to do so. Janice Lester is portrayed as overly emotional and, even in Kirk's body, she is 'red-faced with hysteria'—and the tag line at the end is to the effect that she would have been all right if she had just accepted being a woman. Now that's a pretty heavy load and it's not what you say and we can't really believe that you mean that. What happened?'

It's not an easy question for him, but he gives the straight answer. "Well, I think there *was* some of that in it. I think we're all prisoners of our backgrounds. Of course I grew up in an era in which women were second class citizens who were expected to become hysterical if any real responsibility was thrown on them. I *know* that's not so, but sometimes, particularly in the sixties, that would sneak through in my writing, even though intellectually I know otherwise.

I think that even though on the one hand, although I wanted the ship 50-50 women, and wanted a woman second-in-command, all those things, that *still* in those years constantly those ideas slipped through—and if they didn't slip through from me, they slipped through in the casting, the directing, or the acting or something else. It's very easy to look back now when sexual equality is becoming more and more broadly accepted and it's easy to forget that in 1966 or '65 when we first started, sexual equality was not a term that was used. Women's lib was a trend that was not heard of."

'We think you *did* that, by the way,' we say.

"What's that?"

'We think that you and STAR TREK are responsible for a tremendous amount of that change in attitude.'

"I think we helped. I do. But we—I had my choice. I could have said to the network if you don't make the ship 50-50 I won't do the series. I think you give as much as you can. Some things you don't give on. And then you try for the rest."

'We think it's very annoying, by the way—and you must find it maddening—to hear people with 20-20 hindsight angrily accuse STAR TREK of male chauvinism. For every Janice Lester or "Captain, I'm frightened" in STAR TREK—there were a dozen women who were competent professionals—or rulers, commanders, and so forth. In effect, you *set* the standards by which people are now criticizing you. If they've now gone even beyond *that*—it comes under the heading,

"It's tough to be a prophet." '

Gene chuckles. "Is that it? It's a nice thought. I like to think that we did help. I'm still a student of the times. But as I say, sometimes attitudes will sneak out when I'm not aware of them. No matter what we believe intellectually, there can still be traces. I notice a black for example, walking into a Beverly Hills hotel more than I do a white. Of course part of that is simply that it's still more unusual. To recognize those things in ourselves is the beginning of being able to deal with them."

It comes to very few men and women to have their attitudes, personalities, dreams, fantasies, even errors immortalized—not in stone but in a living reality which continues to be contemporary and relevant to people a dozen years later.

And it takes a considerable courage to admit to errors immortalized in legend—which you and the legend may have helped the world to move beyond.

The criticism is perhaps the highest compliment people pay STAR TREK. They are saying that it still represents the present—and the future.

That's why people bother to criticize STAR TREK.

That the creators of STAR TREK listen, hear, study, think, change, grow—and are willing to admit it—able to raise a chuckle about it—is a sample of what made it work.

The new STAR TREK reflects, in fact, much of what many of the women's lib critics have wanted—a leaning in the direction of unisex and severity, which many who loved the diversity and beauty of STAR TREK may also criticize. But those are the chances that the creators of a legend take.

That kind of creation—in writing, in acting—requires putting yourself on the line—body, mind, spirit, fantasies, dreams, even errors—and standing naked and undefended for all to see—perhaps frozen in that form for all time.

It is the highest wire of all to walk.

Those who do walk it share a certain kinship, for better or for worse.

Whatever else their diversity, they have that in common, and always will.

We return to the Kirk-Spock relationship, Alexander and Hephaistion, the deep friendship—Why does Gene think people find that so attractive?

"Oh, I think for the same reason that most heterosexual relationships are not so much for the purpose of sex as many of us—many of the people even who are involved in them assume they are. Most of us go through life trying to find someone—trying to *make contact* with some of these strange aliens on this planet. . .on this precipice—seeking some assurance that we are not *alone.* That we are not just "bags of skin." That our consciousness will not just be snuffed out and forgotten—all too soon. Sex is—a great part of sex has nothing to do with the physical—the physical act is not so important—unless it affects the other person—but the real reason for touching a person is just to make this *contact.* To hold each other."

We are exploring, too, the idea that STAR TREK may have reached, consciously or unconsciously, the level of deep instincts and archetypes since explored at the level of science. Has Gene since come in contact, for example with Lionel Tiger's work on male-male bonding among primates and men—especially of long-enduring, often lifelong bonds between two dominant males—based on a personal choice at least as strong, although different, as personal choice in male-female bonding. Could something like that be involved in deep male friendships such as Kirk's and Spock's?

"There's no great surprise to me. Male to male bonding is equally as important as heterosexual bonding. You can see it at a bowling alley, in politics, on television. Also in—"

"John Wayne and Ward Bonding. . ." Bill says.

Gene laughs, then goes on. "I think it's unfortunate if men bond with each other because they're afraid of women. Matter of fact—rarely, rarely, just speaking for myself, do I write with these things so beautifully thought out and articulated. More often I write about needs, hungers, feelings, and dreams and so on, inside myself, I suppose. Except for the fact that we do have marvelous literature. History has been weighing these things together. Sometimes it may come out of that, unconsciously. Everything a writer reads becomes a part of that."

We ask, 'Are you surprised at some of the things that are going on nowadays as a result of some of these movements that STAR TREK was a part of? For example, have you read some of the studies published lately— what women find is the most attractive part of a man's body?'

"I have that. Isn't it in *The Hite Report?*"

'It's in half a dozen other places. Do you know what it is? The rear. We keep getting letters all the time.' This one—would you blush if we really went into that? We get letters like that all the time.'

Bill starts to murmur something inaudible.

'What did you say?'

"I play the part by the seat of my pants."

Everybody laughs. 'Does this astound you? That this is what attracts women?'

"No," Gene says.

'What do you think it means? We're afraid to tell you our theory. It might make him nervous.'

"In the case of Bill? They like to see him leaving."

Bill is laughing. "Going out the *door*—"

"For me it's been the belly-button," Gene says.

Bill picks it up. "See *him* coming—"

'*Two* of them,' we say, in the tone of long suffering.

Bill and Gene chortle.

'The thing they love most about yours, Bill, is, they

love to see you get knocked down in a fight. They say you put it up first, and how inviting it is, and they write stories—(Restraining ourselves.) Okay. Because you've got to go.'

"I've really got to go," Gene says. "I've got two writers working in the next room and I promised them a story editing conference. But boy—I've gotten a lot of ideas from *you*." He laughs.

'You want to use our ideas?'

"I knew it wouldn't be dull, Gene," Bill says.

"They've never been dull."

The same can be said of the two men who share the common ground Gene has defined—and who might also be an essay in diversity.

The same could be said of Bill and Leonard Nimoy.

Grace Lee Whitney put it in an interesting nutshell: "Bill's energy would knock you down. I could always tell which one of the men it was—Bill or Leonard—if someone came up from behind and put an arm around me—'cause Bill would *knock you down*."

Leonard Nimoy would not knock you down. *Out*, possibly but not down. . .

Kirk Meets Spock: The Spark

'Is Kirk essential to Spock? What is the essence of the Kirk-Spock relationship?'

Leonard Nimoy: "There was a line in 'Amok Time' which defined that relationship for me: When Kirk is apparently dead and T'Pau says, 'Live long and prosper, Spock.' And Spock says: 'I shall do neither, for I have killed my captain, and my friend.'

You see that, I think, answers your question. I think Spock was speaking truth.

Leonard Nimoy: "How much of Kirk is in Shatner? I think—all of Kirk is in Shatner."

Leonard Nimoy: "There is that chemistry. I've seen it put in a very specific way, about Martin Scorcese and Robert DeNiro—that they spark each other and they excite each other—intellectually, artistically, whatever.

Bill is the only actor with whom I have that spark, that chemistry—to anything like the extent I have it with him. . .When we step into a scene, I always know—something's going to happen. Just amaz-

*ing. Just amazing the tremendous spark of some
kind that he would set off.*

*You remember, Bill, what used to happen in the
makeup department in the morning. You'd come in.
We'd have these screaming, yelling, laughing discussions. Walk out of there exhausted, exhausted—"*

Bill: *(Laughing.) "The day's over. Right."*

Leonard: *"Exhausted, just totally depleted. You
know—how can I do a day's work? I'm aching from
laughing. Just amazing. Just amazing the kind of
spark that he would set off. And I think, as I really
think about it, the idea of working together again on
STAR TREK—it's that thing that I would look forward to most. That happening again. I have no doubt
in my mind that it would. Amazing spark that I get
from him. . . . ."*

The spark fairly crackles between them.

Nobody would have to name it. You could measure it
with a voltmeter.

There is a quickness of anticipating each other, reading each other—as Nimoy is to say "finding each other"
—which finds them finishing each other's phrases, com-
pressing a page of dialogue into a line, a word, an eyebrow.

It's like a pattern of energy, still there after almost a
decade, and now reweaving itself between them, almost
visibly.

What is perhaps more remarkable is that they barely
notice it. It seems normal to them.

This is the first time these two have come together to
confront the legend which that spark and chemistry
created, the first time they have been together for publication since STAR TREK.

We are at "The Captain's Table"—literally, a restaurant on La Cienega Boulevard, Hollywood, California,

Earth, circa the last quarter of the Twentieth Century.

Bill has set up the luncheon appointment with Leonard Nimoy, and we suppose offhand that it is some touch of the Shatner humor which has chosen "The Captain's Table." Still, it doesn't seem quite like something Bill would do. The alternative, let us admit, does not occur to us.

Bill comes in—there's a moment to discuss our trip to California, plans for the book, his work.

Then there's the familiar resonant voice, sounding a little out of place and time in a prosaic Twentieth Century restaurant.

There's some discussion of where Leonard Nimoy will sit. He resolves it—reaching into the booth to put an arm half around Bill's shoulders, and bumping him over with a hip. "I want to sit *here,* by my Captain."

His captain looks a little startled—and quickly bumps over, making room. Not that he has much choice about it. They break up laughing.

There's some chit-chat, greetings.

We start to order—but Bill has us trained. We turn to him and ask, 'What's good here?'

"I don't know," Bill says; he turns to Leonard, "What's good here, Leonard?"

"*I* don't know," Leonard says, "I've never *been* here."

"Never *been* here? Then—why did you *pick* this place?" Bill protests.

There's the lift of an eyebrow, the look of insufferable Vulcan innocence: "It's 'The Captain's Table.' You're my *Captain.*"

His Captain looks about ready to hit him—finally breaks up instead.

Vulcans, of course, have no sense of humor.

We admit that we had thought Bill had picked it. But his look is innocent even of having thought about the restaurant's name in that light. "I thought you *knew* the place," he says to the culprit. A captain's lot is not an easy one.

They settle in for a confab, not looking much like Captain and Vulcan. More like two truants. They fall into shop talk—what each has been doing—laced with an occasional anecdote.

It's a pity the tape recorder isn't on, but what is mainly going on, the tape recorder would not catch—the quick sparking back and forth, the exchange of ideas understood almost before they are stated, the humor, the seriousness, the hint of challenge, the chemistry between these two, the spark.

That spark speaks for itself, but also Leonard Nimoy speaks for it. He has come out for Bill's book—can't resist a little teasing along the lines of, "Oh, Captain, my Captain."

But also it becomes very clear that he has a great deal of respect for the actor who played that captain.

The two meet here now after a decade in which both have voyaged into legend. It is a unique legend, and one they uniquely share. The relationship which they created on screen between Kirk and Spock is without precedent. The response to it has been unequalled. The evidence shows that people who responded to STAR TREK overwhelmingly recognize the Kirk-Spock relationship as the essence of what they most love. In our study, 98% characterize it with some word like "essential," "vital," "the heart of STAR TREK."

These two have become increasingly aware of the response to those roles. Yet they have remained two real men, with their own real lives. They are, and are not, Kirk and Spock—meeting here now to confront their legend, together.

For more than a decade millions have speculated about the reality behind the legend. Who are these two real men? What are they like? What are they like with each other?

There's a kind of calm certainty about Leonard Nimoy in certain moments and certain moods—particularly when he talks about STAR TREK—a certainty which is very attractive, very striking—and very much like Spock. Perhaps it is a kind of gift from Spock, or to Spock. The man who could think for Spock learned a great deal in the process, taught Spock a great deal, and —we are to hear this afternoon—both the actor and the Vulcan learned a great deal from and about a certain Human—captain or actor.

We've come to interview—all four: the real men and the men who are almost more real than reality. Nimoy and Spock. Shatner and Kirk.

Nimoy knows Shatner as an actor with the intensity which could only come from the depth of involvement which they both had in the three years of STAR TREK. They depended on each other for their professional lives almost as much as Kirk and Spock depended on each other for survival.

If either of them had failed to find himself in his own role, if they had failed to find each other, the electric— and electrifying—spark of the Kirk-Spock relationship would never have jumped the gap to create a legend.

Yet it would be easy not to *know* that. Only two first rate pros would know that in their bones.

We've heard it about Nimoy from Shatner and about Shatner from Nimoy.

It is not the same as seeing them together.

* * *

We explain to Leonard that the book is about Shatner, his life, his work, including STAR TREK, and about Kirk—the role, the character, its impact:

'For example we believe that STAR TREK has had a profound impact on many of the revolutions of the last decade. We think that the way Bill played Kirk, as a very masculine man who was able and willing to express his emotions, may have had an important effect on those revolutions—particularly set against the contrast of Spock, and with the relationship between the two char- acters—the star-spanning, legendary friendship. Most people who love STAR TREK see that relationship as developing over the years like a real friendship, from the first season when Spock contended that he had no emotions and it was merely loyalty to a commander, to "Amok Time" when Kirk risked his career and his life for Spock, to third season when Spock risked the ship and interstellar war with the Tholians for Kirk. That friendship has had a profound effect. How do you think that developed? How were you both projecting that?'

Leonard repeats it to himself thoughtfully. "How did that develop. . ?"

'In all our research this is one of the elemental, essential elements of STAR TREK. The relationship between the two of you. Without it there would be no STAR TREK.'

"Yes," Leonard says.

"How did it develop?" Bill says. "You want him to—"

"Great question!" Leonard breaks in.

Bill continues. "—Want him to fictionalize? You want him to—rhapsodize—"

Leonard: "Harmonize?"

Bill: "Or subsidize—"

Leonard: "Do you want me to fictionalize? Or no?"

'Do whatever you want—'

"Okay." Leonard says, "I'll tell you a story. When we did the pilot, 'Where No Man Has Gone Before,' there was a scene where for me the relationship came into focus.

"There was the scene where Bill as the captain was dealing with the fact that a friend of his was becoming a menace—the Gary Lockwood character. And I said to him something about—He's developing this power at an enormous rate of speed, and if something isn't done about it, he'll take over the ship, destroy the ship, whatever.

"And it was in that scene—Kirk's vulnerability, his

dilemma, his ambivalence about what to do, about how to deal with this friend of his who was a menace, that I sensed the beginnings of an insight on what the relationship would be—the humanity that he represented in that scene.

"Does that answer your question?"

Bill cuts in, teasing, "Not as fully as you're capable of doing."

Leonard laughs. "In another hour?"

"Right."

"No," Leonard says seriously. "I really mean it. I thought that that was the key scene in that script for our relationship. That was where it started to—where I sensed how it could go. That there was a human being stuck on the point of a pin, at a point of decision, needing to try to work it through. And all I could do was advise him and say, 'Hey, look, you do what you decide to do, but as I see it from a "non-emotional"—quote— you know, ' "unemotional" point of view, I understand your problem, but this is a menace.' "

'It was a very crucial scene,' we add. 'You were pretty tough about it, too—as if you were old friends of long standing and you could tell him, "You really have a problem here, and here's what you *should* do." Then you reacted to that, Bill, to decide what you *could* do.'

In fact, Leonard Nimoy has pinpointed the scene in the second pilot which *does* electrify fans and which set the tone for the whole relationship. He says about it the very things which people respond to most—Kirk's vulnerability and humanity, and how Spock deals with it. That speaks volumes for Nimoy's understanding of the roles, the characters, the relationship—what makes it all tick.

But it is no surprise. Nimoy had demonstrated that level of analysis before—in the nine hours of conversation and interviews for *Star Trek Lives*. This is a formidable mind and talent—with a great love and understanding of what he and others were doing.

We ask him now, 'How much of Kirk is in Shatner, would you say, Leonard?'

"How much of Kirk is in Shatner? How much of Kirk is *in* Shatner?"

He pauses to mull the question, obviously pleased that it makes him think. You can see all the logic circuits clicking, instantly. Then his face lights with a kind of delight—pleased to be able to give the answer:

"I would say: *All* of Kirk is in Shatner. I don't know any elements of Kirk that are *not* in Shatner. Could *you* give me an example of something that is in Kirk that you think is not in Shatner? I think it's all there. *It's all there.*"

How about the other way—'How much of Shatner is in Kirk?'

It's the point at which he says—in much the tone of Spock—"That's interesting, *interesting.*"—and that he was about to say that there was *more humanity* in Shatner than in Kirk.

"So maybe the answer is the same as the previous question. I think there's a degree of balance, a question of the emphasis on certain characteristics from time to time. But thinking back over the entire three year span —probably the things that I see in *you*, Bill, were actually tapped at one time or another and used in the character—but perhaps not in the degree in which they actually exist in Bill.

"You understand what I mean? I mean, Bill doesn't go around commanding La Cienega Boulevard. You know." He laughs, strikes an imitation. " 'All right, the captain's here—' "

Bill chimes in, also imitating the captain. "I have Fairfax under control—"

"Whereas the character called for him to be a command figure all of the time and everything that he had to deal with as the character was affected by that—all de-

cisions, all attitudes, all—whatever—moments, had to
be affected by the fact that he was in a command position.

"Bill Shatner is not that command figure in that he
doesn't operate an *Enterprise*. So there's a question of
degree. But I think probably pretty much all of his personality was used in the character."

Almost without pause Leonard turns to Bill. "Provocative questions."

"Yeah. Well, they're *good*. Hold on a second. Just let
me make sure that I've got this." The Captain is suddenly very busy with the tape recorder. The actor's face is
not to be read. But it is not every day that an actor, or
a man, receives that kind of matter-of-fact tribute from
the one man who would know best—and who has the
generosity to say it.

Leonard visibly settles in to enjoy the interview.

'What do you think Spock likes particularly in Kirk?'

There's not an instant's hesitation.

"The decency." Nimoy's voice is loaded with intensity. "*Decency. Morality.* The sense of the struggle to do
the right thing—to serve all of the masters he has to
serve. And that struggle—from a Vulcan point of view
that struggle is interesting, because a Vulcan might not
necessarily see the problem from all the facets that the
human Captain Kirk would. There are certain facets
that the Vulcan would automatically eliminate. Spock
would say—

" 'That has no bearing on this case. It's not a logical
factor in this sequence of events that lead to the
decision.' "

The transformation is startling. For that moment it
was *Spock* who spoke—to the last tone and gesture.
Leonard does it, barely thinking about it, as if he summons a presence. Then, as suddenly, it is Leonard again.

"But I think, accepting the fact that Kirk *is* human,
then Spock would tend to admire the fact that he strug-

gles, that Spock sees that internal struggle—which plays back on that first thing I was talking about, that scene from 'Where No Man Has Gone Before'—to have respect for that human struggle to do the right thing. What is *right*.

"A Vulcan might be a little bit more calculating about it.

"But Spock understands the fact that the human has to go through all the various aspects of the case, and the fact that what he is really striving for is not a self-serving decision, but the *right* thing to do.

We say to Bill that there are very few people who have understood fully what Leonard is saying, and yet, whether they have the words for it or not, what he has just been analyzing is what is turning them on.

Leonard chuckles. "Well, let's try to *teach* 'em."

There is something of the teacher in Leonard, as in Spock.

'What do you think Kirk likes in Spock?' we ask him.

But that stops him. "Oh. I don't know. Ask Bill."

'No. We're asking—'

"I really don't know. That would be tough. It'd be speculation. I don't know. Ask Bill."

Bill laughs. "His one-liners."

"One-liners?" Leonard chuckles.

'Come on—have a little conversation, Kirk and Spock.'

"What does Kirk like in Spock?" Leonard begins. "I would say his intelligence, his mastery of his department, control of his department, his—ah—*charm, wit, grace, style. . .*"

We laugh. 'What we would really like is if you would have one of your Leonard talking to Spock or Spock talking to Leonard routines about how Spock thinks Kirk feels about him.'

"Well, if you ask *Spock* the question—"

"I'm *asking* Spock the question.'

"Well, I think the answer would simply be: (In Spock's voice) 'It is unnecessary to pursue that line of reasoning or inquiry.'"

'Oh, he wouldn't get away with *that*. No.'

Leonard says, with relish, "Of *course* he would. Why not? Who's gonna stop him?" He laughs. Bill joins in.

'We'll be here arguing for nine more hours. Do you want that? I ain't movin'.'

Bill says, "You don't have a prayer."

Spock: "I would say, 'That's a typically human need to explore the emotions of a given situation, which only becloud the real issue.'"

Bill: "Which is?"

Leonard: "*I* don't know. Don't confuse me with—"

Bill and Leonard, almost in unison: "Don't confuse me with the real issue."

They break up.

'How would Spock explain his "quite logical concern" for his captain?'

Spock: "Oh, I've explained that many times. It's tough to find a good captain."

'But nobody wants to buy that.'

"It's the truth," Leonard says.

'What do you think Spock makes of Kirk's interesting sexuality? Does he count on it, for example, to help get them out of all the situations when Kirk charmed the ladies out of everything? Do you think Spock is envious in the sense that he'd like to be that way? Do you think he thinks it might hurt the bond between the two of them?'

"I would say from Spock's point of view: (Spock:) 'That's a typical healthy male dealing with the fact that he finds women attractive and they find *him* attractive. He has to work that through. That's part of the Human male—that *kind* of human male who is attractive and attracted to. He has to deal with that. That's what he *does*. That's the way he deals with it. Nothing unusual about that. Nothing remarkable about it. For *him*. I mean, it doesn't happen to McCoy, Sulu, Chekov, Scotty. Not surprising. Interesting. Predictable.' " Spock sounds resigned. Leonard laughs.

'Captain got the girl again.'

"Yeah," Leonard says.

'And again, and again.'

"Yeah."

'Do you think Spock feels any wish that *he* were more like that?'

"Oh, no."

'No? Does he envy Kirk in any way—or wish *he* had that ease with women, rather than the problems he's always having?

"Well—Wait a minute—*What* problems?"

'Well, for example, Leila in "This Side of Paradise—"

" 'This Side of Paradise?' *That's* not a problem," Leonard protests.

' "I *can* love you," Spock says when he finally is under the effect of the spores. Before that he couldn't even *talk* to her.'

Leonard says flatly: "It's not a problem. Spock without the influence of the spores functions the way he wants to—functions the way he *chooses* to. The spores put him in an altered position, where he functions differently because of the spores. But before and after the effect of the spores, he functions the way he chooses to.

'But the essence of that particular story is that the spores released him to express the emotions which he had within him.'

"Well, I dealt with that in the book, *I Am Not Spock*. The point is that what you're saying, the position you're taking is that Spock, if he had the choice would choose to function as he did under the influence of the spores.

'No—'

"Or that he was happiest then. And what I said in the book was that that's not necessarily true. He had some insight into another kind of experience, which was interesting. But that does not necessarily mean that that would be his choice. Given the opportunity, he makes the choice to go the other way. He could, at the end of the show say, I would prefer to be that way, to be in that condition. But he doesn't, does he?"

'Actually, he almost does. He says, "For the first time in my life, I was happy." '

"I wrote about that line, and what I said was that the human assumption would be that that would be a desirable state. Spock is not describing it in a qualitative sense. He's describing it in a descriptive sense. Like you might say, 'For the first time in my life I had a hamburger. For the first time in my life I was happy. For the first time in my life I walked down La Cienega Boulevard. For the first time in my life, I sat down and had lunch at *The Captain's Table.*' It's just a statement of fact of something that he experienced. Humans would automatically say, 'Aw, the poor guy, he can't be happy anymore. He was only happy for that moment.' Spock wasn't feeling sorry for himself when he said that. He isn't saying: (Spock:) 'That's a state of grace that I would like to achieve for the rest of my life.' He's just saying: 'That's interesting. Now I know what Humans mean when they say, "I'm happy." Well, for the first time in my life, I was happy. So, I know, now. It's part of my recorded matter in my head. If somebody says, "Do you know what happiness is?"—Yeah, I think I could say I know what that is. I had that once.' "

Of course, some Vulcan-minded soul may wonder whether being happy is, logically, in quite the same category as eating a hamburger.

But it is an interesting illustration of the distinction which Leonard makes between himself and the separate entity, Spock. It would not occur to Bill to say, "If you ask Kirk." Bill would just answer for Kirk.

We come back to this century and to the subject of Bill Shatner, asking Leonard what he would say if he had to describe his earliest impressions of Bill—and how he felt about Bill in preparing for the second pilot of STAR TREK.

"My earliest impressions of Bill?—Extremely professional, extremely talented, extremely energetic, extremely communicative. I can't give you dates, but shortly before we went into production on the second pilot, I was told he would be the captain. I was very pleased because he had a very fine reputation as an actor and I felt that was a healthy sign about the possibilities. We had worked together briefly once in 'The Man From U.N.C.L.E.' and I was impressed with what I saw him do and the way he approached his work—creativity, energy, stuff—ideas—coming all the time. I was very pleased. I felt relaxed. Because you don't know what you're going to run into. They say, well, we're going to have a new captain. Well, that's just like the crew of the ship, in reality—the crew of *any* ship told they're going to have a new captain. There'd be some apprehension. What's he going to be like? Who's he gonna be? Does he know how to *do* it?"

We mention the contributions both of them have made to the characters—script ideas, bits of business, Leonard's invention of the Vulcan neck pinch, the paired fingers Vulcan greeting sign, etc. and ask what Leonard remembers of things they may have worked on together as a contribution to STAR TREK.

"I think to answer the question in terms of a specific, or to try to, would be to belittle the whole overall thing that happened, and should happen, between two actors who can sense each other. The most important thing was that we could sense each other—that I could see what he was trying to accomplish in a scene and find my place in the scene as a result of that. Because his concepts were

clear, his attack on a scene was clear—you can see what
he was trying to do; you can see what territory he's
carved out for the scene in which the scene shall function; you can see the attack or the area of the scene that
he feels *he* will function in, and then if that's clear, you
can begin to relate to that, feed off of it, use it, feed
back, if possible—pass it on—give him something else of
yours that he can use in doing what he's doing.

"I think that has to happen between two actors. It's
like an unspoken tennis match when there's a very good
volley going on. But it's all mental. It may be totally
unspoken. But the fact that we do, I think, have that
kind of an awareness of what each other is trying to
accomplish in a scene is extremely helpful. And it
doesn't necessarily boil down to a specific incident. It's
a constant, ongoing process, every moment, from the
first time you say the words on a given scene and hear
him say his words. The communication starts to work
and the exchange starts to work—the pace, the style,
and attitude of the scene. And that makes it much easier
—particularly when Bill is playing the command character. He *should* be setting the pace, so to speak."

Leonard refers back to the first pilot of STAR TREK,
with the captain played by another actor. "It would
have been more difficult with Jeff Hunter to play Spock
successfully, because he did not carve out and design a
scene with his acting as clearly and definitively as Bill
does. It's just a different style of acting— I'm not im-
pugning his talent; I'm talking about style. Hunter's
style was to be more internalized, to be more thoughtful,
to be more vaccilating. And for *me*, dealing with that, it
would have been more difficult to play Spock successfully.

"So—it's an ongoing chemical thing that makes it
work.

"Two very talented musicians can sit down to play a
piece that they both know but have never worked on

together. And it may go very badly. It's just not working. They can't *find* each other. Two other similarly talented musicians knowing the same piece exactly as well can sit down and immediately find each other and find a way to put their puzzle together as the piece progresses —do it in a way, you'd think they'd been working together for years—'cause their chemistry is right."

It was perhaps exactly that immediate chemistry between these two which people saw from the first moment of that second pilot—and which sold STAR TREK.

Spock was the only survivor from the first pilot—where he had been fourth in command and without any visible special relationship to the captain. In the second pilot, there were only these two of what was to become the familiar cast. (Except for George Takei as Sulu, but with a very brief part in that episode.)

It was what sparked across the gap between these two aliens which became the essence of legend.

We ask, though, also for the opposite side—the bad moments.

Leonard's answer is immediate—and the same as Bill's: the first story Bill told us about Leonard Nimoy.

"The toughest moment was when Bill's father died. Tough. Brutal, brutal moment. It's impossible to describe it. It was impossible to deal with it. Just impossible to deal with. Overwhelming. How do you deal with *that?*—It's the kind of thing that can only happen in quite that way, I think, in a TV series—that's an ongoing, long-term, relationship. *Maybe* on a movie when you've been on it with the company for eight, ten, twelve weeks or something like that. But most of the time in our line of work you're involved in short-term relationships. 'Hello, good morning. I'm playing your brother today—or your husband or your lover, or whatever,' you know. Tomorrow we may never see each other. It's all over. But under those circumstances, as involved as we were in the relationship, to have *that* happen—overwhelming experience, overwhelming. And I really felt caught between character response and human response. And—what does *he* need? What does he really want? What would be right for him? What would embarrass him? What would be helpful to him? How do you support him without depriving him of his own way of working it through? You know. Tough. Very tough. Very, very heavy day. Heavy day."

'Bill said it was as if you were supporting him with your very physical presence. You were standing close to him. . .'

"Well, I try to do that. Try to do that. It's interesting you should talk about physical relationships. We were joking before about physical relationships. To me, physical use of space is very important. Position, physical relationship. It's quite different if you're standing in front of the person, as opposed to at his side. There's a kind of underlying primitive quality that can be expressed by physical presence. So—that *is* what I was trying to do."

'That's almost exactly what Bill said—and he said that it was an enormous help to him. Bill, you were saying something about the difficulty of that time, the difficulty of communicating, even with the best of intentions—a time when you thought you had hurt Leonard. Do you want to talk about that?'

Bill tells again for Leonard the story he has told us of returning from burying his father, and trying too hard to lighten the atmosphere.

"Leonard, off camera, was trying so hard to help me, acting, perhaps, with even more passion than before the cameras. And in an effort—I don't know—to relieve the tension—or whatever idiocy touched me at that point, I made a joke. And it was really the wrong thing to do. But it was—I never could recall, *re-call*, that moment again. I wanted to get the words and bring them back and choke on them. But it was just impossible. Do you recall, Leonard?"

"Yeah."

'How did you feel about that? Were you—hurt?'

Leonard hesitates a moment, then makes some decision and says it openly. "Um—yeah." And in a moment: "Yeah. It was painful." Then his tone changes. He looks at Bill. "But I think—It's so wonderful to be able to look back and get a total picture of the whole thing—"

"Yeah. Perspective," Bill interjects. "So that the one moment becomes an incident and—"

"Yeah," Leonard cuts in. "But my feeling is that in perspective, what it said to me was: Bill's *okay*."

Leonard laughs, as if the sudden thought dispels whatever lingers of the hurt. After a minute Bill laughs with him.

"That's funny," he murmurs, but he sounds a little doubtful, as if it still weighs on him, still needs to be recalled.

"It was Gene Coon's script, 'Devil in the Dark', Leonard adds, and it was a scene with the Horta. All that screaming and pain. And we had shot some of that while Bill was away, using a double on his back, and then we were in the process of shooting the stuff where Bill had to be there—we had saved some of the stuff to shoot. He was trying to get back to normal—to go on."

On any other morning, it would probably have *been* normal—just one of the famous Shatner jokes.

'Everyone always emphasizes Bill's humor on the set. Do you remember any of that on the set—jokes, puns, the bloopers that he initiated—the ones that wound up on film, and the ones that didn't? What did you think of his sense of humor?'

"Great sense of humor."

'—And, did it help—?'

"Gene Roddenberry said, and he's probably right, that the two of us deal differently with imagined grievances or moments of trouble, or whatever. Bill may have his blowup and then release through whatever—either

anger or humor, and I tend to burn a long time. And—
I admired that in Bill. I learned a lot from that. I learned
that it was possible to grieve at your own expense or
burn at your own expense for a long period of time in a
masochistic sense, that it was destructive.

"Bill has a very constructive attitude—'Let's get this
over and let's get on with it. Let's do what has to be
done.' Very healthy. Very healthy. I think if I had to say
the one thing that I learned the most from Bill, it would
be that. I found myself—we never talked about this—in
the last five or six years, dealing with situations in a
much more relaxed professional way, where I might
have responded much more emotionally, because I
learned that. That you don't accomplish anything. It
doesn't really improve anything or change anything for
the better in any way if you try to grind through and
sweat through and suffer through and struggle through
every moment—and then retain them all as well. You
know. Having done it—you know—if it calls for grief,
fine, give it some grief, if it calls for anger or whatever,
that's *okay,* but the point is, get it over with, get it done,
get it out. Try to move on. Otherwise these things tend
to burden you, burden you. I find myself dealing with
things, particularly career questions, a lot more easily as
a result of that—seeing that procedure, that technique
or personality approach—in Bill."

That obviously comes as a surprise to Bill Shatner.
It's a remarkable achievement for a man to have
reached, but an even more remarkable statement for one
man to make about another—and about what he has
learned from the other. That Leonard Nimoy is able,
and willing, to make it is a commentary on his own
strength, as well as a tribute to William Shatner. And it
is again almost a textbook statement on the value of
emotional openness.

Bill looks startled. It has doubtless not occurred to
him that Leonard would have learned that from him, or

that it would have changed Leonard's life, affected his way of handling career decisions these many years later. They've never discussed it.

They are both wearing the look of learning things from the process of formulating answers, as if they had been waiting for the questions. It's a look of enjoyment, of swift, clear thought, of delight in looking into their own minds, into themselves. It is some part of the chemistry and spark between these two that that is their constant manner of facing questions which challenge them.

After a moment we go on, asking whether that Shatner sense of humor—creating blooper scenes and so forth—ever drove Leonard crazy.

"Yeah. Once in a while." He laughs. "Yeah. Yeah."

Bill laughs in the tone of quoting " 'Would somebody stop all that laughing on the set?' "

We ask Leonard, 'Did *you* ever say that?'

Leonard laughs. "Prob'ly did."

Bill quotes, " 'There's too much laughing going on around here!' "

Leonard, also quoting, " 'Who's that laughing over there?' You know."

'Did you ever initiate any blooper scenarios yourself?'

Leonard intones dryly, "I have no sense of humor. *You* should know that by now."

'*I* remember the nine hours. What I had in mind—Bill initiated a blooper where, on the film, Spock shoots an arrow and the next scene Bill is being carried into a cave with an arrow in his groin. —You never saw that?'

"Spock shoots an arrow. . ?" Leonard asks.

'They cut it that way.'

"Spock shoots an arrow and what happens?"

'And the next scene in the blooper is Bill being carried by two or four men to a cave with an arrow sticking out of his groin—'

"That wouldn't have any bearing on what *I* did. I

didn't initiate that. It was done by the editors who said, 'Well, we have this piece of footage of Leonard with a bow and arrow. . .' "

"What they're referring to," Bill says, "is one rehearsal that they were going to film, I said, 'Carry me in.' And I put the thing there. I made a joke—not knowing there was going to be any blooper film and I made a gag just for the set. But they were rolling and they used it. That's where people would get the impression that we would initiate a blooper situation. But that was the furthest thing from our minds. It was just a gag that happened to get recorded."

'Did you ever do anything like that—any gag like the one he's talking about?'

Leonard laughs. "Stick an arrow in my groin, do you mean? No."

Leonard asks Bill what else he remembers.

"Well, we were devilish." Bill's eyes remember mischief. "We would have moments. . .What really happened most of the time was that we would break each other up while saying the dialogue. I remember one incident where we both came unglued. I didn't know my lines, and I started muttering the lines. And the guy with the boom kept bringing the mike closer and closer. And we began to joke about the fact that it is actually being recorded and they actually can hear me muttering—'cause I didn't know my lines. But we would break up—"

Leonard cuts in: "I remember one day when the two of us heard that Gene was coming down to the set, and somebody—probably you, I think—said, 'Let's get into a big discussion, argument—' "

"Oh, yeah—" Bill says with relish.

"—about certain nomenclature in the ship, because Gene was complaining we spent too much time on the set—wasted time—discussing, rather than just doing."

"I remember that. That was a great gag."

"I think it *was* Bill's idea, as I recall. You said, 'Let's really get into this thing.' So we did. We played a scene for Gene. We had the assistant director let us know when he was coming in the door and we started and played an improvised scene of Bill and Leonard arguing about is this called a class one ship or a Class-M planet or whatever it was, you know—"

Bill breaks in. "And we got Gene involved in the discussion."

"But he was really—Gene got *very* tense—" (Leonard quotes Gene's tone.) " 'Well, uh, I uh—What's going on here—?' " Leonard laughs. "Yeah. He walked in and we were doing exactly what he had been complaining that we did too often."

"*Marvelous* moment," Bill says.

They laugh together.

Gene tells us the same story on himself: "Finally they said, 'Well we'll leave it up to Gene—and *my eyes glazed over.* I never heard of these things either. I just assumed I *should* have." And Bill says to his face 'We got him so good.' "

After a moment when the waiter comes—(Leonard has coffee, Bill orders tea,) Leonard goes on.

"I remember a story—I don't know if we've ever discussed it. It was a hot summer afternoon—and we had a scene to do, you and I, with some stunt men. It was a fight scene—the two of us fighting off three or four guys, and then dialogue, and—"

Bill remembers. His face lights. "Great moment."

"You must understand," Leonard says to us, "when it gets really hot—there's no air-conditioning on a soundstage—and it's after lunch on a hot afternoon when you've been working since seven a.m.—you get a little sleepy. The electricians who run the big arcs—especially when they're left for twenty minutes or so with nothing to do—up high where it's hot—it's not unusual for them to fall asleep up there. In fact, I think there have been a couple of tragic cases when guys have fallen off.

"Every once in a while you would hear a snore during a scene where some guy up high has fallen asleep. Well we had this scene, Bill and I had a fight with three or four guys and after they're unconscious on the floor, we have some dialogue.

"Well, we staged the fight and laid out all the choreography of who's going to hit who and how they're going to fall and then there's the dialogue. We went for a take. We have the fight and it's working, and there's the guys on the floor. We come together face to face and start this dialogue and in the middle of this I hear—" (He makes a muffled snore.) "I could see the look in Bill's eye that he heard it, too. It was at first indefinable. It wasn't really clear what it was. We continued with the dialogue and —a (snore.)"

Bill is laughing. Leonard continues.

"—and my first thought was, one of the guys up high has fallen asleep. Now I must tell you, you have to understand technically what's happening. If there's noise—an extraneous noise outside of a scene, it won't necessarily ruin the scene—*provided* the noise does not land on a line of dialogue. You can have a truck go by in a silence, there's no problem, they can cut it out or they can subdue it on the board. They cannot separate it from a line of spoken dialogue. So if something happens during a line of dialogue, that means you either have to stop the scene—everybody gets mad—or at least re-do that section of the scene to get that dialogue clean. Now I know *him* well enough to know—and I think he knows *me* well enough to know—we're going to try to time our dialogue—"

Bill chimes in. " 'Cause we don't want to do that scene again. I mean—it was a *tough* fight scene."

"Right. We're trying to time the dialogue—so if this thing happens again it'll happen in a silence."

"So we get into his *rhythm*," Bill laughs.

"Finally finish the scene. We're both, like, on the edge of going—on the edge of going—"

"We exit—and become *unglued* behind the set," Bill finishes.

They're coming a little unglued now. Leonard picks it up between laughs.

"One of the guys—one of the stuntmen—had finished the fight, lands on the floor, and I know, in his mind—"

"He's a dead body." Bill continues.

"—he's through. He can relax. 'They've got some dialogue to play'—and he just went *out*. Fast asleep—and he's right at our feet, snoring on the floor."

"And we're talking about where to go next and who —where the monster is, you know," Bill says.

"Now what do we have to do—?'

'Was it *okay*?' we ask.

The two of them answer in unison—almost insulted. "Oh, *yeah. Yeah.*"

"They printed it," Leonard says, and Bill adds:

"It was such a feat—and there was such general laughter that—I think it was Joe Pevney, I have the impression the director on that one was Pevney, said, 'We've got to print it.' "

There's a slight break in the taping. Leonard goes to make a call. We realize later that he's cancelled his appointment to go on with the interview. It was supposed to be an hour over lunch—turns out to be about four hours.

By the time we turn the tape on we've gotten off on something about the Vietnamese war. Bill is saying, "Leonard was very vocal against it. I remember again being impressed by his sense of commitment and thoughtfulness and intellect. It was this fantastic display of courage and integrity. It was not easy during those years."

'Was he convincing to others? Did he change minds?'

"No, he didn't go out proselytizing. He just said, 'In my opinion, it's an immoral war.' I said, 'What do you mean an immoral war? How can America be in an immoral war? This is America.' He was using the words that became popular five years later. He was always going around doing things like that. He was very impressive."

'I remember when we first met years ago, how I was struck by your involvement in politics, ethics—what Bill is describing.'

Leonard nods, remembering. "Well, I started being active about it, I guess it was early '68—you're right it was just about that time '67-'68. It was after the New Hampshire Primary—probably January 1968. And Eugene McCarthy had done well, and the next day Bobby Kennedy announced his candidacy. I had a feeling that McCarthy had been there first and been vocal about that issue of the war. I felt he deserved some support, so I started campaigning for him—feeling that eventually whichever one carried that particular issue, I would support in the Presidential race. And what happened of course was that we were at the McCarthy party at the Beverly Hills Hotel the night of the California primary, and McCarthy gave his concession speech. Kennedy had won the primary that day. I remember going home and turning on the TV set—I was already conditioning myself with the thought that starting tomorrow I'm working for Bob Kennedy—and finding out that he was killed. Amazing years. Amazing years."

Leonard pauses reflectively, then goes on:

"We went through some very interesting times. I mean us in the show—so intensely *involved.* I've never—I don't know if I will ever have that kind of intense involvement in a piece of work ever again. I would *like* to, but I don't know if it will ever happen. We had that total, intense, really seven-day-a-week commitment.

You couldn't do it on a five day a week basis. There was such an overhang of the effect of a week's work and the preparation for the next week's work. You were really at it seven days a week. *Plus* the war, *plus* the assassinations—Jack Kennedy and Martin Luther King and Bobby Kennedy—*plus* the landing on the moon for the first time and the Vietnamese war. Amazing. And—campus riots—Kent State Massacre. Here we are doing this phenomenally intense piece of work which I think has rightly been described as a piece of work that was dealing with a lot of the questions of the time, so it was magnified for us, on a day to day basis, that we were dealing with these things. Amazing period of time.

'We say STAR TREK helped with those problems. What do you think?'

"Well, I'd like to believe that's true. I don't know that everybody would agree with that. I like to believe it's true. That comes back to the question of why STAR TREK is popular. I very pompously tried to answer that question in the book, and I can't answer that. Except to say that we had imaginative production, talented directors, creative writers and *superb* actors."

Bill laughs.

'Agreed.'

"Really, seriously—you can't answer that," Leonard says.

'Look at something like you were just describing—the riots and the assassinations and so forth. Do you remember telling me how fantastic it felt that you could walk into any ghetto, including Watts in those years of riots—and feel perfectly safe, knowing that they would welcome you as Spock?'

"Well, that was true and still is true," Leonard says. "I still believe that's true. But then, maybe some of it comes from a foolish sense of immortality. I mean, it may be like the great gunfighter who believes that nobody can touch him. Then, when he gets it, the obligatory shot is the shot of the closeup reaction on him in a state of shock: 'How could this happen to *me*?' You know. 'Not *me*?' " Leonard laughs.

" 'Honky Vulcan,' " Bill calls out.

They both laugh. "Yeah," Leonard says. " 'Hey, you guys it's *me*.' So, you know, *that* would be the demise of *that* concept." He sobers. "But—I think there's a lot of truth in it. We were and are hero figures to a lot of people—crossing ethnic lines and crossing racial lines—and that's one of the most pleasing things about the whole thing. I think perhaps the thing that irritates me the most is that every once in a while you get some pompous kid or writer or somebody who says of STAR TREK, 'Well it's great escapist fare for insecure people,' or, 'It's terrific for kids,' or 'It's kooks,' or—you know—in some way tries to limit or brush aside the intense interest or encapsulate it in some way so as to put an easy label on it—which I think is an easy way out of dealing with the fact that it *does* cross or transcend a lot of lines.

"And I think that's a proud thing."

Leonard Nimoy speaks of that pride in a level, clear tone, without apology, and it is clear that that tone and the thought behind it is part of the reason STAR TREK could not be encapsulated.

Both of these men have, in fact, accepted what they have done, and for both of them it is a quiet but proud thing.

What they could not expect was the impact it would have—particularly in the way the world saw the relationship between them—a friendship in which either would risk, or even give, his life for the other. We ask how that relationship developed between the two characters on screen—and whether the real men have ever had or wanted that kind of friendship.

It is Bill who answers first, candidly, that he doesn't have any friends like that, for whom he would lose a great deal. The only people he feels strongly about in that way—life-giving—are his wife and his children. But he would *like* to have—No. He interrupts himself as if reaching deeper. No, perhaps he can't say that for certain, because that would mean another source of responsibility. But to have someone who cares for you that strongly—with no family relationship, no support relationship involved—but just the fact that the other person *cares* for *you*—

He looks into some distance for a moment. "But I've never *had* that, and literally never had time for it to evolve, even some semblance of that kind of relationship."

As for how it developed in the series, they both speak of scripts, writers, the unspoken chemistry and spark.

'It looked as if *you* were doing it—*you* specifically. As Bill said to us once, the script is there. It can be played five thousand different ways.'

"Yeah. Yeah. I don't know. I don't know. I'm not sure that I could give you an—" Leonard shakes his head.

'Even something like the episode you told about where his father died, "Devil in the Dark."'

"Yeah."

'I mean *you,* nice peaceful, calm respect-all-life Spock are about ready to *shoot* that thing to protect Kirk. It's he who has to stop you, keep you from shooting it.'

"Yeah. Yeah."

'Things like that—the intensity on your face and the swallowing whenever Kirk was in danger—*that's* not in the script.'

"Did *I* do that?" Leonard says.

'Oh, yes.'

"Swallowed when Bill was in danger?" He laughs.

"Salivated," Bill chips in.

"I should have done something *useful.*"

"Get it *out,*" Bill says, laughing. "He just let it burn inside."

'Fans catch this all the time—the Adam's apple going—'

Leonard turns serious. "You can't—*I* can't consciously deal with all of that on an intellectual level, a lot of that has to happen just as a result of the condition that you put yourself into, and you hope that a creative process is taking place. If it's a totally intellectual process, I don't think that stuff works. And I've had people say to me, 'You did a little twitch thing with your head, which was so clever of you to do that twitch.'" Nimoy laughs. "I dunno I was doing a twitch—you know what I mean, that kind of stuff that comes back to you—People say, 'Oh, the way you hunched your right shoulder in that moment of terror—' Who's thinking about raising my right shoulder?"

"I was thinking of lowering my left," Bill says.

"Yeah. Right."

'That twitch is good. You did it in *Catlow*, too, and everybody yelled, "Spock!"'

"Jesus," Bill says, rather fervently.

"Did I really? Yeah? Really. Really. I wasn't aware of that."

It's true, of course, that much of any actor's art springs from unconscious or not fully conscious sources. It is what Nimoy has defined to us as "open texture"—leaving room for the actor's own subconscious sensitivities to function, and for the audience to be able to weave its own perceptions into the open texture of the design. Even the opposite intention, to carve out and design every element of a scene which one *can* control consciously, which, we have learned, is more Shatner's style, still inevitably leaves room for the unanticipated to function. And both leave room for that alchemy by which elements of the actor and the man become part of the character, and for that chemistry by which two actors, or characters, find each other.

We ask Leonard about the point a great many fans

have made in their writing, comparing the friendship between Kirk and Spock with the legendary historical friendship between Alexander the Great and Hephaestion, so close that they thought of each other as one.

Leonard turns to Bill. "You *played* Alexander."

"Um-hmm."

"In a pilot. It just came back to me."

"That's right," Bill says.

We tell Leonard the Alexander-Hephaestion story in which the Queen Empress of Persia mistook Hephaestion for Alexander and bowed to Hephaestion. Alexander took no offense and comforted her, saying, "*He* is Alexander, too." Meaning—his friend and he were as one.

Leonard nods, "Yeah."

Gene has said that he's designed the relationship as two halves of a whole, as one unit. Does Leonard feel that way about it?

"Could be. Could be. Could be," Leonard says thoughtfully. "Although—I don't really see Kirk as needing—in a functional sense—as needing Spock. In other words, I don't think Kirk is incomplete without Spock."

'Do you think Spock is incomplete without Kirk?'

"Well, I think Spock needs an environment within which to function, to make himself useful. Kirk is an initiator of action. And therefore, if there's a need either way, I would say that Spock needs to have the initiator in order to be useful in the project that the initiator initiates. I think that Kirk needs a science officer, but not necessarily Spock. He needs a good science officer, to run the ship."

It's an interesting tribute to Kirk, particularly from this source, that Nimoy—or Spock—would see Kirk as complete even without Spock, and Kirk as more essential to Spock than Spock to Kirk.

But, truth to tell, the voice speaking has a certain

Spock-like tone, and it is perhaps even Spock of the first
or second season. It is that tone in which he tried to deny
in 'Amok Time' that he had shown any emotion on finding Kirk alive when he had believed him dead—denying
the radiant smile, Spock's first and last, and the
heartfelt, "Jim!" ("Merely my quite logical loyalty to an
initiator of action—who needs *some* good science officer.")

But there is another level to Spock—and to the man
who played Spock. He's not going to get away with that.

'There are many times when Kirk is utterly dependent
upon Spock's strength, control, logic, efficacy in getting
them out of nine thousand and one different situations.
Do you ever feel this when you are playing Spock? That
Kirk needs Spock? What is the essence of that relationship? *Is* Kirk essential to Spock?'

Leonard becomes very thoughtful. "You know—
there's a line in "Amok Time" which defined the essence of
that relationship for me. That line rang a very strong
bell—it rang a bell with *me*. It sounded like a very
honest line. It's near the end of the show when Kirk is
apparently dead, and T'Pau says to Spock, 'Live long
and prosper, Spock,' and Spock says, 'I shall do neither,
for I have killed my captain and my friend.' You see,
that, I think, answers your question. I think Spock was
speaking truth."

It is a statement which we have since read in a preview
of this book to audiences at STAR TREK conventions.
It invariably draws an ovation. There is one line in all of
STAR TREK which has stood for the essence of the
Kirk-Spock relationship in the minds of those people
who love it.

It is *that* line.

To hear it from Leonard Nimoy and know that it
stands for the essence and the truth for him and for
Spock, those people find deeply moving.

And while Nimoy may regard Kirk as more essential

to Spock, Bill has spoken to us of the Kirk-Spock relationship, and the phrase he used was, "undying love." "Undying love, loyalty, what they would give up for each other, their lives, careers—all of that. Sure." Shatner speaks of it as if it is a matter of course, much as Kirk does. ("He saved my life a dozen times over. Isn't that *worth* a career? He's my *friend*.")

The single historical friendship between Alexander and Hephaestion has been remembered for more than two thousand years. But in any generation it has been known only to a handful of people. This one is known to tens of millions.

How will it fare in a rebirth of the legend? We ask them:

'Given all this, given what you saw several years ago and what you've been getting from the fans in response to the friendship between the two, what will you do about it in the movie? Let's say you're given the bare bones. Will you play it up, the two of you?'

Leonard says, "That's a question that I don't think any actor can deal with intelligently until he reads the material. I think we'll go in with a certain history behind us, of *course*. And a certain concept of who we *are*. But it's the script that's going to offer us choices. The choices come from the material. And within that we may make some conscious decisions—or may unconsciously just proceed and say, 'Hey, we know *exactly* how to *do* this'—just walk in and do it as if we'd never stepped off the stage, as though we'd been doing it all these years. The script may, on the other hand, present certain other problems that we can't anticipate, and we may say, 'Gee, I don't know if these are the same characters. Is this the way we used to relate to each other? You know. I mean, did you used to say things like that to me?'

"But what he's saying," Bill says, "is that we'll go in with the historical facts that have *worked* and that we

wish to play, we'll go *in* with them—and then depending
on the material—"

Bill stops. It will, in fact, have to depend in part on
what they are given. But a key element also comes from
these two actors.

In addition to the response on our questionnaire, another independent study of the *general* public conducted
by sampling techniques and reaching more than one
thousand people was reported by STAR TREK fans in
an ad in the Hollywood trade papers appealing to Paramount:

> 80% of the general public said they would see a
> new STAR TREK movie *if* it had Shatner and
> Nimoy, but only 40% said they would see it if
> either Shatner or Nimoy were not in it. (And many
> added that at most they would see it once, while if
> both were in it most would expect to see it several
> times.)

Both studies are measures of the men and of the
effect of the Kirk-Spock relationship.

Moreover, there is much for these two, especially,
which could go even beyond the legend as established
—genuinely into further realms of where-no-man.

We talk for a while longer—some of the questions
which we also asked Gene. But one of them leads Bill
to describe to Leonard the themes of our novel *The
Price of the Phoenix* which Bill read in manuscript
before it was published. Now he says, talking about
the STAR TREK movie, bogged in script problems,
that that novel should be the movie: "Would make a
hell of a movie". It would be, he says, a chance for
the two of them to play something no two actors have
played before—a deeper level of the friendship which
Leonard has just described as "I shall do neither".

We talk about that, about the movie, the script, the

themes of STAR TREK, and as time begins to run out in the late afternoon, get back to some of the sexual themes of STAR TREK: the amazons, gladiators, Vulcan women, aliens, androids, etc., which have proved a mine of themes for fiction, fantasy, etc. 'Bill has said some, or maybe all of these are—interesting—'

"What I find interesting about this," Leonard says, "is that there must have been something that we did in the series that provokes all these questions—*including* the erotic questions and the pornographic questions. I understand that there's a whole underground literature of Kirk's and Spock's encounters with all kinds of females. In terms of your questions—what you *saw* was what we *did*. That's the best answer I can give you."

We mention a few of the specifics—different episodes, scenes, etc. 'In "Plato's Stepchildren", for example, the sexual themes became almost overpowering. Remarkable that that could be done on television in the sixties.'

"Yeah," Leonard says, "but I was very uncomfortable with that script. The idea was 'Let's put everyone up against his limits—turn Captain Kirk into a crawling individual, make Spock cry...' But I thought it was crudely done. I thought there was a script in first season. "The Naked Time" which did that much more effectively and more sensitively. 'Plato's Stepchildren' was third season. I often *despaired* of scripts in the third season."

'In the last script—the last episode ever filmed, Turnabout Intruder, Kirk was in the body of Janice Lester. A lot of stories have spun off of that. What would happen if a person really could be of the opposite sex?—and so forth. What do you think would have happened if Kirk couldn't get back to his own body? How would Spock feel about that?'

Leonard chuckles. "Well, I haven't fantasized about it." He sobers.

"What is easier for me to deal with on that particular script is the knowledge that the *writer* was making a script in which his goal was to prove, quote, 'That women, although they *claim* equality, cannot really do things as well as, under certain circumstances, as a man— like the command function, for example. And it was a rather chauvinistic, clumsy handling of an interesting question. What he set out to prove was that this lady, given command of the ship, would *blow it*. That's really what the script was *about*. Just that simple. You see."

"Yeah," Bill agrees. "The problems were solved without really—"

Leonard cuts in, nodding "That's what *I* was dealing with when we were shooting that show—the knowledge that that was the *concept*. And I rebelled against the concept. I was uncomfortable doing the whole show because I didn't believe in the concept.

"It's a very interesting *question*. But I think that the script didn't really deal with the question. The script set out to prove a preconceived personal prejudice. Didn't deal with—pretended to deal with the question, but didn't, you see. That's what I was pre-concerned with, primarily concerned with in doing that particular script."

For Nimoy to have been aware of that aspect at that time is extremely unusual. It's the same script— a Roddenberry story—that we ask Gene about and which he now sees as reflecting his errors of the time. The episode is criticized especially now for exactly what Nimoy names: not only does it set out to prove a point, but it does so with loaded dice. The woman who makes the switch is not a woman of Kirk's stature, but a resentful, crazed mass-murderer who steals Kirk's body. What she does can't prove much about the female of the species—unless one takes a very dim view of the nature of the female. Nor is it a test of how a *normal* female would command. A more interesting story could have been written around that question, and some have been.

What is still more interesting, however, is that Nimoy, Shatner, Roddenberry had to try to grapple with those questions *then*. And still do.

Even the extended time is running out in the early evening. . .car keys are brought and Leonard is gathering himself up to go, but still lingering to talk. "What you're asking are very provocative and interesting questions."

He stays for a few minutes for pictures with Bill, still talking ninety to the minute, with the gestures which belong to him or to Spock. Then he takes his leave. Bill thanks him, puts a hand on his shoulder for a moment.

Then he's gone. It's very quiet for a moment—it almost seems darker. It takes a moment to place the sensation—as if the electric spark and flow of current which has crackled for hours around the table has been broken.

But that the spark was there, and can always crackle between these two, is undeniable.

Savage Interlude

*Suddenly all of the veneer of civilization left me. I
saw in my mind's eye myself going toward him like
an animal, like a cat, really, my thumbs toward his
eyes, and—my teeth toward his jugular.*   W.S.

We sit in the heart of civilization, a skyscraper suite in
a famous hotel. Flung down below, the riotious fall colors of Central Park, like a wilderness unaccountably
tamed at the feet of the towers of New York. In the
suite, three civilized beings, writers, actor.

But one of them hunts bear with a bow.

He prowls to a window overlooking the innocent park
—which he knows is jungle by night, sometimes by day.

The world he moves in is sometimes not less jungle.
There is, at times, a wary quality about him. Contained.
Alert.

William Shatner moves back to the chair.

"I know I'm perfectly capable of taking care of myself
on any level. I don't feel inferior, nor do I feel superior.
I just know that I'm here sitting in this chair as you are
in that one, and I just know that we're different—but I
don't make it a better or worse difference," he says.

'But what you have done and what you have accomplished *is* superior to what most people have done.
Getting the education and the training, getting the jobs,
making the career, making your life and what you are.
Having the dream. And there *are* some people who will
hate and envy you for that—as if you were a reproach to
them. I know you've felt this.'

"All the time." The voice of the actor takes on a special stress, as if that has hit a nerve.

'Those people don't have the decent reaction which
would be "How marvelous that you have done this, and
I hope I can do whatever I do to the limit of my capacity. Meanwhile, I wish you well." Instead they are consumed by envy, as if your existence were a threat to
them.'

"Absolutely. That's a very big factor in show business. I'm always aware of it. Actors coming up to me
and saying, 'Hey, Billy, how are you—good to see you.'
Well, that's just the surface. What's lurking underneath
is, *'I want, I want, I want,* I've got to *have.'*

' "How is it that you have worked when I haven't?" '

"Yeah. 'How did you get that job when I didn't?' No
question. And I might feel the same way in their places."

'No you wouldn't. That's not your sense of life.'

"But I don't *know* that. But the thing is that I understand where they're coming from, to use your phrase.

"I know that to want to be an actor—there's a certain
involvement in wanting to be an actor. In the beginning
kids want to be actors because in their amateur days
there's a feeling of camaraderie and lonely people go
there—a stock company, an amateur theatrical group.
And they say, 'Oh, we're going to put a play on together
and you're wonderful and I love you and you make my
costume and you do my makeup and I'll act—and
everybody's together. Everybody loves each other. The
show goes on, the show's over. We'll meet for tea next
week, talk about the reviews.' And everything's great.

And if they're part of an amateur group in a city—that
might go on for years. And there are little envies, little
bitternesses and things like that but there's a coalescing
of people.

"Then they graduate from that into the professional
area and suddenly there are people trying to make a *living*
doing that very thing, and now you're down to
primitive emotions, whereby—you get that job, you've
got my bread, you've got my children's education,
you've got my clothes, you've got my *life*! That means
I've got to give up acting and go back to selling ties—if
you've got my *job*. And now it's the law of the jungle.
It's no longer a club and a place to meet because you're
lonely, as it was when you were an amateur actor. I'm
sure that that's what most people get out of amateur
theatricals."

"Now it's—it's *territorial*. The *part* becomes territorial. You stake out a claim that that part is *your* part and
if you lose the part, you've lost your hunting territory—
and you're *alone,* surrounded, savage.

"This is marvelous, though, this is just occurring to
me as I'm talking to you. But—I loved Ardrey's stuff
about males stamping out a little territory there, fighting
other males off, and the females coming because the
males have a little area.

"So, I mean, look how *basic* that *part* becomes to the
actor or actress who is at that point filled with the same
territorial motives."

'That's a beautiful extension of what Ardrey was
saying. The part becomes the territory. When did you
read the Ardrey books?'

"Well, as soon as I found time after you sent them to
me. I haven't finished the second one yet—*The Territorial Imperative*—but the first one, *African Genesis,* is—
magnificent."

'You see what we're saying?'

"Sure. It's shattering."

'We didn't switch all of a sudden to perfectly civilized urbane beings in one easy second of evolution.'

"Well, we haven't, we're *not*," Bill says. "We wear Halston clothes, but we're still dressed in sheepskin rugs —and still—wolves."

There are some of the elemental themes which we've been discussing with William Shatner by mail, phone, face-to-face, with books and manuscripts shipped back and forth—revolutionary studies of the last decade which, in some cases, may have been anticipated by the gut-level themes and acting of STAR TREK.

Charles Champlin in his column in the *Los Angeles Times,* writing about the new STAR TREK movie says that part of the reason for the "numbing" statistics on the continuing popularity of STAR TREK is that "like the western, STAR TREK has the power of parable."

STAR TREK touches universal chords. But also: it has often done so in ways which are original and unique. Did that come from the writing, the acting, both? We tell Bill of the fact that a key episode, "The Enemy Within," in which Kirk is split into two halves is used with healing effect in mental hospitals. He has mentioned the acting challenge in the dual role of the two halves of himself—which the episode calls the "wolf" and the "lamb." He has not known of its use as therapy —the healing effect of seeing even Kirk recognize the wolf within:

"The 'wolf' and the 'lamb,' " he says, "I would prefer to put it as the intellectual and the savage, the intellectual and the beast within man. I consciously looked at it that way."

'We've been looking at it not just in terms of Jekyll and Hyde, good and evil, but the much more interesting idea of the inner enemy as part of our strength. Did you recognize that then?'

"Absolutely. I recognized that the essential human being is that composite of the animal and the intellect.

One cannot function without the other. I tried to portray the animal, going so far beyond the bounds of behavior without the control of the intellect—and the weakness and opaqueness of the intellect without the blood and color of the animal."

'Was that idea in the script at all before you got hold of it?'

"No. I don't think so. No. No. I think what they figured was, 'Let's do Jekyll and Hyde,' you know. But I wanted—more. I don't know how successful I was, but those were my thoughts, trying to make it something more than Jekyll and Hyde."

'You did something very important. You projected that duality—the two halves—the importance of each, even the darker side of the wolf which we commonly regard as evil and try to repress and deny, its terror, its passion, and then the gentleness, the yieldingness of the other half, as well as its proper control. Then—a really astounding idea—you took the wolf back in, accepted it —finally even knew that you had to love the wolf. You hated its excesses and especially its terrors. But you took back in that savage self which we often disown—and on the other side the savage also took back in the gentleness, which perhaps men disown even more often. It was eloquent.'

"I was looking on it as an acting challenge, taking it apart to put more levels and layers into it. It was one of those chances an actor looks for—to say something beyond the words. But I really do believe: anything that is genuinely a part of our natures is something we have to accept—even the animal within."

'And look what the *effect* of recognizing that is. Apparently it works in the mental hospitals because people can see that very thing which you put into it—that the animal is not merely evil and not something we can do without—and that a man can have a "wolf"—that even the best of men do—without letting the beast rule.'

"To what extent it came across, I don't know. I do know that I've felt the animal within myself to the point of knowing that I could kill—by *tearing out a throat with my teeth*.

"So it's there. When Ardrey and the others write about the animal origins still being with us—the predatory hunting ape, the carnivore which was the link from ape to man—I *know* what they mean."

'Was that what you liked most in Ardrey's books? What did you like?'

"Oh, I loved the way he wrote. He wrote scientific fact dramatically. He's a great teacher. His theories are illuminating, and—dazzling to me. But then I'm a layman. But if I were to answer it in a single way, I would have to say, it's the *way* he expressed what could have been dry, scientific fact. He is a dramatist. A playwright. He's a dramatist—and he's a scientist, and that's a unique combination. So it's the way he wrote, and of course *what* he wrote."

'Which of his ideas interested you or turned you on the most or intrigued you?'

"The whole thing. The whole idea of the killer ape. The whole idea of the search for our past. The whole idea of the courage of the men—the ones he calls "the wild men" of South African anthropology—who went against the accepted dogma of the time, and had such a difficult time convincing people that they were right."

Ardrey's *African Genesis* was essentially contemporary with STAR TREK— published in 1965, the first mass bestseller to bring some of the new research on primates and man's origins to the attention of the world. It had not been until 1963 that *any* study of primates living in the wild had been published. (Jane Goodall's chimpanzees.) Since then there's been a research and knowledge explosion. These things normally take time —sometimes decades—to move from science to popular knowledge.

But in the course of discussion for the book, we have defined a phenomenon we call "drama shock"—the mass impact of ideas conveyed by powerful drama through the mass media—movie and especially television.

The phenomenon of drama shock in the mass medium of television is so swift that a sensitive actor may be projecting things from sources no one even suspects. He may short-circuit the gap between scientific study and popular imagination by years.

Today you can see a National Geographic television special in your living room showing dominance and submission behavior in male baboons.

But you could, incredibly, see something of the same thing, on a human level, on STAR TREK in 1966.

There are aspects of the knowledge revolution in animal behavior which Shatner is seeing only now as we discuss them for the book. "It's fascinating," he says.

But there is something in his acting which was there more than a decade ago. Where did it come from? We ask him about it now:

'For example, something which has interested us. Most of the research we are discussing was not known at the time of STAR TREK. Some not at all. None of it very widely. Were some of your gestures on screen planned or spontaneous? One example is "Errand of Mercy" where John Collicos is playing the Klingon Commander Kor, who has invaded Organia and captured you and Spock. Kor is in charge. You're pretending to be somebody from the planet. Very submissive and yielding. And he's not buying that, very much, but he looks you over, walks around you. Meanwhile, you're working very hard at being submissive to this Klingon. You're doing—an incredible bunch of things right out of the animal world. You're backing off, you've got the eyes lowered, you're twisting your hands, you don't even turn to face him as he walks around you, looking at you, you're looking down. It's a perfect job of turning off the other male's, the conquering male's aggression, and showing submission. Now—were you aware of that then, Bill?'

"Oh, yeah," he says. "Oh—yeah."

'Of all those animal signals? You *were*—'

"Sure. Oh, yeah. Oh, yeah."

'—deliberately lowering your eyes, twisting your locked fingers, looking at him from under your eyelashes?'

"Oh yeah. In fact, there's a whole marvelous book written about dog language."

'*Dog* language?'

"The language of dogs, by their body positions. It's extraordinarily interesting. And animals, all apes, for example, you're aware, indicate lack of hostility by not looking eye-to-eye, by avoiding a direct gaze. An anthropologist was able to observe apes by imitating their demeanor. He would sit in a tree and they would come up to him and he would look away. He would never directly gaze at them, because he knew that averting or lowering the eyes was their way of saying, "I am not hostile." *This*—the lowered head and the direct stare in most animals is the look of hostility."

He illustrates—a fine look for facing down a Klingon who doesn't have you in his power. He chuckles. "Oh sure. No—I thought you were going to say some particular gesture—while trying to remember a line a hand got raised or a fist clenched."

'Oh, no.'

"No. No. These things are very carefully planned."

'But it's remarkable that you would *know* that then. It was hardly a matter of common knowledge in 1966. To say nothing of having the kind of mind which would take that in from wherever—even a book on dog language—and apply it, consciously, to a scene like that.'

"Well, that's my *job*. It would be hard for me to identify just when I became aware of which particular idea. I hadn't read Ardrey until we talked about it for the book. But other things—I read all the time, voraciously, any chance I get. Between scenes. Odd moments here and there. So, something had filtered through. And everything is grist for an actor's mill. Those decisions— how to do it and how to get that across—have to be made so quickly that you wonder sometimes, "Is this right? Am I going too far?" But you think it out—and then you walk out and do it. In a play, you get to try it out somewhere out of town—get the audience reaction to it, see how it plays. In television you never quite know —until you see how many people keep watching. Or maybe you don't even find out until years later."

What keeps emerging years later is the vitality and ongoing meaning of that kind of interpretation of a role. The effort to put into it multiple levels and layers, including the elemental, the savage, the necessary wolf, the "blood and color" of the animal, the gentleness but incompleteness of the "lamb"—has resulted in a form of drama which often moves people on an elemental level. That is the most fundamental level of drama shock. The fact that it demonstrably exists for STAR TREK is a confirmation of the existence of the phenomenon of drama shock.

Something which heals a schizophrenic split in a mental hospital, reaches an autistic child, helps a conflict-ridden teenager or adult to think through problems and reorganize a life, saves someone from suicide or near-fatal grief, (as in many letters we receive), is clearly reaching people on many levels which could not be anticipated.

Yet part of the reason STAR TREK and Shatner's performance worked was that the actor was trying to anticipate those levels. One of the most consistent reports of people who watch STAR TREK is that they watch it many times, and each time see some new level, layer, or aspect. Children grow up with it, seeing different values from preschool to college. New people discover it year by year. It does not appear to age or become dated.

It is played in more than 50 languages in almost every country this side of the Iron Curtain—and pirated in Communist China—with Communist Chinese insignias on the *Enterprise*.

Clearly the series and the role were dealing with universals.

But the *risk* of acting the leading role in that way is something which has not been understood. No one has known exactly what Shatner was doing in a scene like the one with Kor (or many other scenes in STAR TREK which function on some elemental level). An actor might well have been doing that out of some instinctive response of his own (which would also be interesting). He might merely have some dim gut-feeling. For Shatner to do it by conscious intention is to make the intellectual leap, from the first fragments of evidence, of believing that what applies to our animal heritage—even as remotely as the language of dogs—goes also for us.

It was not a common belief then.

But if, by the way, it did *not* go also for us, then the actor who took the risk of saying that with his body—in front of tens of millions of people—would look merely incomprehensible—especially when the world tunes in, listening in other languages.

But it is plain that the world heard that silent language, loud and clear.

STAR TREK has had the out-of-town tryout to end all out-of-town tryouts.

And the verdict from the beginning—in million-letter campaigns—was always for revival *with the original cast*.

People sensed, clearly or dimly, that what they were responding to and wanted back was not merely a science fiction show—not even one with a particular philosophy of hope and optimism—but something which those particular actors were doing with it.

The one factor specifically requested in virtually every revival letter Paramount received was: the original cast, especially Shatner and Nimoy.

Our own study reaching 40,000 people, not merely STAR TREK fans but also a wide sampling of the general public, asked about the planned STAR TREK movie: "Is there anything which would make you *not* see it?"

An astonishing 98% said: "Yes." This despite the fact that 99% were indicating that, given half a chance, they would see a STAR TREK movie not once but more than once—most of them many times.

What would make them *not* see it? Some 3% named something amounting to "if the philosophy were changed" or "if Gene Roddenbury were not producing it." 2% said they would have to see it once, anyway, just to see what had been done. The other 95% said: "If the original cast were not in it"—or some variation of that which specified particular members or combinations of the cast without which they would not see it: "at least Shatner;" "at least Shatner and Nimoy;" "not unless Shatner, Nimoy, and DeForest Kelly (Dr. McCoy) were in it;" "everybody unless someone really cannot;" etc.

In the end, Paramount got that message—and staked the biggest budget of all time on believing it. For the first time a television series has made it to the big screen starring its original star—and the entire cast in their original relationships to him.

You could call it the final review of a performance.

In some manner, intellectually, instinctively, perhaps both, the actor was in touch with levels in himself which spoke to the autistic child who knows no other name or face—and simultaneously to the Ph.D.'s, the M.D.'s, the top Long-Range Planner of NASA, etc.

Many of those levels have not yet been explored. It is only relatively recently that anthropologists have begun to study human beings and animals with a view to finding the common ground which unites them. For example, work has begun to focus on the "alpha" male of a primate group—i.e. the most dominant male, with others in rank order of dominance designated "beta," "gamma," etc.

Are there "alpha" males among humans, too? If so, what are they like? How do they establish that? How do others know it? What does it take to be the alpha male on a starship?

Does it take one to play one?

Is there something unique about how *this* actor played one?

There may be.

Some part of STAR TREK's success may well have been that it was a sophisticated analog of certain basic human/animal behavior patterns which are very attractive to us—perhaps from millions of years deep.

Some have been lost or radically modified in our everyday lives, and we may have some unacknowledged hunger for them.

For example, one factor mentioned in almost every response to STAR TREK is the "closeness and caring" —"like a family"—of the crew of the *Enterprise,* especially those closest to Kirk.

That family-like extended network of caring is much like the closely knit groups in which most advanced primates live and which must be our human roots, too.

The *Enterprise* itself and its mission are a highly sophisticated and considerably transformed analog of a very basic primate and human activity: aggression, even —war.

Curiously, Shatner himself saw that very well from the beginning. His model for Kirk was the civilizing warrior-king who conquered a world. Alexander.

As STAR TREK was being cancelled (1969), British scientist Dr. Lionel Tiger, Ph.D., was publishing *"Men in Groups"*—a scholarly study of what he defines as male-bonding is primates and humans: a complex series of behaviors related to defense, aggression, hunting, leadership, social organization, rank order of dominance in groups, friendship, and—war.

"Almost universally, war is an all-male enterprise," Tiger says. "So is politics. So are most sports. So, frequently, are most kinds of leadership, most holding of command of an audience and the means of gaining attention—and. . .human aggression. . .is a propensity of males."

The *Enterprise* is still in many respects an elemental organization for defense, war, hunting—a classic hunting and exploratory group. . .to the stars. But it has been transformed in three major ways:

1. It has consciously outlawed the initiation of force, transforming war-making into the peaceful mission and ever expanding excitement of going where-no-man.
2. It includes women. Not always totally or in the ways that women's libbers of a decade later might want, but substantially and in often surprising roles—including command.
3. It includes within the leading male role-model both the traditional, primordial attributes of the alpha male—dominance, aggressiveness, physical prowess, courage, defense of territory—*and* the usually unexpressed other half—the capacity to express emotion, gentleness, yielding, vulnerability.

Part of the first transformation, an interesting response to the second, and much of the third are due to the actor who played Kirk.

And the interesting question is: how did he, a man growing up in the Twentieth Century, arrive at that Twenty-third Century position?

Where did he find the roots of a unique projection of

the combination of strength with vulnerability—and the acceptance of both as essential to the whole human being?

That projection was extremely unusual—not only in terms of this culture.

Lionel Tiger has even suggested that the inhibition of emotion in males has profound biological sources and was an essential survival characteristic. He believes it was especially crucial for young sub-dominant males that they inhibit emotion in confrontation with older males—yield—and live to become dominant another day.

Dominance commands sexual privilege—access to the fertile females, hence to rapid selection of any characteristic which leads to dominance. Inhibition of emotion may be one.

If that is true, it might point to deep roots for certain forms of male emotional control. That may be the source of some of the response to Spock—and to the aspect of Kirk which also displays that control, but without denial.

On the other hand, while the human being shares biological roots with animal and primitive ancestors, it is the mark of the human to be able to set aside those primitive responses when and if they cease to be life-serving or life-enhancing. One may still need to inhibit emotion in a confrontation with a 20th Century boss or a conquering Klingon, but not in a relationship of love or friendship. Whatever may be the instinctive roots of male restraint, the form of it taught in our culture is merely a *learned* pattern—as evidenced by the fact that much of it *could* break down within a decade.

Our culture has generalized a proper male restraint into the brutal men-don't-cry syndrome, which virtually prohibits males any profound or tender emotion. Ironically, it *permits* the very emotions which young primate males must inhibit: aggression, anger, fighting. But it sets severe limits on male expression of love—and especially friendship, which—irony number two—the primate code *permits,* even requires.

Lionel Tiger also reports the phenomenon of male-male bonding based on personal choice and usually life-long, between two males—occasionally including a third, not as close. It's normally only those males who form a stable bond who become the two or three dominant males in a group and have access to the most fertile females. So, Tiger thinks that bonding capacity would quickly be selected for, and exist in humans, too.

This may be, as we discussed with Gene and Bill and others still another area in which STAR TREK touches on the elemental—with the close bond of friendship between Kirk and Spock and the three-way closeness of both with Dr. McCoy.

All three are powerful role-models, and powerful models of a kind of male love and friendship which is to the death. Each has repeatedly risked his life, career, perhaps even the fate of the ship or the galaxy for one of the others—McCoy once went to certain death by torture ("The Empathy") for his two friends.

The closeness of Spock and Kirk, across a gulf between stars, the closeness of the three, across gulfs of logic, emotion, and Kirk's blending of both—have clearly struck some elemental chord.

Beyond that, Kirk projects an easy male authority, so certain of itself that it is worn like the old jacket. That, also, is something we have rarely seen.

What happens in a somewhat fragmented, isolated society, where few live in anything resembling a primate group or even an extended family, and many do not know on an intimate level anyone who functions like an alpha male, when millions begin to see an actor cast as the archetype of an alpha male: captain of ship and soul —who *acts* like one, even on an elemental level?

Then suppose also that while projecting that image of

the best of traditional behavior, he is also projecting a new model of male openness?

Do people begin to follow that lead?

It does appear that they do.

How many and to what extent can be argued.

What kind of sample of the American, let alone world, population any reasonable study can reach can be debated. The usual scientific arguments apply. Those who reply to a study may be different from those who do not. Short of a strict random-sampling on-the-spot study, one cannot presume to speak for the whole population.

But the same can be said, and has been, of *The Kinsey Report, The Hite Report,* etc. That did not prevent them from being of value as some indication, and the first indication, of what was going on in their areas.

Nor did it prevent our questionnaire on the impact of STAR TREK from giving the first indication in its area —and outdrawing the Hite Report. The questionnaire reached more than 40,000 people, including STAR TREK fans, but also a much larger proportion of general science fiction fans and the general public. The replies had to be stacked in cartons. Virtually all of the replies (99%+) are positive toward STAR TREK. However, another independent study which did use sampling techniques to reach a cross-section of the general public indicates that a very large percentage of the public *does* have a favorable response to STAR TREK. Eighty percent have said they would see a new STAR TREK movie.

So the results of our questionnaire may even be reasonably representative of some large percentage of the general public.

If so, or even if they only represent some significant percentage of the large STAR TREK phenomenon itself, the results are startling.

They indicate that for people replying, STAR TREK

had a *very large impact* on their attitudes toward greater acceptance of diversity, changes in attitudes toward male-female roles, and greater acceptance of emotional openness, especially in men.

Only the most relevant result can be given here—that which directly concerns the impact of Shatner's Kirk on emotional openness. But others will be reported elsewhere.

Question #6 was: Do you think that the way Shatner played Kirk, as a masculine man who was able and willing to express emotion could have affected people's attitudes toward emotional openness in men?

Yes   No   Comment

More than 90% answered: Yes. "No" answers were fewer than 3%. Those qualifying their answer most often said, "It changed *my* attitude, and my impression is that it changed others, but I don't know how widespread the change was."

That is still difficult to answer. But when you read the answers of 14-year-old boys who say, "I know now that there is nothing unmasculine about showing emotion, even crying, and it was Shatner who first made me see that,"—and see substantially the same answer from all ages, both sexes, schoolchildren to every sophisticated profession—you know that for these people, at least, the effect was real and profound.

Set in the frame of STAR TREK, which was explicitly a parable on what was proper to man, that portrayal doubtless had more effect than it could have had in any other setting.

But it had that effect, in part, because people sensed that there was a reality behind it.

If the leading actor had not had that quality which the last decade has come to call "macho"—sometimes almost as an accusation, it is doubtful whether the contrast of masculinity and openness would have come through.

The openness may well have needed the sanction of the masculinity, to reach the people it did reach.

A decade later male emotional openness could be played much more freely—even become the mainstay of shows like "Starsky and Hutch."

When Shatner tried it, the ground was unbroken and much more dangerous.

In some way he had been breaking it since he was six years old—somehow managing to combine both "best kid boxer" with the child who could move an audience to tears, playing football while also doing the plays which were "tantamount to carrying the violin."

We asked him once whether it was possible that he was pursuing the macho sports, in part, to establish his right to the other half.

"Could be," he said, interested. "It might very well be. Although—I *care* to be involved in a sport. I *like* the crisp feel of a tennis racquet impacting with a well hit ball. I like the sensation of skiing, the grace, the skill. But—there might have been an element of that."

There has been a trail of so many and such dangerous sports in his life that the question arises. And if Lionel Tiger is right, sports have some special significance for the male of the species—going back to primitive roots. Were they part of what was essential in making Shatner a man who was clearly a man's man in any terms, even when he risked showing emotion?

We pursued those questions into the area of the most obviously combative sport, karate.

We did not expect the question to lead to the story of the time when civilized William Shatner was ready to kill.

'What led you to take up karate, Bill? Is it the same as we were talking about earlier on the sports? The primitive challenge?'

"Yeah. Listen, I want to be very clear about the karate. I'm not good at all. I've had something like twenty lessons. And I'm not really—my ability in karate has been greatly exaggerated."

'Do you want to do it? Do you want to become good at it?'

"Yeah. Very much. But I just don't have the time. Karate is the sternest discipline of all. It's as much as a ballet dancer's. Every day. Hours. Or certainly three or four times a week. And hours of it, to become any good at all. How marvelous to be able to use your hands in such a manner that you can defend yourself and not be afraid of being hit in the face or being killed by some idiot in the streets—because you're lightning fast. What a feeling of confidence that would be! And the other thing is the discipline of being able to do that is extraordinary. I've met some of these people and they're fanatics."

'Yeah, we've just started it the past few months.'

"To be any good at karate requires a fanaticism which I just don't have the time to do. So I've taken a few lessons and friend of mine is a black belt and one day he was showing me some Katas and we were doing some numbers. And then somebody was coming over and he said, 'Look, with this person here I'd really like to have him see how well I do, so I won't do this slowly because we're really going to go through our number. I'll do it quickly but don't be apprehensive, I won't hit you.'

"And so this other person came over and this guy suddenly stopped being the teacher and became the man he could be if you were going to attack him." Bill laughs. "And I *mean*—he was like me with some six-year-old. I mean, he would have killed me seventeen times over. I went like *that*—and he would have hit me five times. I mean it was—" He makes karate sounds, gestures. "It was with that kind of *waaagh!* It wasn't just—*this*—it was such power and rapidity."

'Had you never seen a demonstration?'

"Oh, I've been to a lot of karate matches, but I've

never looked a guy in the *eye* and realized five blows
went by the time I went like *that*—he'd hit me five
times. I mean it's—it staggers the imagination."

'It's a fantastic illustration that there aren't any limits
to the human potential. There's nothing we can't do or
be.'

"Right—given that kind of time—but I don't have it.
So—"

'My husband started studying karate when we were in
graduate school—he did something once—I think you'd
be interested in. We were out one night with a very close
friend who's about 6 foot 3, 220 pounds, towering over
everybody there. My husband was telling them about
karate principles—you know, you can become a tree—
you plant your feet into the ground, you can feel it taking root and so forth. And Terry said, "Well, that's impossible." Well, Alan demonstrated. There was this
hulking giant, and my husband was standing there with
his arm up like this. Going deeper and deeper, you could
see him concentrating through the arm, this is the limb,
this is the tree, this is the root, it's all the way into the
ground, all in one piece. And this huge guy could not
move that arm—though for the next ten minutes, he
didn't stop trying.'

"That's wild."

'He was putting all his pressure, all his weight—and
there was no budging that "tree." '

"That's incredible. Well, it certainly is all so much a
matter of—everything is so much a matter of the mind.
This same friend of mine who was teaching me is a black
belt and of a really high degree in his particular discipline—3rd or 4th degree black belt—had been a friend
of Bruce Lee's, and I asked him, 'How good was Bruce
Lee?' "

He said, "Well, you know the difference between you
and me? That's the difference between me and Bruce
Lee." He said, "I've never—the man could hold his fist

out like *that* and go like *that*—and I'd be propelled thirty feet back." We're talking about a karate expert.

'It's not to be believed what they can do. You mentioned the idea of not getting hit in the face. We've wondered, did that—you're not aware of it as beauty, but did that—what other people are looking at as beauty—ever get you into trouble?'

"Physically, you mean?"

'Yeah, fights and so forth?'

"I've never really had a fight as an adult. Sometimes I've had to talk my way out. The reason for that is, I lose no matter what. I lose if I lose, and I lose if I win. I can't possibly afford to get into a fight. The only way I could possibly get into a fight would be in my self-defense or self-defense of somebody I love, and then there would be no question. But—a broken face, a broken hand, a toe, a scratch—I mean, I can't deal with those things. Do you know, if I get a scratch on my face—I'm—the way I work I'd be out of work for what? Three, four weeks. A broken nose—forget it—six months. A broken face—and you and I know that all *this* has to do is hit *once* with any kind of force—let alone the force of somebody who's really good—and it smashes your face—it's all over—one blow.

"Everybody talks about you do this, that. Nonsense. All you need is one karate blow to the neck and it's all over. I mean, you know, 'Kick 'em right'—a kick in the balls—I mean, you could *die*—you could be laid up for six months. It doesn't make any—what's a fight? A fight is the first effective blow landed. It's not a fight like you see in the movies, you block that, bang, the guy takes it, goes again—that's *fantasy* time. Reality is—a fight is not a masculine endeavor, it's a killer endeavor. And I as an actor can't afford to be put out of business that way."

'You ever want to fight, if you didn't have those considerations?'

"I've had times when I've wanted to kill people, yeah,

and I've had to really, really get a hold of myself. One time, in a play I was doing on Broadway, I was on stage a lot, a long time, all the time; I was never *off* stage. And this guy who was on for about five minutes, he had two small scenes, and he had a drunken scene in which he hit me on the shoulder—in which he *didn't* hit me on the shoulder. He had a drunken scene. Sometime after opening night, he hit me on the shoulder saying, 'Oh, ha, ha, ha,' and hit me on the shoulder. I let that go. Then I found that every night he hit me on the shoulder, in this long-run play. When the laughs were going well for him, he hit me like this (tap). When the laughs were not going well for him, 'cause he was drunk or something, he gave me a real clobber on the shoulder. So I asked him, 'Would you mind not hitting me on the shoulder?'

"He said, 'No. That's where I hit you on the shoulder.'

"I said, 'It wasn't there opening night.' On a Broadway show, a long run, you're supposed to freeze a play. You don't change anything, because in changing something, even minutely, over a long period of time, that minute change grows to be a *big* aberration in a play.

"So this clobbering on the shoulder began to be a thing. After asking *him* to stop, I went to the stage manager. He couldn't help. I went to the director. He couldn't help. I went to the producer, I went to—Actor's Equity—trying to get him to stop—and nobody could help.

"So—one day I said, 'You hit me on the shoulder again,'—he was a big man—'I'm going to hit you back, on stage.'

"He said, 'You wouldn't dare.'

"I said, 'Don't try me.'"

Shatner paused, wearing a remembered look of confrontation and control—the savage and the intellect, united. It's the look not so much of jungle or gunsmoke, but of galactic confrontation. The intellect had made a

severe effort to resolve the problem within the bounds of
civilization, even taking it to Actor's Equity. But finally
it comes down to *this*. And yet, all the arguments he has
made against fighting went double then. A young actor,
in a hit long-run play. And that was years before he
packed on muscle for the role of Alexander and Kirk.
He had played football, boxed, but he still had that slim
look of an apprentice angel. And still the eyes tell you
that the big man shouldn't have tried him.

"He hit me on the shoulder. And, laughingly, I clob-
bered him. He staggered back. Finished the scene. First
act curtain came down, and he came at me from across
the stage. I ducked and he hit an old man, an old prop
man, in the head. And they broke us up.

"The next day, when we came to the theater, the producer went to see him first to find out what was going
on, then came into my room and said 'What was going
on?' and I told him.

"I said, 'Just, I can't stand that smack on the shoulder
day after day, eight times a week, knowing that it's
going to be bad if he doesn't get a laugh, and knowing
it's going to be light if he does.'

"At which point, that guy came into my dressing
room. Broadway dressing rooms are little cubicles about
12 feet square, with a fire door, which is usually wedged
open. Fire doors are thick and close automatically, unless that wedge is used. This guy kicked out the wedge.
The three of us were locked in a cubicle 12 by 12. And
this guy was obviously enraged.

"Suddenly the veneer of civilization left me, and I saw
in my mind's eye—me, going toward him like an animal
—like a cat, really, my thumbs toward his eyes, and my
teeth towards his jugular.

"I had no interest in sparring two left jabs and a right
cross. I had no thought in my mind of using my legs or
my feet.

"This man in the middle was petrified, understand.

But I was an animal, and I was going to kill him. And when I look back on it, I *could* have killed him, if I had done what I had envisioned in that split second of seeing what I was going to do.

"The man in the middle was able to give us a little breathing time, opened the fire door and got the guy out of there.

"But I realized there that I could have killed somebody. It is within me to kill somebody, and by that primitive means of biting through the jugular vein.

"It was the strangest sensation, because here I had done some boxing, karate, pretty good on my feet—I think—and none of that made any sense whatever. I was going to bite like a cat. I have that within me—and I'm afraid of it."

There is that aspect. The savage. The wolf.

But if you go to look also for the roots of the lamb, the vulnerable human being who longs to "touch out to somebody"—you find those also in Shatner's life, his childhood:

"The moments of unhappiness are mostly centered around being lonely and friendless—apart. I've had to do—I had to do what I could—try to walk beside somebody whom I didn't know so it wouldn't look like I was walking to school alone, not going to movies alone. It was—it was difficult."

'Did you ever want a more idealized friendship? For example, what kind of fiction did you read? Did you ever read fiction where there were two close male friends together doing all kinds of things together?'

"I read all the standard fiction of the time which included *Rudyard Kipling, Tom Swift,* all those things. Whether there was science fiction or—"

'No, I'm not talking about science fiction.'

"No, no. I mean I *did* read it at the time. I don't remember who the authors were, but whoever they were, at that period of time. I read all the kids books—*Mowgli*

—(the jungle boy of Rudyard Kipling).''

'What about Tarzan?'

"And Tarzan."

'Did you like them?'

"Oh, *yes*."

'Did that help you to form a concept of what you wanted to be? Master of the universe, and master of all these sports and skills?'

"I don't know. I read all the Tarzan books, many times. Zane Grey and Edgar Rice Burroughs were big heroes of mine. I read a lot of westerns, pulp westerns. I was a voracious reader as a kid—to the point where my parents would tell me to put the light out at night and I would take a flashlight and duck under the covers and read under the covers.

"So I must have been influenced by that."

'You don't remember thinking how great Tarzan was and wanting to be like that?'

"Well, I must have thought how great Tarzan was, but the next jump—of wanting me to be *like* Tarzan I don't recall. Although up in the country when I was there with a group of kids, we made tree houses, and we'd go to the woods and do all kinds of weird, strange things, stalking—and we did cowboys and Indians in the actual woods where there had *been* Indians."

'Did you have quite a bit of fighting as you were growing up?'

"It was always—yeah, there was always a battle going on between me and the kids in school. I recall them as always being one-sided—there was always a multitude of them—two or three. And I remember the fights used to be where two or three kids would jump me and I'd be fighting them off and a group would gather around and be chanting you know 'fight, fight, get him, get him' against me—for the attackers. But I also have a recollection of being rather good, and not really ever getting badly beaten up and doing more harm than getting harmed. In fact, there came a time when they stopped jumping me, because it was a problem for them."

It's an aspect of growing up which most women would not have experienced—the fighting, even the sports seen as masculine endeavors. The costs of maintaining the duality of both the uncompromising masculinity and the individual choice to maintain the sensitivity of the actor are not easy to calculate. In the face of the loneliness of pretending to walk beside someone, they become almost incalculable.

And somewhere at the bottom of it all is that primitive level which could kill by tearing out a throat.

Is *that,* as Tiger suggests "a propensity of males"?

It's an interesting question of the revolution whether there *is* some fundamental difference between male and female in those areas of aggression, territoriality, defense, dominance. Many researchers and some recent studies have suggested that there is. Part of the difference may even be hormonal, and part may be related to age-old patterns in which the male was defender, sentinel, guardian—and the one who ultimately went, perhaps with one or two other males, to face the leopard.

Has that made a difference to men, to this day—one which ultimately shows up in the biography of a man, in ways not eradicated by the revolution?

We talked about it, ultimately, with Robert Heinlein, the dean of science fiction writers, who has made the argument that part of the highest morality of being a man is to stand and die, if necessary, and that some of the roots of "women and children first" may be bred into our bones—that males have been the biologically expendable defenders of the species.

There is no better argument against a man's being biologically expendable than Robert Heinlein himself. The kind of gallantry for which he and that code stand are still very attractive.

And if you look at Shatner's life—say his urgent con-

cern for his children—you see much of that kind of behavior.

But when we put that argument, later, in briefest form
to Bill, he didn't agree—at least not as a matter of instinct:

"Men are just as frightened as women are of dying. It
is just that up to now they have been forced into situations where they *had* to. Most traditional male courage
is peer pressure. Did you know that? They will die rather
than show each other that they are afraid. A woman
could do that just as well. If that is courage. I think real
courage is a matter of intellect. The instinct which is
more overpowering than anything is self-preservation.
You then have to say intellectually, 'Wait a minute.
That's my wife and child. I *can't* run. I have to stay and
fight.' I don't think courage has to do with instinct or
the animal world, or with males. Courage is a *human*
quality. It is a quality of *mind,* a matter of choice. I think
heroism is a product of intellect; self-preservation is a
part of the gut."

In a sense, that is perhaps the ultimate report from the
revolution, and the ultimate position at which the revolution is trying to arrive: to be able to recognize the
animal or instinctive or hormonal roots of human behavior—and nevertheless to insist on the *human* qualities.

Interestingly, Shatner projected Kirk as, essentially, a
hero of the mind and of the triumph of mind over instinct—even over the beast in man. In another episode
("A Taste of Armaggedon") Kirk specifically makes the
argument that, yes, man has all the killer instincts, and
nevertheless he can make the decision, "We're not going
to kill—today."

It's one of the most powerful statements of the character, and the actor who made it has been there—and
made that decision.

When the revolution has cleared away many of the

traditional notions of what it is to be a man or woman, and clarified much more of what it is to be human, we will probably find that the courage which is the product of intellect is the toughest and most enduring of all. It can choose, even, not to kill. Or—not to cut off feeling or thinking because of some prescription of what it is to be male or female.

That kind of courage is doubtless no monopoly of males. But on some of them it can look very good.

Male and Female

A major wave of the revolution has been the Women's Insurrection.

Possibly the best evidence of its power and of how thoroughly it was an idea whose time has come was the almost instant spread—and instant comprehension—of its most telling language: "women's liberation" (instantly shortened to "women's lib") "Ms." (standard usage in a phenomenally short time), and "male chauvinism."

Not the least issue of the revolution is languge—as we were to see with William Shatner.

One of the attractive surprises of the revolution is the effort of men—some of them—to reevaluate their ideas and behavior in the light of what women have lately been telling them. And sometimes the women even listen back.

It's not a bad way of keeping the war between the sexes from turning into Armageddon.

Not the least issue of the response to Kirk and to STAR TREK has been drawn up along the lines of male and female—and both females and males have seen Kirk in startlingly different ways:

He's the male chauvinist of the galaxy.

Or then again: He has a sexy respect for strong, confident, bright women. Seventeen university degrees and a taste for discussing "sub-dimensional physics" don't turn him off in a woman; they turn him on. Amazons, gladiators, rulers of planets, Romulan fleet commanders, etc., etc.—likewise.

And then there's the etc., etc. He's the womanizer of the galaxy. Casanova on warp drive.

He falls deeply in love.

He bed's 'em, never weds 'em. (Once, not in his right mind.)

He treats women with respect.

He's insufferably arrogant.

He believes in equality.

There's not an equal bone in his body. (What *was* he doing taming the shrew, Elaan of Troyius—threatening to spank her? Does anyone imagine that he would have taken that attitude with the *male* rule of a planet—no matter how insufferable?)

What is "fascinating," not to say revolutionary, is that we *now* recognize such things as questions.

Little more than a decade ago we were essentially oblivious to the problem, let alone any solutions.

STAR TREK and Kirk helped blast through that oblivion, firing the popular imagination with possibilities, questions, an implicit attitude which recognized women as full-fledged intelligent beings.

Kirk, in particular, gave women the freedom to respond to him in many ways, was able to respond to many qualities and ways of relating to him in women.

And still both STAR TREK and Kirk were later damned for "sexism"—a word uncoined and uncirculated before their voyages. Some decades, you can't win.

This decade we walked into a debate with William Shatner—in all innocence—coming at it from our perspective of regarding STAR TREK and Kirk as basically liberating:

'There was the attitude toward women on STAR TREK and your attitude on it, long before we heard about women's lib. How did that happen?'

But he surprised us:

"Well, the attitude towards women on STAR TREK seemed to be more male chauvinist—as I remember—don't you?"

'Well, it had its, yes, moments of "male chauvinism," but then there were also female doctors, lawyers, commanders of ships, Vulcan matriarchs, a queen who kidnapped you as her mate.'

"I think that came from the people who ran the show, rather than anything I might have done."

'But you responded to all of those as Kirk. How did you feel about having to relate to some of the characters on the show—say to the female commander of a fleet?

"You know we were talking earlier—we've been talking since that first phone interview a long time ago—about some of the things Marcy has taught me. I may have been—I *was*—I don't know what the term "male chauvinist" means, but I suppose in all its implications, it roughly categorizes what I must have been in high school and college.

"During my day and age one took a girl out and tried to make a pass and tried to make out—that was the big deal.

"I have come to the point beyond women's lib. Women's lib indicates a movement towards liberation. And usually a movement towards something carries within it the necessities of going beyond reason in order to make the pont—as a radical group needs revolt in order to evolve a change—or so they feel.

"But I really do intrinsically and insightfully believe in the quality of a woman and a man's mind. I do also believe that there is greater upper body strength in a man, that nature gave him more musculature. But while there are those few areas where nature has provided variations in our bodies—I really do believe in the equality of man and woman, and in equal pay for equal work. And I have no sense—not an iota—of looking down on a woman's mental abilities to talk with, to communicate with. There's no sense of I'm a man and you're a woman and therefore—"

Shatner smiles, perhaps stressing that he is, after all, working with two women on a book about his life and his work, his ideas and inner feelings. Once, long ago, he said rather wonderingly, "You know, I'm putting my life in your hands."

But we can hear alarm bells going off among militant liberationists all over the galaxy. ". . . beyond women's lib. . ."? ". . .necessities of going beyond reason . . . radical groups. . . ."

He's going on:

"I—only in one area do I find it a little difficult, and that is: I find it hard to accept a young girl as a newscaster, as against an older man with gray hair telling me the news. I don't think that has anything to do with my disparaging the girl's mind. It is merely that an older man telling me the news of the day seems to be of more importance, and he's had more experience and is able to put it in the proper perspective. In other words, I would rather watch Walter Cronkite than Barbara Walters. But that hasn't got anything to do with Barbara Walters being a girl. I mean, Clare Booth Luce—if *she* were a newscaster, I'd *very much* watch *her*."

The alarm bells mount to a red alert. That's such a charming package of honesty, effort—and unreconstructed backsliding, that it's going to take some time to sort out.

We can hear the letters coming in now:

". . .*girl*?. . .*young* girl?"

But he may be hearing them, too:

"That's really where I'm at.

"I don't even *know* what women's lib is at this point. I mean, I *know* what it is. But it has no meaning for me in that way.

"So that when I'm on discussion groups and somebody says, '. . .and my girl. . .' and the militant women's liberationist says, What do you mean? You're saying "my *girl*." We're *Ms*!—or whatever, *I* don't understand that. What the guy was trying to say was something like 'my baby' or 'my honey.' It was intended as a term of fondness, not as a disparaging thing.

"I've had that happen in a discussion group. But my mentality, *my* personal mentality is now in this state of total equality. I don't even think of it in terms of, 'Aren't I so great that I am granting them equality.' It's totally —so totally accepted."

And we can hear the letters saying politely or not so politely:

"In a pig's eye!"

Somebody's going to say he wouldn't call a male newscaster "boy" at any age, that Barbara Walters probably has at least as much "perspective" as one William Shatner, if not Walter Cronkite, and that the argument is "illogical," not to say male chauvinist. And that even "my girl," "my baby," "my honey" are something of a problem. He's still very fond of calling women "sweetheart," "dear," even "you little darlin'." On him it looks better than you would think.

But it's plain from the whole context of our knowledge of him that he's both absolutely sincere and quite aware of most of the issues involved. He's doubtless heard those very arguments before. In fact, his language shows that he's heard a few. He's just resistant to one or two of them. And he has a point.

And he *may* be not fully conscious of one or two others—which is a point we set out to pursue.

On one point of resistance, language, we share a certain part of his resistance. And it's for certain we're going to share the flák for what will be called the "sex-ism" of "where no *man*."

But we also own a piece of the other side. See some of our fiction.

Which goes to show you how complicated revolutions can get.

We keep getting letters in response to *Star Trek: The New Voyages, The Price of The Phoenix,* or *Star Trek Lives* with some variation of the following:

Dear Ms. Marshak and Ms. Culbreath,
    Thank you for excellent editing of *New Voyages.* The stories are evidently selected to reflect the under-standing of the characters and ideas which came through in *Star Trek Lives.* The emotional and "logical" quality of the stories is unexcelled, possibly unequaled even in aired STAR TREK. You even man-age to include some humor, always a saving grace. There are even a few women who do something useful and don't fall apart.
    I do have a complaint. Please consider for your future editorial standards the matter of language.
    Sexism is pervasive and pernicious, even when not so intended.
    For example, "manning" the ship. Why not "person-ing" the ship? Or, Scotty is trying "manfully"—why "*man*fully?" The use of "man" where what is meant is "person," "mankind" or, better, "humankind" or even "sentient being" continues an ancient tradition which is nonetheless harmful. It excommunicates half the human race.
    My half and yours.
    I am, therefore, trying personfully to persuade you to person your battle stations and fight like gentlebeings.
            Live long and personalize,
            Ms.

That last sentence is the letter's saving grace, and also

the illustration of why, as writers, we are not too keen on the argument. On the whole, we've tried to make the stories revolutionary; the language—English.

If it is not the English of the next century or even the next decade, we're aware of the problem, but we haven't yet figured out how to person the battlements. Possibly the time will come when the substance of the issue will be settled so thoroughly that the language will take care of itself.

Meanwhile, we found ourselves arguing the substance with one William Shatner:

'What are the differences between men and women? Should they just treat each other as two persons?'

"The differences between men and women, besides the obvious physical differences, you mean—are *none*. Except that two people having a dialogue between them—either emotional, verbal, social, sexual or whatever are conditioned by their psychological biases and if one prefers to be led by the other, that's their—meshing —of their psychological needs. And that goes between men and men and women and women. They're still equal, but if some emotional needs of one are met by the other that doesn't indicate an inferiority but merely a—compatibility.

Which, if you stop to think about it, might be a sophisticated justification of a variation of male chauvinism—or a rather profound and possibly revolutionary thought. Or possibly even both.

Recent research indicates some of the factors in male-female differences may really exist and be inborn, even physiological.

'Then you really believe there are no innate differences—mentally or in ways male and female should relate to each other? All the things we've heard for years: men don't show emotion, women are more sensitive, more empathic, more yielding, more tender; men are more aggressive, more dominant, more warlike, more sports-minded, impassive, strong, silent—the two aspects most people think of as masculine and feminine

—you don't buy that?

"Well, no. I don't buy that as a genetic characteristic. It probably is an acquired characteristic, or set of characteristics, in this society, or in any societies. But certainly in a matriarchical society that isn't true. So I think the differences, if any, apart from physiology, must be taught.

'But then there is physiology, and it's becoming more apparent in things like *The Brain Revolution* book I've mentioned and other new research, that the body affects the mind. Have you heard about some of the new research showing that the male hormone is connected with greater aggressiveness? Even that it makes certain changes in the brain especially before birth, so that if you took away the male sex hormone or increased it, you'd reduce or increase aggression? Also, the male sex hormone increases sex drive in both sexes, and aggression in both. Some of the new physiological researchers, as well as people like Lionel Tiger are saying that this is part and parcel of our heritage from animal days—and that most aggression is essentially a male phenomenon.'

"Yeah, I've heard a litle about that and that's possibly true. If so, therein lies a difference which I hadn't noticed, but I'm trying to make a point about sexism, which is not in me at all."

'So when you meet someone or deal with someone you would relate to that person just as a person—never mind male or female? You'd decide, for example, whether to be more leading or less leading, how to "mesh" with that person just on the basis of that 'person's—'

"—of their mentality and their emotional needs."

'So when you start out with a man or a woman, it doesn't make any difference? You don't come into it with any different behavior?'

"My bias is for equality. If I have to act a role in order to satisfy their needs, it will perforce to be a short term relationship."

"Is this just something you've been doing recently or since Marcy—?"

"I think that it probably—my tendency is to think I've always felt this way. My *actions* seem to indicate differently. Not always but in my adult life. I don't remember the turning point, if there was one. But I—Marcy must have had a huge influence.

'You do do things, by the way—just as a point of interest—we're writers, we're supposed to be observant—you do things which are not quite what you are saying they are. The first time I met you in New York—about the second time I saw you after our first talk, you did something. Now there's no way that anybody in this galaxy can characterize me as a passive person who needs to be led. Would you agree with that? That's fairly obvious?

"I would—I would think so."

'And yet one thing which you did which was very intriguing—was you went like this, Bill. (Indicating taking her chin in hand, lifting and holding it for a few moments.)'

"I chucked you under the chin?!"

'What exactly did *that* signify?'

"A magnanimous gesture—?"

'It was adorable.'

"Well, maybe *you* were adorable."

"(Chuckles.) Well, it isn't exactly man to man—

'I mean, it's true. If you were adorable I might have chucked you under the chin. But I wouldn't. . . . There was an Indian Ambassador in Ottawa when I was playing in a repertory theater in Ottawa. An *Indian Ambassador!* I didn't know. Who cares? We were at a party. And there was this guy and we were standing around shaking hands and he had little round, brown cheeks and they glistened. And I went up to him—I was a young actor—and *I pinched him on the cheek*—and when I realized what I was doing—! But have you ever seen someone whose cheeks were just—chuckula-mumula? Have you ever? I mean, there are people who *look* like that. So I mean that didn't have anything to do with whether he was a man or a woman. It was the *cheek*.

'Well, I don't think it's the same kind of thing. It's an intriguing aspect of masculinity. I found that very attractive—in you.

"Well, don't also mistake the fact that there is a duality going on in an actor. To get up and do a one-man show—can you imagine what doing a one-man show for two hours is *like*?

Can you believe that you're standing there and people are looking at you to be amused and to be entertained? I mean—just the thought of it sometimes is very—you have to have such a tremendous ego to say—"Of *course*, I will entertain you." And at the same time you're saying, "Oh, shit." You know." He laughs. "There is this duality going on. So if sometimes I come on strong, that apparently is part of my personality. On the other hand we both know that that isn't *all* of my personality.

'But it made a statement right then and there. There are very few men in the world who would dare chuck me under the chin." (He laughs.) It's true. You did it with such a naturalness that it was—extremely alpha. If you met my husband for example—I am *sure* you would not chuck him under the chin. I *promise* you, it would never occur to you to do that to him. So there is a difference. I'm trying to point out that there is a slight difference about how you approach a man and a woman. It's not exactly equally.

"Okay."

'Okay.'

"But then don't forget the Indian Ambassador. I remember—I can still remember that he was staring—he was staring—the little brown eyes—"

'Somebody should have filmed that.'

(Ever wonder whether that Romulan fleet commander wouldn't have had him for breakfast someday for that faint trace of a "my dear girl" attitude when she became his captive? He chivalrously but somewhat patronizingly proposed to treat her as his guest. But she was Vulcanoid, you know, sharing an ancient ancestry with Spock—and a human male's "upper body strength" might not go too far against that. But that's another story. . . .)*

As a matter of fact there is an avalanche of stories, fantasies, letters, phone calls, artwork, etc., which pour in to us reflecting different aspects of Kirk's multifaceted capability for relating to women, love, sex.

The avalanche shows that one of Kirk's chief appeals is that he is not a man with a fixed program. He doesn't respond only to submissive dolls—or only to Dragon Ladies. He's quite capable of relating to both, or neither, doesn't try the same tactics on one as on the other, isn't above tactics if it's war, but knows how to declare peace. He has an eye for the girls, a head for figures, and a taste for a piece of the action. But also, most women see, he has a capacity for deep feeling, deep love—and for expressing it openly.

It was women, predominantly, who first understood the impact of Kirk shock. That was not so much because women had a special revelation or superior genius, (although that is always a "logical" possibility), but because they had special hungers—and a couple of clues from the revolution which was beginning to brew.

They were starving for that very emotional openness in men.

And they were starving for the image of a first-rate man who could respond to the different kinds of women they were just beginning to realize they were capable of being—and even some they could *not* be (at least, not yet.)

STAR TREK was the first concrete portrayal in dra-

---

*See *The Price of the Phoenix* and *The Fate of the Phoenix* by Marshak and Culbreath, Bantam Books, 1976, 1978.

matic art of the *spectrum of potential* of women.

No, it was not complete or exhaustive or free of error. It was the first. And it was swift, bright, sharp lines of color from parts of the whole range of the spectrum. Women also were: Heroic. Villains. Murderers. Kidnappers. Soldiers. Gladiators. Amazons. Innocents. Immortals. Gentle souls. Shrews. Shrewdies. Scientists. Security guards. Engineers. Yeomen. Officers and gentlemen. Aliens. Androids. Vulcanoids. Witches. Bitches. Doctors. Lawyers. Indians. Chiefs. Commanders. Rulers. Matriarchs. Queens. Kings. (Well, language *is* a problem. "Queen" doesn't cover the territory. Show us a king tougher than T'Pau of Vulcan. Show us *anybody* tougher than T'Pau.)

And that's just for openers.

The catalog of STAR TREK's women, even of Kirk's women alone and the kinds of relationships he had with them, would be an encyclopedia of possibility.

And the fantasies which spin off from it should come in a plain brown wrapper. (And frequently do. Usually to our mailbox.)

The fantasies make it plain that STAR TREK, explicitly or implicitly, presented the whole spectrum and smorgasbord: sex, sexiness, love, tenderness, anger, enmity, equality, inequality, contest, challenge, dominance, submission, role-reversal and role-breaking, tradition and the unprecedented, the familiar and the outside-the-square, yesterday, today, tomorrow, and where-no-man-woman-person-being.

Men see Kirk as a possible model to be transformed and transfigured into qualities they can use in their own lives, or as the embodiment of how they might relate to the various kinds of women now emerging in reality—or whom they might meet or like to meet in where-no-man fantasies.

Even women will see him as a possible model for their own character—as women have seen male heroes for years—once as almost the only decent models of what it is to be *human*.

But now they will see him as even more.

Kirk does represent mankind and *man*—a very good, tough, tender, strong, vulnerable, dominant, yielding, successful, impatient, troublesome, charming, irritating, delightful, hot-tempered, cool-headed, bright, foolhardy, egalitarian, chauvinistic, boyish, full-grown, and unadulteratedly gorgeous specimen of the species. To whom a certain actor does bear a close resemblance.)

But Kirk is in a slightly different situation.

Having those qualities—and risking his interesting anatomy all over the galaxy, Kirk is a perfect specimen to be taken for captive and mate by a Scalosian queen— or to be taken as a provocation to thought, among other things by Terran women, circa the Twentieth Century.

What do we really want in a man? In a man-women relationship? Is it really, in truth, equality? Androgyny? Sex-blindness in the same sense as we used to talk about color-blindness—no awareness of the difference?

Or do we really want, perhaps, to delight in diversity?

Maybe we want Tarzan back. Maybe we want Tarzan *with* emotional openness—alias James T. Kirk. Maybe we want Tarzan not so much with Jane as with the tough, no-nonsense Queen—La of Opar.

Some of us may even want Jane back—or Jane with a lesson from La.

The universality of symbols like Tarzan—translated into almost every language in the world, filmed in end- less variations, printed in uncounted editions, filtering down to comic books, gum wrappers, jokes, graffiti— constitutes the best evidence of the power of a really first-rate archetype of a vision of the ideal man. It is through such archetypes, worked and reworked through the mechanism of fantasy, from our earliest childhood fantasies through our most sophisticated sex fantasies that we shape our real selves, our real lives, our wishes and desires for what we want to find, or create, in a man or a mate.

That is the kind of archetype Kirk is becoming, even more rapidly. The kind of permanent engraving on the world's consciousness which Tarzan took decades to achieve, Kirk is achieving within a single decade—and this time with the face of mind of a living man who is seeing it happening, and getting the feedback from the shocks it's touching off.

It's mind-boggling.

But neither Kirk nor Shatner boggles very easily.

Love Story: Part II
The House on the Hill

Marcy Lafferty Shatner:
I could be a chameleon. I know now: that's not
unique to me. We've all learned how to put on our
best dresses—or our best skins—for whomever we
were with. I was great at that. But what happened is:
Marcy got lost somewhere.

Now—I can't believe that somebody would allow me
that freedom—that he *would encourage me not to be*
the chameleon, and just to be me.

There is one person of whom William Shatner says
"for the first time to any human being, I began to open up
and reveal what I really am, what I feel, things that have
hurt me."

It is that story—the other half of the love story which
was born in the crucible, which we have come to pursue.

It turns out to be a trail of surprises, which may not
only be the story of one man and one love, but in some
sense, the story of us all.

We drive up to the house on the hill.

Somewhere we hear the remembered echoes of the familiar voice: *"the house—has become the essence of both*

of us. . . . It's—private. It's—protected. It's—a haven."

It is.

The high gate opens for us now. A steep drive rises to spacious grounds. Wrought iron and space and height are the guardians of privacy. It is as remote as any castle-keep, and as necessary.

This Camelot could be too vulnerable. Even to love. Especially to love.

The private address is strictly for private friends, family, those few who need to know, and for no one else.

The height itself is privacy, protection, a sense of expanded horizons, looking not so much down as *out*— over a wide sweep of city which stretches to every horizon. By night the view is a tapestry of space-black velvet scattered with jewels of light, flung at the foot of mountains, and rising to their heights. By day, the straight-lines of purpose reveal the hand and effort of man, the Earth-born city of angels, climbing casually to build on mountains.

This height is perhaps as close to stars as the hours of a man's life can buy.

Somehow we can't help thinking of another house which was furnished for three hundred dollars.

He has bought this house with more than money.

Here are the years of the crucible, transmuted into the gold of peace and privacy by his effort. Here is the territory he has won, the height he defends, the home he has made for his family and for the woman who walked through the years of the crucible with him.

Today we are to meet that woman, see the home he has made for her—and the home she has made for him. . . .

It is the first time we have met Marcy. ". . .*The beauty which she has physically is nothing to the beauty of her soul. . .*" we hear the voice saying.

The first word we hear in the voice of Marcy Lafferty Shatner is "Kirk!" It is not a time anomaly or a private fantasy. A command: addressed to the male of a pair of splendid creatures who do not appear to be dogs, nor of this world. They are ravening at our throats, but obey at a word. They do not look like Dobermans, but are of the red color. They look like rare alien sculptures, as if they should come from some other planet. The male has the look of a stallion, of the prime male thoroughbred he is —a champion of champions: Kirk.

Marcy welcomes us graciously into a home which bears the look of being cared for by a perfectionist and with love.

After a moment she steps out to the kitchen to bring coffee, tea, and Bill comes in wearing a dark blue running suit, a glow, and much the same look of being cared for.

"Bill's not *safe*."

It is Marcy's estimate, too. We are talking about his acting: what does she think about him as an actor? "The best." It is unhesitating.

"Because—he's very daring, extremely courageous. This is over and above his acting ability. That *obviously* has to be there. We're not even talking about that, right? Like—a dancer who can do steps is not necessarily a *dancer*. It's a whole other level, if someone can *dance*. Mostly it takes courage for an actor to take the risk to make something *happen*.

"Laurence Olivier himself always said that an actor walks the finest line between making a total fool of himself, and having to have the great courage and great humility to the work he is doing to *try* things—to be not just *good* and not just *safe*. Bill's not *safe*."

Marcy Lafferty Shatner is, in an interesting way of her own, also not "safe." She, also, is a performer—an actress, a dancer.

She is the daughter of Percy Lafferty, for years network programming manager for CBS. She's grown up around actors and acting, has acted on stage, screen, and television herself. That world was not new to her when she met William Shatner—and she had never seen him in STAR TREK. She saw it in reruns—after she met him on "The Andersonville Trial."

"I didn't miss one then. I thought they were fabulous. I thought he was tremendously talented." She smiles. "It was just part of the package. It wasn't that he was a star or actor. I've been surrounded by that all my life, so that was not the immediate thrill. But it was *him* and *he* was the actor."

She says unequivocally: "I think he is one of the greatest actors."

And of Kirk and STAR TREK: "I don't want to put it down by saying, 'as television goes, it was good.' I think it was very fine stuff, in any terms, and challenging —very challenging to the actor, especially when you take into consideration the short amount of time, and really the *depth* of many of the episodes and the versatility required. I really think we shouldn't underestimate just how much he could show there. Great versatility. Great daring. We always joke about 'Captain Perfect,' the complete hero. But—it *worked*."

There is something in this house and this woman which has worked too. We do not know the woman, yet. But we know from the man that in at least one very fundamental way, Marcy Lafferty did not play it safe.

("Marcy hung in there.")

She made her choice and she backed her play. It was a risk. She put all her chips in the pot, and all her love in one basket, for a man who, by his own estimate, was "insane—the way an animal is insane."

Later she is to tell us about that: "I didn't stay because I knew I'd get the brass ring if I stayed, and I don't want anyone to get that impression. I stayed because I loved him—and it was just more good than not good."

The good and the not good, we learn, probably were

both where-no-woman, and where-every-woman: the
highs, higher; the lows—perhaps—lower, but the problem much the same as everyone's: a quest for love and
trust across the gulfs of loneliness and longing. (*I'd stay
away for days. . . For the first time, to any human being,
I began to reveal myself. . . I don't know what I would do
without her. . .*").

We ask about it, sitting in the elegant, comfortable
home on the hill—with that man settled in, happy as a
reformed clam, on the other end of her couch.

We tell her of some of the things he has said about
her, ending with '. . .that you're his "conduit to the
world"—which is a gorgeous phrase.'

Bill cuts in, in the incorrigible tone,

"Or—half-wit to the world."

'How you've transformed his whole life. We find that
an extraordinary testament of love.'

The look between them is also a testament.

Marcy has not read "The Crucible: Love Story"—nor
any of the manuscript. She returned from a trip to New
York only late last night. And as we are to discover, Bill
is letting her come to the interview fresh, setting no limits on what she is to tell us, taking no edge off what she
might say. She has no idea what he's told us or what
we've done with it, nor of what he would expect *her* to
tell us. But she knows him for a very private man. It's
not the easiest spot in the galaxy for the wife of a practicing shellmouth.

We ask her about the beginning. "Andersonville". . . .

"Probably I remember more about it than he does,
'cause I was much more interested in him than he was in
me." She was production assistant to director George C.
Scott. She too, starts with the story of running lines with
Bill. "He had most of the lines, anyway. We'd sit during
lunch, and I really had a terrible crush on him, and he
didn't even look at me. Hardly. And then one day he
started looking a little more. He looked up at me from

his script across the room—" there's just a slight break in her tone—"and we became very good friends and we had fun together."

("...I gave her my 'look'—and I kissed her....")

She is not shellmouth Shatner's wife for nothing. And maybe she shares a little of the shellmouth persuasion on her own *("Marcy'll kill me if I tell you that story.")*.

But she speaks with a certain candor and irony of her own feelings. "It's really not one of your great romantic beginnings, because he was going with someone else at the time. It was a pretty low time in my life. It was about two weeks after the show, and I had really given up hope he would call—and then the phone rang.... And in the beginning the love that grew I think was mainly mine. We didn't really know we'd end up this way."

Her glance includes house and home, the man on the end of the couch. There is satisfaction in it, perhaps a trace of lingering astonishment, possibly something of the proprietary and territorial.

"As for saving him and all that—" (it is not a phrase we've used to her—and she hasn't read it; she says it as if it is familiar and accepted between them) "—I feel the same way: that he did that for me. Isn't that what love is?"

We want to go into that. What *is* the love which was born in the crucible?

We start with the attraction. What did attract her to him?

"Oh! I don't know how you can even define such an attraction. His energy. His *energy*—that's him. He loves life and he really knows how to squeeze every drop out of it. I think he has tremendous animal magnetism—and perhaps I'm more spiritual. I love life as much, but he brings that out in me—managing the world."

Did any of that—say the animal magnetism—come through to her on screen, before she met him?

"Sure."

Just emphasized again?

"Because you make me think about it—that is obviously so, because he just has so much energy. What do you call it—sexual, dangerous energy—and risk—the dangerous qualities that I guess, if you *make* me define it will be the essence of the sex appeal. And I'm sure it came across to me, but I didn't have a crush on him before meeting him, or anything like that."

It hit when she met him?

"Uh huh. Yes."

Right away?

"Yes, it did. I really had a schoolgirl crush on him."

How would she define a "schoolgirl crush" as opposed to falling in love at first sight?

"Maybe when you get older you don't believe in falling in love at first sight—or else some people call what I'm calling the great crush falling in love at first sight. It's exciting and interesting and it's fun and heady, and *you* may call it love—and it may *be*. It's just not what *I* call love. I really do think love takes a long time to grow. Or maybe it *is* love. Maybe it's just semantics. Maybe it's another level. Because, it didn't fit any dream. I never carried around a dream of what I would want to have. Except when I was very young, and that was really based on a lot of false information and was not really workable. And once that got shattered—you start living every day, and I just never had a grand scheme."

We mention a theory that one level or basis for love is an attraction to one's mirror-image—the reflection of the basic essence of one's soul.

"We just bought a painting that I am calling 'Bill.' It's modern abstract expressionism. And when Bill saw it he thought I wouldn't like it because it's just—awhhh! It's just so much energy—it *jumps* at you. I walked in and I said 'wow!' I loved it because in one word, if someone had put *him* on canvas, that would be it. I know you'll laugh when you see it, because there's no form or figure."

"No they won't." Bill says.

Marcy continues: "But it is so much that joy and that daring—there's such a *risk* involved in this painting, and there's so much energy, and I think of all things, I'm not sure that's my mirror image. I think that's another case, where your image would be—complementary."

"Is there some aspect of you, perhaps, that would *like* to be like that?" We ask.

"Oh yes," Marcy answers immediately. "Absolutely no question. I would *love* to be."

She says it easily. The tone is simple admiration. And in some way it is recognition and acceptance of diversity. She loves him for that energy—would even love to have it herself.

But there is a kind of luxury in the fact that she doesn't *have* to have it; he has enough for both. He is notably protective of her. She is perhaps, in other ways, even more fiercely protective of him *("Sometimes I hear her on the phone. . .she guards me. . . .").*

She does not look like a fierce guardian. Except for something in the green eyes.

Marcy has a certain look which is almost translucent, delicate, perhaps even fragile. She is soft-spoken, rather deliberate in speech and movement, capable of stillness, able to sit quietly, laugh softly. Her face is clear, young. Only a certain look of the adult woman in her eyes would tell you that she is not a young girl in the first blush of maturity. The eyes tell you that she is a woman grown, with a certain blend of her own vulnerability and strength.

She is doubtless not a porcelain doll, despite any Dresden look of fine translucence. She is doubtless not in any real sense fragile. Still, he guards her energy (—is she tired? Does she need to rest—?) as carefully as he spends his own careless abandon.

("I'm taking days off the end of my life, putting them in front.")

It seems normal to *him*. Perhaps it is. Perhaps it is a

cost only he can count. More probably, it is both. We
have seen how even under stress or in the worst of times
he can nearly always muster another level of energy—
sparking a new project at the end of a killer day, still
another idea, another story, another joke, carrying people along with him.

It is a remarkable enough performance at any time.
Some of it was immortalized on the STAR TREK
"blooper reel"—even when the fires of the crucible were
already burning.

By the time Marcy met him, they were white hot. He
had hit bottom—the days which he can't remember. . . .

Yet she has said that when they started to go out, they
had "fun together—really good times."

What was he like in those days? We try to get at it.
'Everybody has heard about Bill's sense of humor on
the STAR TREK set. Did he show any of that side in
"The Andersonville Trial"?'

"Well, he didn't play any of the jokes that I've heard
about. But he has a *great* sense of humor."

'Did that turn you on?'

"Yes. It still does. I'm sure it always will. God—if I
have to give up something—if I could only keep *one*
thing, between the humor and the energy—."

Marcy breaks off, shaking her head, looking at him—
indicating the magnitude and flat impossibility of the
choice she started to set.

How does his sense of humor manifest itself around
here?

"Oh, he's a clown, but he's also very ironic. I mean
he's cynical, too. But it's not just practical joke humor.
It's just the ability to laugh. I guess you know him more
as that funny joker of all those funny—"

Bill turns to her almost protectively. "You've never
seen them. That side—."

"I've never seen that side of Bill, so when I talk about
his humor—"

"When I said side," Bill says, "I meant also the blooper film."

"I've never seen that. I'd love to see it. I've heard so much about—I mean, he's *wild*. Everything I've heard I can absolutely picture. It's not surprising to me."

She should see the reaction to it at a convention, we say. Five or ten thousand people—hysterical. 'You know, Bill, we've noticed that after the first conventions a few years ago when the bloopers were first shown, there was even a deeper caring for you. It would be interesting to try to analyze exactly why.'

"Because I think—people like to *bag* you," Marcy says. "If you're strong and brave, you can't be funny. Or if you're villainous—if you're dangerous, you can't be good. People like to put us in niches. But I told you from the beginning, he's fun—and that's a tremendous factor. The most *fun* person I've ever known."

It's probably one of the tributes he'd most like to be paid, and the full reality of it includes, also, some image which comes to us: sunlight glinting with quicksilver brightness off of troubled water.

'He went through a very bad time,' we say. 'Divorce. The ending of STAR TREK, financial and family problems—was any of that apparent there at "The Andersonville Trial"?'

"I didn't know any of those details," Marcy says, "because, again he never talked about it. But I thought there was a quality of sadness and bitterness, and when I saw him—before he ever met me I saw him once, when he did the 'CBS Playhouse' that I love so much."

She looks at Bill. "You were standing alone." And then back to us. "I just saw part of him. A friend of mine was working on the show. I was walking past a set. And he was standing at a chair—I remember with his hands on the back of the chair, just looking out over the top of the chair. And I stopped. For the longest time, I just looked at him, and I thought he looked so sad and angry. And there was always that quality to him.

'What did that arouse in you?'

"I just wanted to make him feel better. I felt bad for him."

'You're talking about before you met him—that moment on the set—?'

"Oh, what did *that* arouse in me? Nothing. It was so strong that not knowing him, I remember, it was just a moment—it was *that* strong. It was like, 'Oh!?' " (The exclamation is a question, a comprehension, a lament. It is the tone of finding a bird with a wing down. An eagle.)

'Do you think that had anything to do with how you responded later, when you did have the overwhelming reaction—the crush, whatever you want to call it?'

"No, I think I put it out of my mind. And when he talked about his children, I think I remembered. Like, I would say, 'Do you have children?' and then we would talk about them, and he'd be in a great mood, with such love that it was so sad. But I didn't ask him or poke around about it because he was very private."

'If you could describe your developing awareness of him after the beginning—what did you start to see in him after you saw the magnetic, he-can-take-over-the-world animal magnetism? What, then, did you see?'

Marcy laughs, not so softly. "Well, *that's* pretty good, isn't it?! I mean—what else *is* there?" She sobers. "I think, just a deepening of those things, and the fact that they were *real*. You really run a risk when you get to know someone that you think is marvelous, but they either don't live up to it, or—"

'Right.'

"His tenderness, his gentleness became even more apparent after that. He's very *kind*."

'Could you give an example of why you thought he was tender and gentle and kind?'

"There are so many," she says. "Mostly in terms of myself—of understanding really very delicate personal things that required a great deal of listening.

"And also—" Marcy adds, "the ability to apologize, which I find very rare in so many people, especially in a man. And I don't mean to sound like I'm castigating all men."

'That's rare. And the more alpha a man is, the more powerful—"

"Alpha? I'm not quite sure I get the picture—?" Marcy says.

"There sits an alpha male—" indicating the other end of the couch.

Marcy laughs. "Oh. What's a beta male?"

"A beta male?" The other end of the couch is heard from, in a tone which draws laughter even before he starts. "A *beta male?*" More laughter. "Requires fifteen cents."

Marcy: *"See!"* She breaks up, indicating: incorrigible —thank God.

After a moment:

'We're just defining alpha male in terms of dominance —the leading male figure, say, in—'

"Yes, I understand. Now it comes back to me—in the animal world."

'The alpha's the one the others follow, submit to—'

"He would be that. Yeah."

More laughter. Slight pause. She's been candid about her own feelings, a little reserved about anything touching on him. We haven't had much of a chance to indicate that the shellmouth game isn't what it used to be. It's only fair.

'He's told us a little about that beginning—when you first kissed.'

She looks at him, a little startled. She laughs. "You *told*—?" Then to us. "It's a funny story. I mean—it's not particularly *romantic.*"

Bill has a smile in his voice, teasing her a little. "Why don't *you* tell it?"

Marcy laughs. "You see, I don't know how he told you. . . This is very *interesting*. I don't know *who* he's ever told these things to."

"Why don't you tell it as you remember it?" he says.

She laughs, perhaps remembering too well.

"It was just total—" For a moment Marcy turns to Bill—"I think like you told it—" Then back to us, the words tumbling out, "It was just *tremendous physical attraction*. I was eating a *hamburger*—which I don't eat anymore—and *so* nervous. I *jumped* up and—(she laughs) 'anything—what do you want?' I was having a *hamburger*. And he *kissed* me and I just turned to jelly— as they say in all those terrible books, my knees buckled, and I couldn't think of a thing to say—" she pauses a moment, saying openly, with emphasis: "It was terribly *romantic*. And I was just crazy about him—and that's the whole story. He sat me back down." (She smiles, laughs.) "I was a peccadillo in his life."

Bill says instantly: "I'm a hen-peccadillo husband now."

'Yeah, huh? *Everybody* can see that.' (To Marcy) 'Do you think he would have this devastating effect on women in general—that kiss, I mean—?'

"Of course." Marcy says. "He *has*."

Bill chokes on that, laughing, getting out some strangled protest that ends in—"for heaven's sake!"

'I'll tell you, Marcy, I think you're very kind, that you let—now *my* idea—I would like very much to put a cloak and cape around my mate. I've often said this, and he won't go along with that. Do you ever have that temptation—to do that with him? Nice cloak and mask?'

"No, I mean—I know what you're *saying*, but—actually—I'd like to put him in a box and never let him leave the *house*!"

She ends forcefully, and we chuckle. 'Yes, I know.'

"I hate it," she says seriously, the lingering hint of

laughter vanishing. "You know, what you find attractive in somebody, most of the other people find attractive too. You can't think it's only for you. And I think that's very territorial and very normal—'cause I really think we're very, very much—animals. It's something I try not to dwell on, 'cause it's very upsetting."

'I get the impression you were holding yourself back and weren't going to fall in love. This so-called crush or physical attraction or whatever—you were going to call it *that*. When did you start to see him in terms of love as opposed to crush, and "this is my mate"—hopefully for life—as opposed to—'

"I *never* thought 'this is my mate,' " Marcy says. "Because, you see, Bill didn't *want* that.

"I was perfectly happy the way things were for a long time. He made me *happy*. It wasn't *ideal*, but *nothing* is. I had no grand marriage scheme—there just came a time that I didn't feel I could continue to give so much of myself, if he didn't share my deep-laid feelings. I knew I just couldn't go on like that, that if I did, I'd finally *not* like him.

"I didn't want *that* to happen. And I did *not* think he'd ever want to be married again. And I didn't blame him. He *had* his children. He'd gone through a painful divorce. Why would he want to be married? I didn't take it personally. But I also knew that I probably would have to be married.

"So I *said* that, in essence, to him. And he said that he really *did* want to get married. And I was so *surprised*.

"And then he started just laughing. I said—'I mean—do you have any idea *when?*' You know," Marcy laughs.

"He said—'In the next five years.'

"And then I said—'I'm sorry, I can't wait that long.'

"He said, 'The next free weekend, then.' "

Marcy puts a sigh, a laugh in her tone—the tone of confronting unbelief—with resignation: "I came home and I told my *parents*—"

Bill is laughing. "It's the truth. That's exactly the way it was."

"And my father said 'sure, sure.' I mean Daddy *never* thought we'd get married.

"And I said, 'Well, he *said* the next free weekend. I think it's about three weekends from now.'"

Bill and Marcy laugh together.

'And that's what it *was*?'

"Yes," Marcy says. "And I think he was really very scared. But I *knew* it would be terrific. Also, it was like having the best medicine. As soon as it was over, I think he liked it."

Then Bill says, "It's interesting because at one point during the ceremony—I haven't said this before—I heard a sob coming from someplace. I turned around— 'who is that sobbing?' And it was *me*. *I* was sobbing."

'What were you thinking, Bill?'

"I don't know. It was terrible."

"No," Marcy says, "It was very moving. It was really beautiful. And—I'm sure he's been happy."

He has laughed, softly, perhaps the word would be ruefully, telling the story on himself. But he is not embarrassed. He tells it now with a kind of ease.

But it was only much later that these two began to come to grips with something else. It is not only "men don't cry" which can keep people from being real to each other. It is a trail which Marcy opens up for us, with a candor and level of analysis of herself which we find increasingly remarkable, as she, too, opens up.

After a moment we ask Marcy now: 'What do you think he saw in *you*, Marcy? He's asked us to ask you.'

Marcy laughs. "I think that's *mean*. You mean he asked you to ask me because he didn't answer, right?"

'No, he answered. He answered two volumes worth.'

"Did you answer, Bill—?" She asks him. He nods. "Did you say you *did*—at that time? Or in retrospect—?"

"Well—probably in retrospect," Bill says.

"I *can't,* because—"

"Well," he says in a tone that is somehow protective, "the question really is: what do you think are the qualities that I saw in you?"

"That attracted you to me?" She laughs. "I think it was entirely a physical attraction. What did *you* say?"

He smiles, teasing her. "I said your legs."

She chuckles, a little acidly. "Yeah. The first day I wore a *skirt*. That was the first big breakthrough." She sobers. "It was funny—the beginning. I don't know. I guess I'm—I think I'm—funny. And—things surface in me rather easily. Perhaps that was a big attraction. Perhaps the biggest attraction was that I cared so much for *him*. But I do think it's awfully difficult to say what somebody else sees in you, without sounding terribly self-serving."

Or, possibly, terribly restrained. She is doubtless better off to let him speak for herself ("*. . .a spirit, a saint. . .the soul of an angel. . .and I really mean the goodness. . . .*").

Nor would he define what she saw in him. She has no difficulty about *that*.

'He's told us about the house furnished for three hundred dollars. Tell us something about your feelings about that, that he had to do that—especially after the triumph of all the other years, and of STAR TREK?'

"I *loved* that house, although it was rather simply furnished. But I—when I found that *out* later, my feelings were—I hurt for him. That's really too bad—" She turns to Bill, realizing what she is getting into, surprised, checking. "Did you get into all this for the book?"

Bill nods, confirming. "I talked about it, yes."

At that moment the phone rings, a peremptory summons, and he is on his feet, moving quietly, excusing himself.

She is already speaking as he goes out, as if the con-

firmation and permission has released a floodgate.
"What I hated most was what he had to do work-wise.
That I *hated.* As bad as those other things were, you've
just got to go on. It requires so much negative energy,
too, to harbor anger. Some people, of course, it enables
them to survive. I'm really not like that. I think it's just
totally depleting and degrading. It's unfair and cruel and
sad and all those things, yes, but that happened, and it
all happened for a reason, I believe. The only really immediate thing that hurt me continually was that he—
because he's *so* practical. That's a side that I don't *know*
if you know?"

'Yes.'

"He's so very *practical.* He had children to support,
houses to support. And he didn't do what so many actors have done after a series—in fact—price himself too
high? I think he *underpriced* himself tremendously. And
I think that's one big thing, perhaps, that I've done for
him. 'Say *no.* Say *NO!*' He couldn't say no. He literally
could not afford to."

"And for many years he did every show that was offered to him—and *did his best.* I mean, that's so
marvelous. He can *phone* these things in. He really *can.*
There's so little quality stuff. Endless guest shots, quiz
shows. He worked so hard, all the time. He *never*
stopped, *ever. Sundays.*

"*That* hurt me. And I think that when you work that
hard, and you're that *good*—it really is selling yourself
cheap. He never *felt* that because he looked at it as his
responsibility for something else."

The look in her eyes is plain admiration, and more—
something close to worship. She goes on, as if to be able
to say it before he comes back. "Another thing I didn't
add is how much I loved him for his ability—perhaps
this is where I saw his kindness first—was with his children. He adored them—really, not out of guilt or not
being a Sunday father. He truly just adored them, and
they adored him. And that ability to give love in its truly

most unselfish form—there were times when he'd break his back—it's very hard to maintain a family relationship when you get a divorce. And I think it is a triumph of his determination, which is, like, *unbelievable*, and his will, which is endless, that they are all now just fine.

"I think that was one of the—probably the biggest reason—he loves me, because I helped him so much with them, gave him a home that they needed, made a lot of things possible."

It's an extraordinary statement for her to make. We begin to understand more of what this woman is and how she was able to hang in there through the crucible.

'He said he was *insane* in those years.'

"It was *horrible*. But—it's all worked out very well. And I do really, really believe that all our pain is for a purpose."

'Do you think it's caused by something? Are you talking about something which is either spiritual or religious?'

"Well, I don't think it's put *on* us. Sometimes you do it to yourself, and sometimes you feel like you're an innocent victim. But I really believe anybody who experiences something negative, if they can make it positive, is on a whole other level than somebody else. And that is your gift, your enlightenment.

"But we do like to be comfortable, so it's hard, because that kind of growing process is so painful. It's my personal belief, and it keeps me going, and it's impossible to justify or explain. There is a kind of justice. Sometimes you get thrown for a loop and you can't answer, and then it's just faith. But I do believe you have to turn everything around and make it positive. What are your *choices?* Either to go with it and be hurt—and be nowhere, and be blind—or to learn. And that's what I mean by "positive"—I don't mean you can make everything pleasurable.

'How did you feel about the fact that he would *do* all

those things to keep his family going? For example, I find it very attractive. If he would do *that*—then if he's on a desert island or a plane crash, he'll do whatever he has to do to protect his family.'

'Absolutely. He's a survivor. That's one of his most attractive qualities. That's *him.*'

We describe what he has said about his emotional state in those years—"insane the way an animal is insane" because he'd lost his kids, lost everything, was scrambling, clawing to get it back. How did she feel about his emotional state then?

"You must understand that because he felt those things, he closed himself off, rather than ask for help, so that I could not actively know the depth of all that, because he did not wish to discuss it. I didn't know until after I knew the children. I didn't really know them for two years. Just met them after six months, but didn't get to share things with them. He kept them very separate. He kept all that to himself and that pain was his, and it was not something that he wanted to share. It made him wall himself off. I just felt tremendously frustrated.

'He's said "Marcy hung in there." In fact, he's said you say now something like, "I hung in there, you bastard." '

Bill comes back from the phone to hear the last of that. "Was that what it was?" we ask him.

"Um hum. That's right," he says.

"Well, I *did*. That's *right*," Marcy says with vigor, laughing—a tone of triumph. She chuckles. "If the water wears away the stone—. Perhaps there's another way of putting it. Drip, drip, drip. No. I said I wormed my way into his heart. It was just—he who laughs *last*, laughs *best*."

She laughs. Best.

"But I was able to do that, because I was getting what *I* needed," she adds.

'What were you getting?'

"Just—emotionally I was sustained more than I was not sustained."

It's the point at which she says that she didn't stay because she knew she would get the brass ring.

"But there was a point there where it really had to come to a head," she says. "It *did*."

'There must have been some bad times.' We start to say. 'He's said, for three years, if it hadn't been for *you*. . . ."

There's a sudden shattering sound—it's a bark. Off the Richter scale. The ravening monsters have crept in soundlessly and fallen asleep. Now they leap up. "He hears something," Bill says softly. "What is it, Kirk? What is it, baby? Okay, Kirk. Now lie down. It's okay, Kirk, down. That's right."

The great Doberman comes, and after a moment of ecstatically collecting his rightful due at the hands of god and man—wriggling like a puppy under the ruffling and caress of the man's hands—lies down obediently at his master's feet.

It's only a moment. A man and his dog. But there's something very simple and very touching about how he is with the dog. It's a level of love which he has had for a long time, spanning any other love, never failing him, never betraying—(". . .but never the *kind* of dog, or the *way* I wanted a dog—with some inchoate longing. . . .").

The inchoate longing has been satisfied now, at least with the kind of dog and the way he wanted a dog. And perhaps other inchoate longings, too. . . .

"It was horrible," Marcy says, picking up the thread of the question again as the dog subsides under Bill's hand. "I wanted to share that, but I couldn't. You can't *force* someone to let you share."

"What was the question?" Bill asks.

"About your pain. . ." Marcy says, checking.

"Go ahead," he says quietly.

"There was always so much anger, and pain, and

fighting, and evidence of difficulty, and it was very awful. And then—it just got better."

'Were there times when you thought you just wouldn't make it?'

"You mean Bill and I?" Marcy hesitates for a long time. It is the first time she has really paused over a question, allowing a silence to fall, not looking at Bill, looking, perhaps, into herself. And deciding what she will say to us. "Yeah," she says finally in a low voice, reluctantly, but firmly. "There were times. Because I didn't think that he would allow himself really to need anybody, to open up. And you can't force that. I'm not talking about after we were married. I'm talking about those first couple of years."

'Did you ever get the feeling that consciously or subconsciously or unconsciously Bill was testing you?'

She nods. "Yes."

'For what? What was he trying to determine?'

"I'm not sure. I don't know—for whatever his needs were. But I did feel he was testing me." She pauses a second, murmurs: "I must have passed." She laughs.

'He said that he learned to trust you—and opened up —for the first time to anyone. Did you know that he had never opened up to anyone?'

"No," Marcy says. "I still find that so difficult to believe. I really do. For someone who had the capacity to give so much—I mean, I *believe* him. It's just hard to imagine. But I think that question of trust—was probably the test.

"And it was very joyful when he did start to open up. I felt very happy. The more you can give, the more you can open up, the more risk you are willing to take—the better and deeper the love is."

'Did you ever feel that before that you were, and perhaps he was, too—"psychologically invisible?" We feel that there is a human need to be visible psychologically, to at least one other person—who will know what you *are*.'

"I'm *sure* there is. I never thought about it actively but now that I *have* it, I would say that's absolutely true. But I never felt the lack of it, because I pretty much could present myself in any role to please anybody— whatever they wanted. Change myself to fit *their* needs—"

It's the opening chord of what is to become the chameleon theme—and it is cut off when Bill, who has once again left the room with the swift strides of answering a red alert, calls her to the phone, then answers another one himself.

It is like that *all the time,* we see as we return time and again to the house on the hill, this trip, and again in a few months. The phones never stop ringing. Later, when we are working with Bill, on various projects we see him scoop up the phone, accept or reject some offer, resolve some professional question, work out some complex problem—and return to the middle of some interrupted sentence without missing a beat. He seems to handle it with ease, but the strain must take a toll. There may be two, three, five calls in an hour. There are five on the first hour of tape, perhaps ten or twelve the first afternoon. "I *hate* the phones," Marcy says later. "There are times when I think—if I hear *one* more call—" But she does, and she shields him when she can. More often than not, however, he takes it, shielding her. It's not hard to see what she means about his energy.

When they come back, they find us getting acquainted with the dogs—pussycats, now that we have been accepted by the master and mistress.

There's some conversation before we turn on the tape —Marcy on how Bill has changed her life. Then:

"How could you explain how somebody brings you out just in every way? He's just tremendously supportive. In any area, areas I've had problems in, work areas, everything."

'He said that when he opened up, the feelings welled up for a while, and then they went away, or at least he could handle them. We've talked to him about the old idea—"men don't cry"—how we believe the way he played Kirk helped to break that down. Were there times when he *did* cry with you?'

"Oh. Were there times when he *did* cry? Well—Bill?"

She's caught on the dilemma again, looks to Bill in appeal.

He laughs, appreciating her difficulty, teasing a little. "That's *great.*"

"I don't know *what* he's told you." She looks at Bill. "I don't know what you want me—what I *should* tell—"

Bill chuckles in sympathy, smiles at her. "I understand. I understand your problem. Say what you want."

"Well, *yes.* He's very open. There *have* been times. I just won't tell you *when.*" She smiles as if the secret is worth keeping. It's not a bad shellmouth compromise.

Bill chuckles, murmurs something appreciative.

'How do you think that you were projecting the fact that he could trust you? There must have been a time when you didn't know you could trust *him.*'

"I think—I just *decided* to trust him," Marcy says.

'Part of what I'm getting at is, Bill has said in those early years that you were lovely and pretty and delightful, someone who cared for him, and so forth, but he's said he didn't really care.'

"Right," Marcy says. "Of course, I'd like to believe that that's not entirely true. We'll never really know because it was never tested. I never took that risk of, say, leaving. But if he says that's true, it's probably true. I didn't believe he didn't care. But—I'm committed to whatever I do, with a great passion—whether it's bathing the dog or—"

"I mean," Bill cuts in, "she *really* bathes the dog—with lanolin and oils and brushes."

"So—there never was a point when I said, "Okay, *now* you get the good part of me, because you've earned it.""

That also is a rather extraordinary testament.

We turn to the more general question of emotional openness in men—was she aware of that as a question? Did she see that potential in Bill? And explain what we have suggested as the effect of the way he played Kirk on breaking down the men-don't-cry syndrome and on the revolutions of the decade. Do some of Bill's comments reflect discussions with her—for example his comment on "male chauvinism" in STAR TREK and in himself?

"Yes," she says, "but I think what women's lib is really about is that if somebody really loves you, they must let you *be*. Men have through the ages—" She shakes her head, "This could open up—I have to keep this simple, because we could talk for a *month*—"

"But there *is* a great deal of this in the book," Bill says. "If *fact*, it's a central question. Why don't you answer this as fully as you can, and then have another session?"

Marcy takes it up eagerly. "When women become more independent, it really tests a relationship. It's like creating your own monster. If man encourages you to develop yourself, and you *do*, you become more independent, and that can be very threatening. So I think in the whole male-female world usually women *have* been subservient. And you don't change your nature. I mean, it gives me great pleasure to *do* things for Bill. But they're not mutually exclusive. I can also have opinions and be strong, and disagree, and he may not like it at the moment. He may not like it *a lot*. But he likes the *idea* that I *will* and *can*. And I think the intellect has to take over at that moment. Because we all get threatened. We think they'll leave us and abandon us as we think of independence, but I don't think that's so. I just don't think you can keep anybody tied to you with need and have any deep love come out of that."

'Bill, do you want to talk about the focus of the book —tell her about it?'

Bill: "Well, this book does have a big focus on male-female relationships, and their theory is that STAR TREK and the character of Kirk helped to promulgate the feelings of emotional openness in men and concurrent female independence, as part of the whole syndrome. And, how it is reflected in our personal life? That's a thread that runs through it. And I've given my interpretation of it, and you're in the process of giving yours."

Marcy nods. "You see Kirk—it was television, it was film, it was make-believe, and so you could have the perfection of this incredibly domineering *conquistador* man who also believes in women's independence. And in reality, Bill *is* like that. But it's not that simple. . . . There are times when you're threatened, and you work those things out. But basically that *is* what Bill believes.

"That there are snags now and then along the road is because we're two people who didn't come from perfectly perfect backgrounds, and we both have insecurities and needs, like everybody. But if you honestly have the well-being of the other person in mind, then that requires some amount of sacrifice—which is not always the easiest thing for an alpha male. You strive and you work it out all the time."

"There's another factor for us, too," Bill adds. "I have three girls, three girl children, and they're just becoming young women. Part of the intensity of my appreciation of women's roles in our society is due to the fact that these three girls are about to enter society, full-fledged. And I want them to have the best education and to have a skill that is equal to any man's. One of the girls is thinking about marine biology. Ten years ago that would never have been thought of as a woman's job. And the others are into psychiatry or psychology. And I want them to emerge as totally functioning human beings—not as *women, per se,* but as functioning human beings who can make their own livelihood, have independent thought, and therefore approach their partners in life as equals."

Marcy says, "But as a *man*—and as the woman who lives with him, he may have emotional needs that are not always hand in glove with his intellectual—um—"

"Statements," Bill finishes.

"No. Real endeavors. And that's when the conflict comes. But who is that not *in?* You cannot be such an alpha male and not have those—"

Bill cuts in, "But I think that there is another whole aspect of that, and that is the individual personality. Not women against men. It resolves itself down to: two people living together have to conform in many ways to each other's personalities to make it work. There are critical questions that arise.

"The main one to me, the litmus test of a male-female relationship could be: if both of you were offered very good jobs, one in New York and one in Los Angeles—I mean the woman's in New York and the man's in Los Angeles—and you're married and you live in Kansas City—do you head east or west?

"And *that* is where the whole relationship revolves. Whose needs, in that area, need to be satisfied first? Traditionally the woman would say, "Let's pack and go to Los Angeles." Nowadays, it's possible, in rare instances, that they pack and go to New York City.

"And it's probably even more feasible, plausible, that they say, "We'll see ya someplace in New Orleans," Bill laughs. "And *that's* where it's about.

"To me it's not now a matter of man and woman, but how two people living together—they could be in a homosexual relationship—and that decision would still have to be answered.

'How do *you* answer?'

Bill answers without hesitation.

"*My* job. I'm the breadwinner. And it's just perforce that Marcy must come with me if I go on location as I would go on her location if I wasn't working. But if it's to take us away for weeks or months—to keep our marriage together, Marcy must come with me, because I *must* go on that job. Which is not to say that Marcy shouldn't go on location on a show that she's on and I would go with her if I could.

"But when it's down to a conflict, not necessarily all the time, but I'm talking about the polarity now—not a gray area where it's more important for her to have her job than for me to have mine, because of the evolving career or whatever, or my show isn't really that good and so I can give that up. I'm talking now dramatically. *This* or nothing will happen for me again."

Marcy says, "So hypothetically you just take each one and there's really nothing—"

"Well," Bill says, "the *problem* would be if the two people had never really discussed it and each one assumed, "Well, of *course,*" and when that question was asked we both interjected—"Well *mine*" y'know—at the same time."

His "my job" is unequivocal, in the simple tone of "that's how it is"—without apology or wavering. That very practical streak and sense of responsibility, perhaps of honor, which will work day and night, Sundays, never stopping, to be the breadwinner, support his family— has its price.

He's very aware of the revolution. It has changed his thinking in many ways. On this, for him, the line is drawn here.

'One thing which struck us, Bill, was some of your language, like "upper body strength." Does that reflect some discussion the two of you have had at one time or another?'

"*Who* said upper body strength?" Marcy says, interested.

"*I* say that," Bill admits, "about three times in the discussions for the book—talking about one of the differences is the 'upper body strength.' I kept using that phrase. I might have read it the day before and it struck me, or something—"

Marcy laughs, "Probably because girls don't do push-ups."

'It doesn't sound much like a phrase he would have used. Does this reflect discussions that you've had down through the years about male/female differences?'

"Well, sure, we discuss it," Marcy says. "It's fascinating. I just think that there *are* differences. I think we're meant to be complementary. You know, you can't make everybody alike. I think it's a mistake. I've totally supported the women's movement. I think it's absolutely so important. And it's so *sad,* to me, how many women have had no chance to fulfill themselves in *any* way. I don't mean necessarily by getting a job, but by being treated just as a human being of self worth, and being congratulated on running a home. The more I see, the more I realize how lucky I am. We have to have this revolution to give women a sense of their own worth. And I think when that finally comes down, instead of threatening a man, it can only make things better. I think it's too bad that people are going through this time of trouble—I'm sure men are *extremely* threatened by the women's movement.

"But a male being so dominant and having so much expected of him, I can't imagine was always easy, or that all men wanted that, or couldn't help but feel that they'd failed somehow. I think this will make it just better for everyone. We discuss it all the time."

'Do you argue about it?'

"We don't argue much about it. Isn't that *boring?* I think the only arguments that may come out of that is that we've both lived and been brought up one way, and yet intellectually you are striving for and believing something else. Sometimes you have a tremendous emotional clash. It's not always easy. But—it's never a big deal. We are really very much in accord.

'Is a lot of your focus the traditional male/female role?'

"What do you mean? *Was* it?"

'Was it and *is* it? Has it changed?'

Marcy speaks thoughtfully, "Yes, in many ways the traditional male and female roles. Yeah. Yes, but also I like to work, and I don't think they're mutually exclusive."

Bill says, "You must *define* traditional male and female roles. Marcy's pointed out that what women have not had was the chance to fulfill themselves even in the traditional male/female roles. If what they independently *want* is to take care of home, husband, children, and make the home pleasurable for both, then this is their fulfillment. That's really what pleasures them more than working in an office as a secretary—or as a boss. They do it out of fulfillment, not out of duty. Do you see? So what may appear to be a traditional male/female relationship may indeed be a *new* male/female relationship based on independence and fulfillment.

'What we're getting at, Marcy, is the idea that there are actually two halves to each of us. What is commonly called the male—the dominant, the aggressive—

"Yes, I *know* what you're doing. I mean the show where he was split down the middle—it was very good."

'And more generally—what's commonly called the feminine side, the more submissive, the more yielding, and so forth. But actually both are in all of us. Now we suspect that you can't be fully developed to the optimum unless you can actualize both potentials, both halves of the whole.'

"*Ideally.*"

'So—how does this work with somebody like this who is such an alpha dominant male as you've said. Can you actualize the other half of *you?*

Marcy pauses, "Yes. I *guess* I do—"

"That's an interesting question," Bill says.

Marcy nods, "In a way it would have to be answered no because that would mean if I had to go conquer and to work all the time to be fulfilled—perhaps if we would extend that, then I'm not *doing* that. But I think in ways that are important to me—"

'No. You don't have to go *out* and conquer the galaxy.'

"I think with Bill it's more like he's *brought out* the other half in me—the more manage-the-world qualities.

At that point the phone claims its due again.

The afternoon has passed. It's getting late. Marcy has a prior obligation for the evening, guests to prepare for, she's overstayed her time with us and still wants to go on. But Bill calls a halt for her. (—are you all right?). We set a time to meet again with Marcy. He takes us to go over his notes on the manuscript, to show us the grounds, to play his album "The Transformed Man" for us.

We walk out to see the grounds—beautiful. Fruit trees planted that will mature in a few years. A view sweeping down and out to wide horizons. A heavy stone bench by the pool which he wants to move nearer to the edge of the view. "I need another 'upper body strength'" he laughs. There is his gym by the pool. Assorted equipment, a heavy punching bag. We try it. Might as well punch a wall.

We go to the guest house, just up above the main house, partly the girls' domain, also a study where we hold several work sessions. Now he wants to play the record. A sunlit room with books, a few pictures or posters from Bill's career, the six photo and clipping albums which Marcy has compiled as a gift to him, and which we go through later for the book.

Perhaps the most notable feature is a bearskin on the floor. It is a Kodiak bear of the kind that stands nine or ten feet tall. This one would have. We don't ask about it

now, but at a later session, yes, it is the one he killed—
with an arrow—his hands illustrate about two feet long
—and he wishes now that he hadn't. He regrets it very
much, almost wishes that the skin were not there, but
keeps it.

It is in this same sunlit room, later, that he rehearses
for us "Whales Weep Not"—a complex, daring poem
by D.H. Lawrence which he performs at the Hollywood
Bowl to save the whales.

He goes over his notes on the manuscript—one or two
things to add, a couple of items from clippings to
change. No complaint about the end of the shellmouth
game.

The manuscript notes bring forth a couple of interesting stories. Clippings in the Lincoln Center Drama Collection have said that Shatner played Henry V at the age
of twenty-two in Scotland, to a standing ovation. We
puzzled a little over the time and place, but it was in
several clippings. Turns out the story was even more interesting than that. He tells it now—and a few days later
we read what he did not say in a drama critic's account
written the next day.

It was in Canada, the Stratford Shakespearean Repertory Theatre. What no one had said was that the young
Shatner had gone on to play Henry V *as an understudy*
—on a couple of hours notice, unrehearsed, early in the
season when most understudies would not even have
known the lines, and there had been no opportunity for
an understudy rehearsal with the company. But
Shatner's contract called for him to understudy the part.
Characteristically, he had come prepared to go on—on
the thousand-to-one chance that he would be needed.
He was.

It's an enormous part, one which carries the whole
play, one of the most difficult, fiery, and heroic parts in
all of Shakespeare. The drama critic writing the story
felt constrained to point out the difficulty and majesty of
the part—and could not find enough adjectives for the

young Shatner's performance. He stepped in for the famed Shakespearean actor Christopher Plummer, who was carted off to the hospital with a sudden illness late that afternoon. A notice was posted that Shatner would play the part. No one asked for a refund. Shatner went on. He carried it off, getting through the great speeches, the eve of Agincourt, the battle scene ("once more into the breach—").

Finally he was over the hump, only a lighter ending scene to go, the audience in his hand.

Suddenly *he couldn't remember the line*.

No one to prompt him. No one quite realizing that he was in trouble. He looked around for some way to save the situation—suddenly spotted the actor who was playing his brother, crossed the stage towards him. . .

"Now remember this is an understudy in front of a company of players who had played the role, played the play many times in rehearsal and quite a few times in performance. And suddenly they all think I've gone crazy, 'cause I was breaking the mold, the pattern of the choreography of the play. I walked over to my brother, I put my arm around his shoulders and I said to him (in a whisper) "What's the line?" and he looked at me and went (Bill illustrates unintelligible garble. He laughs, illustrates whispering again, in some desperation) "What's the *line*?!!" (garble again) and went, "Oh Jesus, he's not going to be any help to me at all," and I started to walk away, trying to think of where to go next. Now meanwhile, looking back at it now, I realize it was a marvelous piece of staging. Henry V, depleted and tired after the battle, goes to his brother seeking some kind of support from his brother and then walks away. Now, looking back, it was a marvelous piece of staging. And as I walked away the line that I couldn't think of came to me. I said the line. We continued on with the play. That's the story of *Henry V*. Not in Scotland, but at Stratford, ok?"

Okay. But that's not quite all the story. The drama

critic reveals: the audience rose in a standing ovation, overwhelmed by the young actor's performance—as was the rather tough-minded critic. He praised its fire, its passion, its intensity, the young actor's fine talent—already magnificent and promising greatness. . . .

In a moment that actor gives another note on *Suzie Wong:*

"Now I say I forced people to stay in their seats on *The World of Suzie Wong.* When I say I forced people to stay in their seats, I think that needs a little clarification, 'cause it sounds like I made *Suzie Wong* run. Whereas, in fact, I did change the running time, cut twenty minutes out of the running time. What I meant when I said I cut the running time, I lightened the play, and when I say I willed people to stay in their seats, all I mean is—I think this is where it needs clarification—I was so determined that whole rows would not get up anymore, that I found myself pulling every trick of my trade out. Both that I knew—that I'd heard of, that I instinctively thought would work. Variation in pace, variation in volume, energy level, and the willing them to stay in their seats was not so much metaphysical as it was physical. I mean—if I heard the slightest sound, I'd open up on it. Turn around and aim the guns of my voice and looks—so that nobody was allowed to *cough.* And that energy level, that increased the pace—that was almost self-energizing. And people were swept up in the —caught up in the pace of it, so that we then got the play to run. Okay?"

We finish with the notes and he plays his album "The Transformed Man" for us. It is dramatic readings and spoken song. With special meaning for us now because of the story he's told the opening is from *Henry V,* and we can almost see both the twenty-two year old Shatner who played it, and this one. There is Shakespeare, Cyrano, popular songs—a Beatles song, then "It Was a Very Good Year."

The album moves from contrast to contrast, drama, humor, lightness, depth—the voice, the man, transformed, transposed, always in a new key, without benefit of the music.

His face follows it now. When it is over, we say, "Bill there have to be fourteen men on that record, and every one of them is you."

(Later someone asks us to ask him about a query letter which has come in. The writer is arguing with her boyfriend that all the voices on the album are Shatner. Her boyfriend says it's impossible, there have to be a bunch of different men on there.)

The letter would please him. He conceived of it that way, played it that way. It's a remarkable tour-de-force. He's been nominated for a Grammy for a record (reading Isaac Asimov's "Foundation"). He would have liked it if it were for this one. "This, to me, is a work of art."

Yes.

Toward evening Bill backs our car around in the tight space and takes it down the steep driveway, then leads us down the shortest route in his car while he goes to an appointment.

There's a lot to be said for that aspect of having an alpha male around the house.

And the woman who has him around the house on the hill has already said a great deal of it. But it is barely a beginning of the love story, and the mystery, which lives in that house.

The Chameleon Effect

When we come back to the house on the hill a couple of days later it is again Marcy who greets us.

But this time she has read the manuscript. The first words out of her mouth as she leads us in are astonishment.

"I just can't *believe* that Bill told you some of those things. What he said is true. I *know* that I'm the only person he's ever talked to about some of those things—until now. I can hardly believe it. But he *did*."

It's clear that has changed her attitude toward us. She was gracious before, but a little reserved. She's more relaxed now. Somewhere she says, "You know, it's so hard to talk to the press, to writers. They always get it wrong, distort, do something terrible. And you try to trust, and trust, and trust again. But it's usually really terrible, and you stop. But now—Bill was so *happy*—"

We are still talking about the book, about what he said about her, when we switch on the tape. "I was so surprised," Marcy says. "I was just misting up reading it."

'Everything that's in there—he *said*—those are his exact words,' we say. 'And not only that, but he's never said anything *else*—it's *all* had that tone—everything he's ever said about you from the beginning.'

"Well, he wouldn't say anything bad," she says. "Bill wouldn't be unkind to anybody. He just wouldn't say anything.

"But it isn't that he isn't saying anything—he's saying everything like that all the time. It's an intriguing kind of focus. Many men would not do that.'

"Everybody needs strokes," Marcy says. "My *God*."

'We want to talk about how Bill has changed since you've known him,' we begin.

Marcy answers without hesitation, "He got the inside out. I'm sure there's been a big outward change, but he didn't *change*. He just got it out.

"The fun didn't change, 'cause that was always there. And the drama and the great highs and certain things like that were always there. But the softness and compassion and the kindness—*that* came out—and I don't believe that I taught him that—I just don't believe you teach someone that age *that*. I believe it's either in you or it's not. 'Cause it's not an awkward thing that came out. His inside just came out and he wasn't all guarded, and he wasn't all tugged by so many tensions and things, so that all these things could blossom.

"It's been a slow, inch by inch type of thing. Nothing magic. Slow, slow, slow. And it's just so *fabulous*.

"I can't believe that it's so good, and I'm *sure* it will be snatched away from me—that I can't have it because it's so—*so nice*—and I'm expecting something bad to happen.

"Which may be, again, a commentary on our society and what we're taught—that if it's good it can't last. Why *can't* it? WHY CAN'T IT BE GOOD AND LAST? You know? Why does it have to be taken away? I really feel that. And that's very frightening.

'How do you deal with the feeling that it can't last?'

"I say: you can't dwell on this. What will I do? I'll get sad, panicked. All negative things, and if I keep thinking about them, they'll take all my good energy and they'll only make me unhappy and I'll probably bring it about. Because I really do believe what you fear the most, you will bring about. So I just—my mind goes: 'Come on, if something bad is in store for you, where you're going to lose Bill, why don't you make the most of it now?' That's the only way Bill survives, by living the most positively now.

"It's like the person who loves deeply and has a great loss, I think is capable of loving again. The one who doesn't I think probably won't. I mean, the one who doesn't have that kind of passion.

"If you believe that everything happens for a reason, and you just have to deal with it when it happens. . . ."

Marcy breaks off.

'I'm familiar with the feeling that if you have anything good, somebody is going to snatch it away. But you're the only person I've ever heard articulate it like that.'

"Oh, yes." Marcy says, "I'm thinking of anything good—anything I go: "Okay, now I have to pay for it by being super—"

"I hate that most of all, that feeling, because it never allows you the total joy just to go with it.

"Listen, what do I have to do to pay for this goodness? You know, to earn it, to pay back for it. I don't feel other people have to pay back for it. Just me. What do you do? I have to force myself to, as the song goes, 'accentuate the positive.' "

She is silent for a long moment. It is a time to go to something else entirely.

'Are there still ways in which he's a little bit unreconstructed as a male chauvinist?

Marcy smiles. "Yeah. But that's him, too. I disagree with you, um—if Bill was totally fifty-fifty, I would not have been drawn to him. That may be perfection; that may be like Socrates was—balanced. But often the most intriguing things about us—our energy—comes from a certain imbalance.

"I think you run the risk of taking away things you like if you try to get too much harmony. He *is* an alpha male. So the fact that he can cry—what you said, yes, but in other ways he's going to drive you a little—no, not drive me crazy, because it doesn't."

'No? He doesn't?'

"No. He really doesn't. He's very fair. He might, at a given moment, be struck stubborn and willful, because you don't, as I say, remove that incredible stubbornness and willfulness. Willfulness can also be on the bad side too. But there has not been *one* time in our most, you know, moments of real loggerheads, where the next day he has not been able to sit down and talk with me about the very thing involved in the fighting before. There hasn't been *one* time. There were times when I thought, 'Well, *this* is the one time—THIS TIME I CAN'T GET THROUGH!'

"And—that never *happened*. He will always have this remarkable ability to come and listen. So—the intellect may be a little late, but it's *there* and that's what's important.

"There are not things, say for instance, that *every day* I can count on—" (her voice illustrates what it would be like to have some daily disaster to count on.).

"He's really very generous. By generous, I mean— isn't it funny that I should *think* that? You see, I don't think it's my *right*. I think it's being generous. And that is—that expresses so much myself. I wish I had had more sense of self-worth myself. He really *gave* me that."

Suddenly there's a shattering noise. Marcy speaks without interrupting a breath. "Kirk, come here! Lie down. You will please note that I'm talking to my *dog*, not my *husband!*"

'I don't know, it sounds kind of cute.'

"I have *never* called him Kirk."

'Do you tell him to lie down?'

Marcy laughs, *"Yes."*

'What are some of the things that you do run into loggerheads about? Say whatever you want.'

"God, I *can't*. I don't think I can think of any. Let me try. There are no big issues." (She reaches down to the dog. "Kirk's supplying the sound effects while I'm thinking. He's groaning.") "I honestly can't answer that because I'm not holding anything back. I *would* tell you.

"We don't fight or come to loggerheads very often. It's very rare. I *hate* it. I hate to fight, and he does too. *Sometimes* it'll happen, but it's so *rare*. I cannot give you big issues. In the big issues we're very much in line on one track.

"It's usually something small. Something probably where I'm asserting my independence and he's asserting his—if I had to give you broadly—and the other's feeling threatened, to let the other do it. And you just go off. I think that's what I would trace it to.

'How has he changed you?'

"Oh, I'm *so* much more *sure*. It's brought *me* out. My independence came out and my ability to take control, and all those things—now that you *say* it—the way you phrase it—were the alpha qualities in me—brought out.

"Sometimes he'll say, 'You know, you're getting awfully bossy,' and I'll say, 'Well, you created your own monster.' And it's true. I didn't. He did. In little ways that we laugh about. But—it's really beautiful.

"It's the ultimate turn-on. 'Cause I can't believe that somebody would allow me that freedom and encourange me not to play a role and just to be me. I still can't accept it sometimes. I'm sure I often stop it, because I can't. It's just such a *heavy* experience.

"Now I'm much more sure. I've always had a lot of friends and gotten along well with people, and I like them, and I think I'm a nice, kind person."

Marcy pauses, then goes on very thoughtfully.

"But I've often role-played. I could be the chameleon. I know now—I've been to some women's groups and

I've heard them speak, and it's not something unique to me. We've all learned now to put on your best dress for whomever you're with, sort of—your best skins—to reflect what *they* wanted you to be. I was so *good* at that. I was *great* at it. But what happened is: Marcy got lost.

"So, I was great at making people feel good, but then *I* wasn't feeling good myself. So, that balance was all screwy—that was all *wrong*. And I've started to learn now, really that *that's* no good—to go to the other extreme, 'cause you lose yourself and the best of yourself."

It's a remarkable statement for a woman to make about herself. And it rings some bell with us which keeps going off over the next few days—the image of a chameleon who changes color, skin, essence—and loses self. . .

'What do you think *is* you?'

Bill comes in.

Marcy laughs. "Oh, I'm so *glad* you walked in at this impossible question."

Bill chuckles, in the mode of Captain Perfect. " 'I'm here to answer it.' Hi, darling, how are you? Hi, dear."

"Well," Marcy says, "I think their car is blowing up."

"No. It's probably just the radiator," Bill says.

Marcy says firmly, "Will you just go look at it?"

He goes.

"How can I answer that question?" Marcy says. "I can't. To get me to talk about me is harder than to get Bill to talk about him."

'What do you like best about yourself?'

"Yes. That's better if you ask me questions. What do I like about myself? I think I have a rather humorous way of looking at difficulties. I believe in the essential goodness of people. I think I have the ability to bring that out. It's probably one of my greatest talents, I think —my compassion, 'cause perhaps I've *felt* pain—we all have. We're not really nice to each other. And if I can spread a little happiness—maybe that's the biggest achievement I'll ever do.

"What I like *least* about myself is, I'm not as aggressive as I think I should be. I bog myself down by thinking maybe someone will be offended if I take a very positive, action-type role. I get angry and wish I could go beyond that. I can't, most of the time.

"So, maybe Bill and I will end up with me running everything and him fulfilling all those qualities that I've done always. One total reversal. Gone full cycle."

She has spoken with relish, pursuing the thought, laughing—and serious.

" 'Cause you can see where, in your ways of looking at things—I could trace our relationship: I was so chameleon and gave him what he needed, so he wasn't threatened, and he began to trust and trust and trust.

"And then he began to love me, and I began to come out *me*, and be less, all the time, the mirror and the sponge—which brought out in him a certain softness and ability to open up. And we really brought those things out in each other.

"Now we're sort of—" (she illustrates with her hands) —"if *this* is the peak—we might *cross!*

"I mean that would be funny.

" 'Cause that *is* essentially what you talk about—those 'other-half' elements in ourselves. So that would be the other extreme.

It's an interesting analysis—particularly the thought that her being so chameleon could give him what he wanted and bring him out—whereupon the chameleon began to stop being the chameleon.

We are to think about it again on the last day, when he, not having heard this, tells a story about a chameleon.

Now we ask Marcy: 'How do you feel about that just as a fantasy projection?'

"You mean, would I *like* it? No, I really wouldn't. I just want to have *enough* of *me* to be able, *able* to do that.

"Because I'm obviously drawn to those qualities in him. I just don't think you change nature. And I don't really *want* to change it. I know where Bill says totally there's no difference between men and women. There's plenty of cultural difference and where do you draw the line on that difference? I'm not sure I agree with Bill. But I don't have the knowledge to back that up."

Bill comes in as she is saying this.

'You're saying you don't agree with his saying there are no differences between men and women—?'

"I think there *are*," Marcy says.

'I don't think deep down in your soul you believe that either,' we say to Bill.

"Well, there are obvious differences. . . ."

Marcy says to him, "But you said in the book, and I was struck by it, that taking away all the cultural, socio-economic—*all* that—if you could start fresh—"

"Brain capacities, talents—" he says.

"Well, I don't just mean that, 'cause I don't think there are differences there, I think the capacity of the brain and talent are the same. But I do think—"

"That's really what we were talking about," Bill says.

"Emotional stamina, I think, perhaps," Marcy says. "I don't mean to quibble with all the liberationists, but after a point, doesn't heritage *become* biological? And even the experts are not clear on that. Where do you say it's just completely cultural—or biological? Something we've lived with for five hundred thousand or a million years. So—it *is* part of us.

"I just think men and women are complementary, as opposed to totally equal on every level."

We ask Marcy about what she would want to do most in life. Essentially what she *is* doing, she says. Maybe a little more in her career. But mostly just to learn to love what she has. "Your book just made me sit back and go, 'Wow!' We get upset about little things, and *we have so much*." She wants to do more good parts, but recognizes "the time to have really pushed and hammered and done all the things, really concentrated on myself, was out of school after being in all those plays—and being totally selfish and concentrating on yourself. I never did that.''

In some sense, whatever happened before, that also is part of the stack of chips she shoved into the pot these last seven years, part of the price. She has made her choice, and stands on it, but she knows what it means. "Joanne Woodward once said she wanted to have *everything*—a career, her great love, all the parts she wanted, a happy marriage, ten kids—in a way I feel the same."

'What about children?'

"I don't know. We don't want any now, and I think now is all we can deal with. I feel as if those children are mine. They're a huge part of our life. There is no time now to have a baby. It would only take away from the little time we have together. I don't want to miss out on childbirth, that whole romantic thing. I would love to have his child. But I don't know. We have time."

We are interested in what she said about the dream that failed. It may be that she is referring to a first marriage which also ended in divorce. But it may be more general than that. Our dreams, visions, and heroes are often the most revealing part of us.

'Marcy, is there any character in literature, history, or whatever, that you have the most affinity for—say, someone you would like to have been?'

"When I was young, Scarlett O'Hara was my be-all and end-all." She laughs. "I'm probably *so* far from being Scarlett. I would think that I'm more like Melanie, if you really got down to it."

"She used to *play* Scarlett O'Hara in real life," Bill says in the teasing tone. "I accused her of it. In her defensive mechanisms. She's Scarlett O'Hara."

She just gives him a look. "Margot Fonteyn, 'cause ballet was my love. I think it's the ultimate expression. I adore her; she is the essence of great talent and great humility." She goes on. "Eleanor Roosevelt, Jackie Kennedy, Cleopatra."

'It doesn't have to be a woman. Could be a man.'

"I've never wanted to be a man, so I couldn't say that I thought of being Alexander the Great or somebody else I admired."

'Which men have you admired or fallen in love with?'

"Men I've studied—Socrates. Others. Gave me food for thought. John Kennedy, Bobby Kennedy, Alexander the Great, the Greek heroes. I've always been drawn to Greek mythology and history, and the Athenian concept of the perfect man, the concept of the balance. The Athenian gentleman was the warrior but also the intellectual.

"I'm not negating what I said before. Ideally I do think balance is what you go for. But maybe on an emotional, living level, the one who is slightly imbalanced, unbalanced, is creating a great energy that I find very attractive. It draws *me*. 'Cause I was balanced the other way."

'And in marriage—if one has that tremendous intensity—'

"If you both have such intensity, I don't think it would work," Marcy says.

'What do you think about what she's been saying?' we ask Bill. 'What are you in the marriage?'

"What force am I?" he says.

Marcy says (in the exaggerated tone of a schoolteacher) "Check one of the above: the high energy level, or the lower, balanced energy level?"

We all laugh, but when we ask if he sees it that way, he says, "Well, not entirely, because Marcy is full of programs and things to do that wouldn't occur to me. She's really an instigator."

"Like what?" Marcy asks, "If you say that."

"The exercise, the diet changes, the weekends—all kinds of things."

As we follow up on it in that and later sessions, we learn something of what he means. In the last few years they have virtually revolutionized their diets—especially cutting out sugar, white flour, going for more natural foods, better nutrition. Marcy is a vegetarian and has stopped eating meat completely. She does prepare meat for the family. Bill eats some meat—but we have also seen him make a meal of fruit salad.

They both feel healthier, and the results of that, plus the exercise, the jogging, swimming, tennis, scuba diving, riding, etc.,—all of which they often share—are very apparent. Clear skins, a slim youthful look, a glow. Coming in wearing a light blue running suit and a hint of sunburn, Bill would practically glow in the dark.

The fitness, the appearance, are partly a tool of his trade, partly a matter of health. He's always felt a responsibility for that, has worked on it, against the constant enemies of tension, pressure, stress.

He never drank, doesn't smoke, tries to jog even when he's on location.

We ask about the weekends—does he mean something like encounter weekends?

"Almost," he says, "but just between ourselves."

Which says a mouthful.

"We ski and swim," he adds. "Mostly we talk, we read—we read a lot *together*. We have many mutual projects. Dogs. Horses."

"We don't go separately to have fun," Marcy says. "There's only one thing we don't share that Bill loves to do. Motorcycling. Because I'm afraid of it and I really can't get over the fear. He taught me to ski, to skin-dive. He goes to ballet with me. We share more than any couple I know."

Bill cuts in. "I'd rather go *shopping* with her than do anything by myself. In other words, what we do on occasion is to go out shopping. Whether it's grocery shopping or for clothes, or just to lounge around. I try to share her life as much as she does mine, as far as possible."

"We *learned* a lot together," Marcy says.

We ask *what* ideas, other than women's lib and some they've mentioned, have influenced their lives.

"Oh my God—every idea that's come down the pike!" Bill says. "Every aspect of our *lives* has changed in the last ten years. Our *cells* get rejuvenated—you cast off all the cells of your body every seven years. And all our *ideas*. The meaning of life. Your priorities change. What is essential and what is not essential. Just the passage of the decade in your own life makes a difference. You begin to see your own mortality."

Both time and revolution have touched them. They have been more conscious of the revolution and more involved in it together than many couples.

There is another level of the marriage which we explore a little through Kirk, Shatner, and the fantasies about them: the level of territorial defense and possession:

'Millions of women have fantasies about Kirk, and Shatner. Do you have any feelings about women's having these fantasies, Marcy?'

"I know I've got girlfriends who ask me the same question. I've never thought 'I've got William Shatner—I've got Captain Kirk.' I don't think that way."

'Never mind Kirk, just William Shatner. We have boxes of letters coming in saying how they've followed him for years—everything he does. Intelligent letters. Articulate. Then you can hardly believe the fantasy that comes out.'

"Well, so they're not having these great fantasies fulfilled in their lives, and here is this handsome, attractive, sexual, talented—all those things man. His name is William Shatner, who happened to have played a role that really reflected all of those qualities of himself. So it doesn't seem illogical to me at all to have fantasy about him. It's not strange to me that some women have these fantasies. Why not?"

'Do you think *you* might have if you hadn't met him?'

"Well, I didn't."

'Did you ever have fantasies about Bill or Kirk or a combination after you met?'

Marcy laughs, "No. Why would I have a fantasy? I've got the real thing."

'Did you have fantasies after you knew him but before you were married, that weren't happening?'

"Yes. A fantasy is hoping that someone will do something or become something. I would hope that he would open up and let the inside out. Which is what happened. You may not mean that, but that was my fantasy."

'Do you feel possessive of him?'

She speaks and there is the sudden sound of jungle, "*Yes*. But I don't let it get through to me. That is just *me*. I *can't*. If I thought about it I would be *consumed*—with all these letters and things."

We are again impressed with her candor. There is a kind of unsparing quality about it which is very attractive.

The barriers are down now, and she, too, has said things to us which we would not have expected her to say.

There is much more, in several sessions and repeated trips to the house on the hill, more than a dozen hours on tape.

We touch on STAR TREK. "I really do think that Bill is Kirk. That is true. You say it very well in the book, that he's such an alpha male and yet he has all the tenderness that a woman dreams about, and letting a woman express herself and encouraging that, and taking over. And benevolence. Leadership. They've created a perfect man. And Bill's just stepped right into that role."

She's also very moved by Spock, especially by the Kirk-Spock relationship. "It was such a great relationship. You felt such love between the men. There's one show I watched again recently that got to me every time. I mean, I would start to cry when Spock bends over Kirk and goes 'forget, forget' ("Requiem for

Methuselah"). It was such an act of love."

'What's wrong with androgyny?' we ask. 'There might be a lot right with it, but if it's taken to mean obliterating the difference—'

Bill: "It won't work. The differences exist."

Marcy says: "But we don't really know what they *are*. *Now* with the revolution, they're finally beginning to train the girls like the boys."

One view of sex, we say, believes that there is an element of conqueror and conquered: no matter how powerful the woman may be physically, emotionally, intellectually, she still wants to feel the man's strength power and efficacy. 'The argument is that this is almost biological, because the sex act finally depends on the male—no erection, no sex. So, we may be set biologically to want to experience that relationship—the strength and the yielding. But the more alpha a man is, the more he wants a woman strong enough to appreciate his strength.'

But immediately we run into an argument.

"I don't go with the concept of conquering," Bill says. "I know a lot of people do. I used to be shocked at the girls in high school and in college who used to say, 'You're going to boast about me.' "

'We're not talking about that kind of conquering, Bill.'

"You're talking about sexual conquering."

'Yes, but not anything like boasting of "conquest." We're talking about the powerful man conquering someone who is his *equivalent*.'

"Well, wait a minute—'conquering'—is that the sex act?"

'It will *culminate* in the sex act, of course.'

"But everything else is designed to lead to the sex act —isn't that a definition of 'conquering'? Is it or isn't it?"

'We're talking about her willing surrender out of admiration.'

"Yes or no? Are we talking about *sex*?"

'Well, it's a little hard to see a fantastic, romantic, conquering relationship which would not climax in sex.'

"But the word 'conquer' is—" Bill begins.

"—is sexual," Marcy finishes.

"Is sexual," Bill concurs. "The word 'conquer' means: 'I stand astride you and have conquered you.' It doesn't mean we are two people in a beautiful, beneficial relationship for the two of us, which at some point evolves into sex."

"Let's just take a one night stand," Marcy says. "You can't conquer and *give*." "That's right," Bill cuts in."

There's a kind of exchange of looks around the room —cross purposes, as if no one had ever spoken of "this incredible conquistador male" or of playing the game of "pretended rape-acquiescence, power, virility."

'All right. I'll be more specific. That view was mine before I knew it was anyone else's. I've since recognized that it doesn't cover the whole complexity of the subject. But my view then was that I had to work to become the best that was possible to me, to be worthy of the best possible man when I would find him. I waited a long time while I was looking.'

Marcy: "And that's *your* way of looking at something, I mean, I could see how you could think that a man was tremendously attractive, and for no other reason than that you wanted to, go to bed with him. That's different than what you're saying."

'I'm talking about when I was 18—not saying that that philosophy represents all of what I feel now, although much of it still does. I've since recognized more the possibility of other people's diversibles. I'm trying to make a *point*, William.'

"I'm trying to *understand* your point."

"Sex is a celebration. It's a celebration of your essential self. When you get a new job or achieve something fantastic, you want to celebrate—you have a party, say.

How the hell do you celebrate when you've created what you think is the best in yourself? Sex is the most intense pleasure anyone can experience. So it's proper that that should be the celebration. But how can you celebrate if you think you've created something great within yourself—unless you find someone who can match that? Then you *do* find someone. He's conquered you by the greatness of what he *is*. *That's* what I'm talking about. Does that make sense to you?"

"—dimly perceive where you're leading to—" Bill says, not helpfully. "But—what are you *asking*?"

Then he cuts in to answer himself. "Would the conquering of a superior woman be better than an inferior woman—is really what you're asking. Would—*bedding* —a woman who was—majestic—be better than someone who was a—proletarian? Is *that* what we're asking? Well— *Certainly!*"

'How much karate do I know? Not enough, huh?'

"You see, the *word* conquer is the problem," Bill says.

Marcy nods. "Honestly. I'm not being difficult. That's terrific how you look at it, and I look at it, perhaps, differently. [I'm not sure that—] the only way I can think, the way you make it sound, is someone who'll have sex for power. Like a man who's really powerful. *That's* a turn-on. Or someone who's really rich."

'No, that's not involved at all.' The response may be almost on an instinctual level, to the man whom a woman feels is capable of taking on the galaxy. And—*her*. Maybe that's part of the attraction of the alpha male. It is to me. I've been working since age eleven, doing all kinds of things. That set up certain character traits in me. And I've wanted someone to match that. Many people do feel that.'

"Well, then, *good for them*," Marcy says. "I just don't think of somebody as 'are they good enough for me to give myself to.' I just don't think that."

The argument itself is perhaps indicative of what is

going on in the revolution. For at least a decade now people's most fundamental ideas about sex, love, romance, marriage have been torn up at the roots. Occasionally we may have thrown the rose out with the thorns. There may be aspects of male-female relationships which are rooted a million years deep and are not easily torn out—by a decade.

We ask: 'Apart from Marcy, Bill, what kind of woman appeals to you?'

'Oh, Bill looks as if he is enoying that thought.'

Bill does a Humphrey Bogart accent. "Frankly, sweetheart—'' He laughs, then says, "UM—a woman. . .Well, she—the ideal woman has to be pretty —or handsome—or striking."

'That's the first thing?'

"Well, probably that's the first thing I would *notice*. Then, a good figure is the second thing I'd notice."

'What's your idea of a good figure?'

"The Greek ideal. Venus de Milo. 36-24-36. The Greek ideal is a definite measurement. Did you know? Yeah. Although I don't know whether that's the number. *Then*—she has to be in touch, and aware—''

"Then?"

"Well, I'm talking about—''

'Yes, I know.'

"I'm *going*—the *door* is opening. . .''

"You don't see her *mind*," Marcy says.

"Right. You see her body. You see how she's dressed. Now, you can read a great deal into the way a person stands, looks, carries herself. You can read a great deal from the way women dress, the way they wear their hair, their eyes, how they look at you.

"*Then* she's got to have that magnetism.

"If a woman is *not* pretty, but she has that magnetism, that special something, it can be dynamite. And if she's pretty *and* she has that special something—that's wild.

"*Then* she has to have the personality, the intelligence.

"*Then*—she has to be unselfish, 'cause selfishness is something that turns me off in a woman, totally.

"*Then*—well, there can be a lot else, but that's what I look for, that and the capacity to be herself, to grow and develop."

The story in the house on the hill may not be merely the story of one couple or one crucible, but the story of us all. These two have each survived a divorce to face in this marriage the central question of the revolution.

It is, in fact, the question of emotional openness, of being able to say, as Bill put it to us once: "Here I am, as I am. Love me if you can. But at least *know* me."

Marcy has touched off a chain of thinking in our minds which leads us to an idea: the other side of "men don't cry." On the last day we are prepared to present it to them. We are not prepared for what happens: 'This isn't so much a question as something we are trying to get to. Perhaps a theme, Marcy, from something you said—for the counterpart of "The Crucible" chapter' Bill and Marcy lean forward attentively.

'Marcy, you said you were a chameleon. You said: "Marcy got lost."'

'Is the Chameleon Effect perhaps the counterpart for women of "men don't cry," for men?'

'Women have been more free to express emotion, so long as they tailor their emotions—and themselves—to the person they are with, adopt a protective coloring of what that person wants them to be. Men don't cry, women don't make waves.'

'Are many women as emotionally closed as men, but in a more subtle way? Is that how *you* felt, Marcy?'

If we had wondered what response would be, we had our answer: immediate, electric *interest*, excitement—from both of them.

Marcy: "You've *got* it! You've got it very well. The Chameleon Effect—it's a tremendous idea. The way you explained it—women as emotionally closed, but it guises itself differently. I think the chameleon thing—having been freed of *that* is the most precious gift I have ever been given."

She looks at Bill, but he is already leaning forward, his face lighting up.

Bill: "I think it's a *marvelous* idea. I really do. I think many, many women prostrate themselves emotionally. Probably from male domination. They become anything that the man wants them to be. If he wants them to be happy, *be* happy. Sad, they're sad."

Marcy: (Pursuing the thought) "Because we *learn* to read people very young, because of the way we had to express ourselves. If you were good at it—man or woman—you gave what was wanted."

We are impressed. It is a rare woman who would have spoken openly of having played the chameleon herself. It is a rare one who would respond to the expanded idea of the Chameleon Effect with intellectual excitement, taking it up and elaborating it.

As for Bill, he looks as if he has been given a new toy —maybe a new planet. But we would have expected that.

It is then that the unexpected begins to happen:

Bill: (His face lighting from the inside, with the look of delight—and of walking the wire) "That would be a marvelous idea for a story, though.

"A Chameleon. A woman Chameleon. Literally someone who changes shape, coat, size, fit. And then you have anything you want. You want to have a pet? Here's a little dog."

Shatner's whole body has come alive. With some small, controlled movement of the actor's body, the expressive face—the little dog is *there*!

Bill: "Wouldn't that be funny—? Wouldn't that be a science fiction story? The woman who can become anything. You want a huntin' dog? The total companion. Punching bag?"

His shoulders create the punching bag.

"That would be hysterical. The Chameleon Effect. The perfect woman."

He starts to let it go at that, but his eyes are still working on it. 'What else would she be?' We prompt. He takes it up again—and this time the excitement suddenly takes a serious turn:

Bill: "She could be a car. Oh boy, I'd love to drive this car. A steamboat, an airplane—a staircase so the man could climb to the stars. . .

"She could be anything.

"She's the cloud that he soars around.

"She's—nothing.

"He never falls in love with her because he doesn't know who she *is*.

"And she tries to become herself, and takes away all the things he loved about her.

"And he hates her.

"That's the end."

Marcy breaks in: "Oh *no*—you *can't* let it end that way! He *has* to fall in love with her."

"No." Bill says firmly. "He says 'I hate you. I hate you for having taken all those things away from me.' "

He has startled himself. He had never intended to complete the story—but the writer's imagination took over, while the actor's body created and demolished each chameleon role in an instant. He did it in one swift sweep of thought, without pause or hesitation, building in the drama, the language, the concept.

It is the kind of performance for which no award exists.

The logic of the concept took a turning which perhaps even he did not anticipate. But it *was* what the concept implies. He lets it stand. But it sounds the ominous note of what is, in fact, the danger of both the Chameleon Effect and "men don't cry: *"He never falls in love with her because he never knows who she is."*

No one can fully love someone who is in hiding, or who has no self to hide.

For a long moment, Bill and Marcy look at each other, perhaps realizing the enormity of what they have been fighting—on both sides.

Marcy is not happy for his fictional chameleon woman. But she knows that they have taken up the fight against both the Chameleon Effect and "men don't cry."

After that moment we call them back.

'Marcy, what was that dream you mentioned to us?'

"Oh, it was a cliché—the old romantic dream. It was unrealistic. We're brought up on it. It's not nearly as important as this other thing—the chameleon effect."

"Oh, but that's what it *is*," Bill says. "We were brought up to do all those things. To act in a certain manner and do certain things. Either you were brought up that way or you acquired the knowledge in school or —wherever it was, there inhabited inside you the chameleon." He smiles at her. "And now you've turned into a fire-breathing dragon." He chuckles.

'She's a fire-breathing dragon?'

"I'm trying to draw a parallel."

"I tell him he's created his own monster, and he *has*," Marcy says. "But it's better. It's much better. For him, too."

'How do you think you are better for him?'

"Because I have a stronger identity. There's more strength. There's more to give and it's not out of fear. A *desire* to do. That's a tremendous difference. The actions may be the same—but I think the quality would be different for him."

"Oh, it *is*, definitely," Bill says. "I can't *force* her to do something."

'You can't?'

"No. She does pretty much—I mean, we both do what we pretty much want together, and she'll, like, cede to me in many ways, but I can't *force* her."

'How do you feel about that?' We ask him.

"I like that. I like it. It's a cause for *respect*."

He weights the last word with emphasis.

There is more that we talk about that day—and much of it refers back in one way or another to the chameleon theme—its effects on everything from sex, to love and marriage, to male and female roles.

The Chameleon Effect finds its way into almost every topic. They are taken with it.

Marcy: "Beauty is a two-edged sword. You're loved for it—but then you feel the terrible fear that you are loved *only* for that. And you are expected to be even more the chameleon, to make yourself over and live by your skin."

Bill: "Sex—you can't have the optimum in sex without a real emotional relationship with someone who *is* real. Role-playing, being what you *want* her to be, being the chameleon, doesn't help. You never know *her*. And *you* have to be real, open. As much as you can. Otherwise, it's just an orgasm.".

The last thing Bill says is "The Chameleon Effect is a perfect theme. It's perfect."

Marcy agrees, elaborates it in half a dozen ways, develops it further along the lines that it can affect men as well. The Chameleon Effect is not merely a woman's problem but a human problem—whenever people are expected to play roles. Including the role of "men don't cry." The man who is hiding behind a stiff upper lip is also playing the chameleon.

What is perhaps most fascinating is to watch these two elaborate the concept, tossing it back and forth to each other, and to us. There's a kind of fearless exploration here, even though it touches close to their lives, even close to things that have been painful.

And that is a love story in itself.

There *is* the story of the decade here, and it is no fable

or fairy tale, but the honest story of two human beings who have fought the two halves of the battle of the decade: against "men don't cry" and the Chameleon Effect.

As an actor, this man became the symbol of that battle to be real, to be open, to make *contact*. He became an example of that to people who adopted the fight in their own lives. Many of them, both male and female.

Both men and women can suffer from both aspects of the problem. There are male chameleons and females of the don't cry persuasion. And there are those who are neither.

But that is always a battle not lightly won.

As a man, this man has been making that fight and making headway—with this woman at his side.

That is the real-life love story which brought them through the crucible, to the house on the hill.

It is a part of that love story that the last thing Marcy says is about Bill, and the reality of what we have all been talking about:

"I like what you've done in the book. Because you've *caught* him. You haven't said what has been said over and over again. You really *talked* to him. And I will *tell* you: what he said is what he really *is*.

"You've captured him—a part of him that has never been captured."

Shatner: Where To?

STAR TREKKERS alone *can make the difference be-tween a future in which we sink into a new dark age and one in which we go upward, outward, to the stars. . .*
>   Robert A. Heinlein

I take STAR TREK to be our longest range plan.
>   Jesco von Puttkamer
>   NASA's Program Manager
>   for Space Industrialization
>   and Advance Long-Range
>   Planning and technical ad-
>   visor to **STAR TREK: THE
>   MOTION PICTURE.**

The emotional openness—yes, I sense a change in the dec-ade. I see it in myself. And without that we are doomed. No question about it. I do think that was in Kirk, and Shatner put it there. Bill created that emotional effect, and it hadn't been done before.

It was him. He made the role.

And also I don't think anybody's written roles since that would give him the scope to do that.
>   Theodore Sturgeon
>   Award-winning science fic-

> *tion writer, author of STAR*
> *TREK episodes ''Amok*
> *Time'' and ''Shore Leave.''*

The parts which would tap the whole range of William
Shatner have not been written.

> *Arlene Martel, leading guest*
> *star of ''Amok Time'' (as*
> *Spock's Vulcan wife,*
> *T'Pring.)*

He walks onto the bridge of the ship.

It is the first time in almost ten years.

Everything is strange, familiar. The captain's chair is still at its center, but somewhat redesigned.

He surveys the ship slowly, as if taking possession of it again. The memories are there. The chair is still—or again—his.

It has been a long decade.

He walks over and sits down in the command chair, his hands touching its controls.

A hush falls over the people checking the control consoles, acknowledging the moment of his return, the meaning of it, the intensity which is in his own face.

There is a low murmur of satisfaction, as if some center has returned to its rightful place in the universe—and on the bridge of the *Enterprise*.

Then the murmur rises almost to applause, welcoming William Shatner aboard the soundstage set which is the bridge of the new *Enterprise*.

For a moment the fusion of role and actor is almost complete. It might indeed be Kirk returning to command of the real *Enterprise*—the scene Shatner will film first for the movie.

Later Bill says that he did infuse Kirk's response in that first scene with "Shatner's own intensity of emotion on returning to everything that this has meant."

The moment of that return is also a landmark of the life, and a turning point for its future.

We began this book with questions: What, really had been the reality of this man's life—as actor, as man, as legend?

How powerful had been the effect of the role in which he voyaged into legend—on the world, on him?

What was the reality of his life now, after a decade in which he had lived through revolutions which he and the legend had in some way touched?

That moment on the bridge set of a multi-million dollar mega-movie is, in its way, an answer to some of those questions.

For that set to exist, with the chair still his, is the bottom-line on his creation of the role of Kirk.

In 1965 Shatner first stepped aboard an *Enterprise* bridge. The role of Kirk has spanned more than half his professional life.

Then it might have been merely a role. Now it has legend to live up to.

This is the first time that any man has returned to re-create such a starring role, after such a lapse of time.

In the decade, the role, the phenomenon have gone where-no-legend.

After five years of uncertainty, **STAR TREK: THE MOTION PICTURE,** became a reality in that moment when he stepped onto the bridge. The movie promptly became the prerelease blockbuster of all time: booked into a biggest-ever 1,000 theater release, for a longest-ever sixteen week guarantee. (Previous record, *Superman:* seven hundred theaters, twelve week guarantee.)

And that's only the American release. Where, by the way, the old STAR TREK still plays 383 times per week in 134 markets—after ten years.

Worldwide, the new movie will reach millions never reached even by STAR TREK's translation into 51 languages in over 67 foreign countries. Countries which do not have networks to play STAR TREK have theaters which will.

Paramount has options with Shatner and the rest of

the original cast for sequels or other follow-ups. It is also the first time the *entire original cast* of a long-"dead" production has returned for its rebirth.

Ironically, the show which died an untimely network death ten years ago is now one of the hottest properties ever in network bidding.

ABC has offered $15 million for a package including two plays of the STAR TREK movie—*and* an option for a *television series.*

Whatever form the future of STAR TREK will take, it is now certain that it will *have* a major future. And it is certain to be part of William Shatner's life for a long time to come.

A startled Paramount, even now only beginning to get glimmers of the full magnitude of the phenomenon, is billing the STAR TREK movie as:

> The most eagerly awaited film of all time. *Starring the original cast,* headed by William Shatner as Captain Kirk. . .

He steps onto the soundstage, and the ghosts of ten years are with him. . .

For five of those years he walked through the crucible, alone, not sane—a raw mass of pain and savage hurt, love gone, kids gone—even this, gone. The starship would fly no more. And the role to which he had given himself, putting his best on the line—had been rejected. Cancelled.

The verdict appeared to be: one more television show, come and gone.

The dream which he had reached for in the crunch of the snow—the dream of being a great actor—which seemed within his grasp as the golden boy—was hollow, even shattered.

Kirk was dead.

There were nights, moments, when William Shatner wished that he could die, moments perhaps when he risked it—not really wanting it, but tempting the gods of bear-hunting and scuba diving.

Of what his life had been before, nothing remained—not even the fifteen dollars to cash a check. Only the daughters who also were torn away, and for whom he still drove himself, never saying "no."

Of STAR TREK it did not pay to think. He had to face the brutal fact that the show was dead. Forever. There was no thought or question of anything else, no hope of revival. No revival of that kind had ever happened.

Nor was there even a major critical estimate which said: yes, this was greatness.

Finally, after the worst of those years, the ultimate critical opinion began to come in—from the thousands, then the millions. But of that he could not know, then.

Certainly there was nothing which reached him in those years which said: *what you did has made a difference.*

If there had been, perhaps it would have made a difference to him in those years of flame. He was fighting the kind of typecasting which has destroyed actors before and since, sometimes to the point of suicide.

Shatner's reputation had never depended on a single role, but the identification was at least as strong. He didn't complain. Just dug in and furnished the house for three hundred dollars, took the jobs he could have phoned in. Salvaged a month here, a time there, to do "Andersonville Trial" or something else he found of merit.

And he kept on keeping on—sane or not.

For his own hurt—from the days when the boy had walked beside strangers, not to seem alone—he knew how to maintain a shell—and a shellmouth.

Few people have seen much beyond that shell. By his

own account, no one, until very recent years.

Those who knew him in the crucible years, even in other years, have known in some sense another Shatner. Not necessarily the one who has emerged these last years.

Some part of that Shatner is related to the way he played Kirk, and to his slow acceptance, over his own resistance, of what that has meant.

He steps onto the bridge. August 7, 1978.

The ghosts are lively now. The entire original STAR TREK cast is gathered to launch him on this new voyage—where no star has gone before. Not in anyone's wildest dreams ten years ago when he stepped off a bridge set did any of these people expect to see him in command of an *Enterprise* again. Nor did they expect to sign on again with him.

Now they celebrate the moment of their return.

They are all there: even Leonard Nimoy, who does not have to film for another week, comes to wish Shatner and everyone well on the first day of filming. Gene Roddenberry, who cracks a bottle of champagne over the bridge railing to launch the ship. The old cast, the new—Persis Khambatta and Stephen Collins. The nearly one hundred people it takes to prepare and film the scene. Robert Wise, one of the most famed film directors, with four Oscars—best direction and best picture on *West Side Story* and *Sound of Music*. The bridge itself, courtesy of a bigger investment than a few episodes of the old STAR TREK. Also courtesy of NASA and the space program—with advanced state-of-the-art working technology. (Hence, tight security, involving even the FBI.) Also courtesy of NASA: its top Long-Range Planner, Jesco von Puttkamer, as technical advisor—to a science fiction movie.

It is old home week, a family reunion, an impossibility suddenly made real on a soundstage.

Even Shatner's family is there. Marcy, his three daughters. It is a moment not to be repeated, for Kirk or for Shatner.

Cameras roll. The man who moves to take the captain's chair is touched, moved—perhaps more than he quite wants to be.

He plays the scene, he says later, not only with Kirk's intensity, but with "Shatner's intensity."

Looking at the film again, months later, he thinks that if he had it to do over, he "would have played it differently."

It is immortalized in celluloid, not to be redone. Perhaps that is just as well. It stands as a monument to the decade.

In that decade, he has gone even beyond the role he created as Kirk, and more recently, beyond acting.

Few people know, as he walks onto the bridge set to begin **STAR TREK: THE MOTION PICTURE,** that he is deeply involved in projects in which he is not only star but creator, originator.

He comes in through the STAR TREK offices at Paramount and stops to murmur to one of us, "They want it!"

He's talking about *Star Traveller*. We've just had a conference about it and another project at his Century City office, where he has been showing a demonstration of *Star Traveller*'s special multi-media effects to backers. He's conceived *Star Traveller* as a multi-media science-fiction stage show using latest lasers and concert technology.

As the movie starts production, we work on that project, sometimes coming for a working session in his motor-home dressing room over the lunch break, sometimes staying to talk further between takes on the set.

This is a man who is at the studio filming from an early makeup call to late in the day—sometimes 5, 6 o'clock, sometimes later. He has to be there, in full

makeup and uniform, all day—often for virtually endless retakes.

He's lucky to get home by seven or eight o'clock. He
has lines to learn, sometimes other appearances to
make. Dozens of phone messages to catch up on.

And in the midst of that, he is, in effect, in pre-pro-
duction—acting as producer, director, creator, co-or-
dinator, businessman, etc.—on what grows to amount
to a multimillion-dollar production, *Star Traveller*.
Phone calls on that alone are staggering. He works over
lunch—brown bagging a small peanut butter sandwich
or something equally exotic. The uniform goes to be
cleaned and he holds conferences in slacks or a robe.

He is somewhat inclined to take on projects which
would drop someone else in his tracks.

This is not the first time that he has developed and
produced his own material. *The Transformed Man*
album was his concept, his material. So was the one-
man show which he played to tour audiences of more
than 100,000 people. The album *William Shatner: Live*
from that performance was his own production, through
his company, Lemli Music,* named for his daughters.
Over the years he has bought and put development money into certain properties, looking for writing of quality.
But this is his most ambitious project.

Star Traveller, first conceived as a second one-man
tour show to be played alone on stage, has grown and
changed in concept, possibly will still change from this
writing. By the beginning of the STAR TREK movie it
had grown to a major multi-media show with sophisticated modern laser-concert technology, still with almost
a one-man show focus.

By shortly after the end of filming, it had developed as
a planned multimillion dollar production coliseum show

---

*Inquiries on any of these should be directed not to the distaff side but
to Lemli Music, 760 N. La Cienega, Hollywood, CA.

—with all the attendant changes in script, format, content.

Negotiations over who would produce the show in what form, with what creative control, became a major project in themselves, continuing throughout the filming and beyond.

Meanwhile, **STAR TREK: THE MOTION PICTURE,** opening with a twelve week shooting schedule, rapidly began to demonstrate that that estimate was an instance of the famous optimism which springs eternal in STAR TREK.

Bill went in for script conferences, planning sessions on the movie.

Seven months later. . .

For the final wrap-day of principal photography, only Shatner of the regular cast is in the scene. But his invited guests, studio people, a few friends and guests are there to celebrate the final wrap.

Ironically, the filming is of the very first scene of the movie—Kirk crossing a concourse at the United Federation of Planets Headquarters, brushing shoulders with the routine aliens and casual infinite diversity which are his world. He meets a Vulcan science officer who has been posted aboard the *Enterprise*. Not Spock.

It is a brief scene—the space of a short walk on screen, a couple of lines.

But the meticulousness of Robert Wise takes the filming into the late afternoon, then into the evening.

Bill moves with solid professionalism, apparently untiring, as he always seems to be on set. Between the twenty odd takes, when there is time, he moves off to chat with his guests, discuss a project with us, greet a long-time fan and writer invited by the STAR TREK office. Then back with unruffled concentration to walk through the scene again. "Lights, camera, door, Bill. . . Action. . ."

What is not seen is the effort he talks about later. In

the film, this scene must be followed immediately by the first scene, "scene 64"—Kirk's first scene on the bridge —which he played on the very first day of filming, seven months before.

He has seen again the shots of that scene—which he played with Kirk's emotion and his own, on that day when everyone returned to the legend.

Now months of his life have passed in a day-by-day progression of making the movie, living his life, doing other projects.

And now Bill is here alone, the rest of the cast gone, filming a moment which must mesh with that first-day intensity.

Indeed, it will be the first moment which must mesh with the intensity of millions who will have waited for it for more than ten years—the first new glimpse of the world of STAR TREK and of Kirk.

As such, it was an acting problem for the professional actor who played Kirk—to be solved with that professionalism which is the actor's craft and art.

But for the man who played Kirk, both the opening day and that last day of filming were also landmarks of a life, a monument to a role, and a decade.

Even most of those who were on the STAR TREK set —that opening day do not know how far Shatner has gone in that decade, nor in what direction, nor through what fires.

Perhaps it would have helped in the years of the crucible if he had known that this landmark lay ahead.

It would have helped if someone could say: That dream of greatness as an actor did come through. If there had been nothing else but Kirk before or since, it would still stand as one of the great performances. More than that, people have paid the ultimate tribute to an actor: they have believed that the performance was real, and that it was relevant to their real lives.

Ultimately someone did say that.

In the long run, enough people said some part of it, in some form audible to Paramount, to make that bridge set a reality, and the captain's chair still his.

But when we began the first planning sessions for this book, it was a different world. No movie. No likelihood of one. The very idea was at best a gleam in someone's eye. For Shatner, the years of the crucible were barely outlived. But even so, there was a kind of hollow space where STAR TREK had been, and part of his heart.

He had just started to appear at STAR TREK conventions. There was, clearly, love there. You could cut it with a knife. But what was it *about?*

To suggest more than four years ago the basic hypothesis that television drama could make a difference, that the phenomenon of drama shock existed and could change lives—was also a where-no-person venture.

To say that an actor's performance of a role could have influenced people's actual thinking and behavior on a matter like emotional openness, was another.

By the time we interviewed Shatner and Nimoy together, the orbital shuttle President Ford had named for STAR TREK's *Enterprise*—in response to a massive campaign by STAR TREK fans—was aloft in the real skies of earth.

Roots had played to a record audience—and the question of the serious impact of television drama had become obviously a legitimate question.

A STAR TREK movie was planned and script writers and directors were working on it.

And before that movie was to fly, STAR TREK fans would have taken a direct and successful hand in reversing expected cuts in budgets for the real space program.

Holocaust would have played to *one hundred twenty million* people in America, and caused political crises in West Germany and elsewhere.

The question of whether drama shock could exist was

no longer academic, and in fact has been answered on the face of things by the mere existence of *Roots, Holocaust,* and the response to them.

In the case of STAR TREK, the legitimacy of considering a serious impact may be less clear. Many may be inclined to dismiss it as "just entertainment."

But if a documentary of the past can have clear impact—what about a documentary of the future?

Those who remember the '60's, when STAR TREK was filmed while it appeared the world might burn, remember a sense of nightmare doom.

Bombings, burnings, war, the threat of doomsday war. . .

In some way, that sense of doom has lifted in the decade.

The facts are not so different. We still possess the capacity to destroy ourselves.

But the attitude has changed.

Most people do seem to sense that it *has* changed.

On our good days, at least, we think we're going to make it.

Why and how can be argued. No one would want to attribute it all to STAR TREK. Some would dispute attributing any of it.

But the fact is, STAR TREK said: There will be a future, and it will be man's proper future—to the stars.

And it was STAR TREK which became the phenomenon. Not any other show. Not gloom and doom. Not even mere science fiction—which has been tried before and since, and never had that impact.

Cumulatively, STAR TREK has had a far larger audience even than *Roots* or *Holocaust*. It is a seventy-nine hour future, played fifteen years deep.

Institutions which were carved in stone at its beginnings are gone: the whole structure of institutionalized racism has been dismantled—despite any problems which remain. The South is safe for Uhura—and for her contemporary counterpart—whom Nichelle Nichols has met—the black woman newscaster who has her own television talk show in Huntsville, Alabama.

The women's movement, not even born in 1966, staged its first major demonstration in the last year of STAR TREK—and has since become a revolution.

Man has reached the moon—in the year STAR TREK was cancelled.

Maybe it was that moment when the world saw STAR TREK as drama—set against the living-color of man on the moon—that the world went where-no-man.

Perhaps it was even at that moment that the sense of doom lifted.

Certainly over the years some substantial number of people have been quite consciously affected by STAR TREK, as our questionnaire shows.

How many they represent can be argued.

That they exist—and in substantial numbers—is attested by the Orbiter *Enterprise*—and the new *Enterprise* on the sound stage.

The hypothesis of drama shock has, in one sense, already been verified by the mere existence of those two new *Enterprises*.

In another, it will be confirmed further by the box office receipts of **STAR TREK: THE MOTION PICTURE.** Paramount and the world may even yet be surprised by the magnitude of the phenomenon.

Long before it was certain that the movie would fly, at almost the moment when the Orbiter *Enterprise* first flew, Robert Heinlein, the man who is considered the dean of modern science fiction, spoke to us about Shatner, STAR TREK, the future. Heinlein is, among many other things, a man who has *been* the career naval officer Shatner plays—a part of the thin golden line of defense which stands sentinel between the wolves of a world, or a galaxy, and—home. As such, Heinlein was profoundly moved by Shatner's portrayal of Kirk, and

by the vision of decency, love, courage, hope, achievement, triumph which was the essential message of STAR
TREK.

Robert Heinlein never wrote for STAR TREK, has
no stake in it except the stake of a man who believes in
the power of ideas to move people and to affect the
future.

It was out of that conviction that Robert Heinlein
told us:

> STAR TREKKER's *alone* can make the dif-
> ference between a future in which we sink
> into a new dark age, and one in which we go
> upward, outward, to the stars.

It is a strong statement to make about the response to
a television show. Yet if it *is* true that drama can have an
impact, can change people's minds, lives, feelings, actions—then mass-media drama on the scale and with the
message of STAR TREK may well make even a critical
difference.

There are delicate balances of all kinds in our choices
of possible futures for ourselves and for the world which
may be tipped by a powerful vision of what is possible.

If even a modest percentage of those who have
watched or will watch STAR TREK implement only a
fraction of its ideas in their lives, it will have made a
difference.

And if that is true in areas like support of the space
program or acceptance of diversity or greater acceptance of changes in male-female roles—as our results indicate, then it can also be true in an area like emotional
openness.

The results of the questionnaire do confirm overwhelmingly that Shatner's portrayal of Kirk reached
and moved people on that issue.

And if many have been moved on a conscious level, it
stands to reason that many more have been moved on
that unconscious and subliminal level where much of

our actual behavior begins.

If so, it may well, in fact, have been a breakthrough role.

In the long run, it has to be the premise of every writer, every actor, every creator, that the effort can make some difference, if only to entertain. But at bottom there is the wish for some lasting substance and effect.

We recognize it fairly often in the case of authors. To contend that an actor can have had an effect is much more rare.

Shatner did have an effect, was it coincidental, or an aspect of his art?

That cannot be answered in a vacuum, nor, necessarily, even by the actor. We went to those who were in a position to know.

That it was by no accident that Shatner did it, and that it was he who *did* do it, was the independent conclusion of every professional colleague we talked to who saw him do it in those days—from actors to production people to writers.

Theodore Sturgeon, whose name you will also find on almost anybody's list of the three top writers of classic science fiction, was in a unique position to observe that. He was also the writer of two STAR TREK episodes, *Amok Time* and *Shore Leave,* one or both of which are on most viewers list of favorites. (*Amok Time,* the top favorite of many, is the episode in which Spock must return to Vulcan to mate or die. His betrothed wife T'Pring, chooses challenge, making Spock fight for her to the death—against Kirk. By contrast, *Shore Leave* is almost an idyll, in which lethal dangers turn out to be—an amusement park.)

Not many even among STAR TREK fans know that Theodore Sturgeon came west and set up shop in the STAR TREK offices in the early days of the series. "Gene believes—'In the beginning was the word,' " Ted says. "One reason STAR TREK worked is that it was a writer-oriented show. I was all over that lot. Wherever I wanted to go, I was free to go. I studied the actors. I wrote Kirk just exactly the way Bill spoke. Leonard spoke Leonard's own language. There was a fiendish design in my doing that. My lines weren't changed very often."

But in the case of Kirk, Sturgeon is first to acknowledge that there was more there than "the word."

"I didn't see a tremendous amount of originality in the *concept* of Kirk. I don't mean that we had done this before, but that *kind* of protagonist, as conceived, had been around before. But then Shatner did it as well as it could possibly be done. He was just right for it. He was awfully good at what he did. And *then* he began to put more into it. There were things like the emotional quality, and the humor, and the relationship with Spock, the protectiveness of each other, say, *that* came out of Bill's character.

"Do you know that he—that all of them—got so far into their characters that they would *speak their own lines?* In *Amok Time,* for example, in the last scene where the doctor was so pleased to see the sudden flash of humanity in Spock, where Spock suddenly came up with this brilliant smile and said, 'Jim!' when he saw Kirk alive and had thought he was dead—and then was still denying having any emotional reaction, at all, and Dr. McCoy said, 'In a pig's eye!'—that was *De.* (De-Forest Kelly.) That wasn't me. De put that in his very own self. They all did that from time to time. Bill certainly did. And when it worked, they let it stand, because that was one of the things the show had going for it.

"Plus, Bill would fight for any change he thought was needed.

"And the combination of *that* with the generally very good level of writing, plus the unheard-of themes we've been talking about—it's never been done, before or since.

"I think you're right that Bill created that emotional effect, and it hadn't been done before.

"It was him. He made the role.

"And also—I don't think anybody's written roles since that would give him the scope to *do* that."

Ted Sturgeon is one of the relatively few people who would be in a position to judge to what extent Shatner made the role.

And Ted is the kind of writer who is perhaps uniquely able to judge what he argues in that last statement.

Ironically, it is an argument we have also made, and had—with William Shatner.

We had found a man who questioned himself. Had he followed his dream of greatness? Or betrayed it? What, really, had he achieved?

"Laurence Olivier is a great actor. He has had the great material to work with. To compare me in the same breath with him is ludicrous."

There is a painful truth in that line about the great material, which Theodore Sturgeon and a number of others have sensed.

Apart from those halcyon early days on Broadway and live television when some of the great and some of the very good material did come Shatner's way, and with the major exception of STAR TREK and certain other fine parts, there has been a scarcity of really great material.

It is not something which merely affects Shatner. Other extremely fine actors spend most of their lives in the deserts between the rare oases of great or even good roles. Most do not even work.

But for Shatner there is also another level.

We had suggested to him that even apart from anything else he has done, the role of Kirk stands as a classic in itself.

But more, there is a sense in which that performance has moved many people in a way that even Laurence Olivier has not.

People's general, and appropriate response on seeing an Olivier performance is: What a magnificent actor.

People's general response on seeing Shatner's performance as Kirk was: What a magnificent *man*.

And if you think about that, it is the ultimate tribute to an actor.

People think of Kirk not so much as a role Shatner played but as the man they believe he is or would like to be, and often as the man, or person, they themselves would like to become. Even women, perhaps especially women, have found Kirk a liberation from what they also have been taught in a hard school: the best don't cry.

That kind of tribute in real lives comes to an actor so rarely, if ever, that there is no name or award for it.

But what it does reveal is a capacity which even the role of Kirk could not fully tap.

In a New York hotel room we argued once that the parts had not been written yet which could tap it.

But Shatner, always reluctant to overestimate, is nothing if not stubborn: "The challenge is there, the great classical parts, Shakespeare."

'Which takes up the same problems everyone has been looking at for four hundred years. What's the real challenge? It's been interpreted, reinterpreted. Today we're up against a world of revolution—of Future Shock—new problems all the time, new solutions. The knowledge revolution. All the revolutions. Where is the great drama which is being written about *that?* The media give us the capacity for drama shock on a scale which can move the world. But where is the level of drama which would tap what you have shown in Kirk—and beyond *that?* Where is the great new drama? The new themes? The parts aren't being written."

It is an argument which Sturgeon and others are also to make to us: the roles which would give Shatner scope to *do* that have not been written.

"It's too bad," Sturgeon adds, "because we *need* that."

Sturgeon goes on to say that he does sense a change in emotional openness within the decade. "I see it in myself. And without that we are doomed. No question about. I do think that was in Kirk, and Shatner put it there."

If it is possible for this actor to do that with one role of scope, where is the material which would have given him scope to go beyond that?

It is something which others have also sensed about Shatner, and it is something which perhaps is best appreciated by another actor. Most of the STAR TREK cast has spoken of unexplored, unexploited potentials in Shatner.

But it was seen also by other actors who have worked with him from time to time and watched him over the years. And there are aspects of it which can only be appreciated by a woman. Arlene Martel, also a fine actor whose range is seldom exploited, is remember by STAR TREK viewers for her flawless performance as Spock's Vulcan betrothed wife, T'Pring.

Without prompting she said to us:

"I don't think Bill has had a role *yet* where his own essence has been able to emerge. The roles have relied on his equipment as an actor—his voice, his movement, his skills, his intelligence—but not on his sensitivity, his sexuality.

"STAR TREK touched on it. But only touched.

"I feel him trying to reach *beyond* what he is given, to give it a value which is beyond what it has. He should—no, not *he* should—*they* should have to be *writing* the things that have value in order for him to be in them.

"I don't think that has been done. The parts which

would tap the whole range of William Shatner have not been written."

In the end perhaps it comes down simply to that.

STAR TREK opened up a role of scope and breadth, gave it a basic direction and a unique setting, plus very often the kind of writing which offered possibility. Into that Shatner infused elements, both consciously and unconsciously, which made the chemistry and unique message of Kirk come alive.

Now he has returned to the role and legend again, a decade older and more liberated by the revolutions which he has touched or which have touched him.

What translation he has given that decade on screen will be seen by the millions when the movie opens.

And even before it does, he will have and has gone on to other things.

Some may be fun. The play *Otherwise Engaged,* which he began rehearsing shortly after the movie, opened to rave reviews:

"The funniest show in town, quick, hilarious, stunning." (Gardner McKay, *Herald Examiner.*) "Witty, entertaining, excellent. A wonderful cast." (Ron Pennington, *Hollywood Reporter.*) "Wise and witty, extremely fine." (Sylvia Drake, *LA Times.*)

There is a footnote on that. Charles Impaglio, the senior publicist at KLET, the Los Angeles Public Television station where Shatner filmed "The Andersonville Trial," gives us permission for pictures—and a spontaneous review of *Otherwise Engaged* which he just saw. "It makes you remember what a fine actor he really is—with the classical training, Shakespeare. I saw the play in New York with another actor who played it very cold—and the role was nothing. With Shatner there was *somebody there.*"

There is a morning shortly after the movie filming when we go to meet him about something to do with *Star Traveller,* at the Beverly Hills theater where he is rehearsing *Otherwise Engaged*. It might be a title for his life. He rehearses 11:00 a.m. to 8:00 p.m. Mornings, 8:30 to 10:30, except today when he meets us at 10:00, he rehearses a new presentation for an expanded *Star Traveller*, deals with stacks of phone calls, then comes home to learn lines, makes other appearances, makes more phone calls, considers new material.

His plan, for when the play opens, he says casually, is an old dream—play the play at night, make movies during the day.

That's over and above working on *Star Traveller*, or plans for a STAR TREK sequel.

Okay. And now from the reality of the rebirth of STAR TREK, he is certain to get more of the things which he should be playing.

And yet the question remains: Where are the roles which would tap the full range of the man we saw take an audience flying with him?

Once we suggested that he might have to develop them himself.

That appears to be a direction in which he is moving. *Star Traveller* is a bold concept. The form it will ultimately take remains to be seen. That he would conceive of putting it together is a statement in itself.

We had predicted some years ago when we were beginning this book that ultimately he would create his own opportunities to do the unusual, as in that first one-man show—to go beyond where he has gone before.

Increasingly, over these years, that is what he has done, creatively, and in his life. Now and then an image comes back to us, kaleidoscopes into another:

A man with a drawn bow, facing a bear which towers ten feet tall.

Same man. Same bear, now a memory in his sunlit study. There he performs for us what he will perform for an audience of 18,000 at a STAR TREK convention—taking a bigger risk than hunting bear: "Whales Weep

Not." "They say the sea is cold, but the sea contains the hottest blood of all. . ."

It is a strange but appropriate choice for a STAR TREK convention.

He knows it. ("I want you to tell me what you think. I need your advice.")

He stands without prop or preamble and does it, there in the sunlit room with the great bear he has killed. He now wants to make a plea for the life of the whales: aliens of our own home seas, which we are about to destroy.

Strange, sensuous, loving beings who call to us in an unknown tongue—not from an alien world. If we cannot hear their kindred kind, how will we know a brother from the stars. . . ?

"Listen to them calling. . ."

There are people in that STAR TREK convention audience who do weep. Some of them are men.

And the man who stands on stage is, and is not, the man who hunted bear. Is, and is not, the boy who moved an audience to tears.

It is Shatner himself who has pointed out that every molecule in our bodies changes. And almost every idea.

We began with the question of whether he has changed during the decade—in emotional openness, in other ways.

We were to put the question to him directly. "Is it possible that the openness you projected in the role of Kirk was your dream more than it was your reality? Could it be that you learned that you could permit yourself to express emotion mainly or only in your work—so that acting became where much of your real life was lived? Was that, perhaps, one of the chief appeals of acting for you?"

And in a limousine on the way to a one-man show, William Shatner's eyes lit with that look of thought. "I *knew* you would do that!" he said. "And—it should be your observation as against mine—it's dramatic, it's interesting—but, yes, I would agree."

It is one thing to project openness on the screen. It is another to fight for it in your life.

Particularly if you are born into a world which precedes the revolution, where the lesson *is* don't cry.

Where he comes from, where more of us come from, a few decades ago, the standards of what it is to be a man are, in many ways, dead-set against that talent which he sensed was his birthright.

There are millions who would have given up the talent, perhaps never fully knowing that they made that decision, to fit the image of a man. There are a few who would have fought for the talent and more or less given up on the other half of what people defined as a division.

In some way, clearly or dimly, Shatner sensed from childhood that it was essential to him to fight for both. The child on stage, moving the audience to tears, the boy who could still go out and swim, wrestle, compete—became a theme of his life.

Whatever else sports came to mean to him, there was some sense in which they were always the other half of the fight for wholeness—to be the athlete and the artist, the man, and the human being.

We ask him about it once in those terms. Was there some sense in which his ability and interest in sports paid the freight, gave a legitimacy to that more sensitive side which could express itself mainly on stage?

"You mean—*because* I can throw the football, I can carry the violin case? Yes, I suppose there *was* some of that."

It was not a fight which had a name in those days. Still doesn't, for most men. But there are boys growing up now for whom the issue will not arise in that form—partly because of images like Kirk.

That image could not have existed if Shatner had not made his own fight.

If he had merely been the sensitive young actor, if there had never been the football or the motorcycles, the pilot's license and the bow hunting—the projection of Kirk wouldn't have come off. This happened to be a man who could have gone and done it if he had to—and even enjoyed it—and he had to know that in every scene.

It came through. The audience knew it, too. And knowing that, they could accept the emotion.

There is some sense in which by winning his fight and proving his right to that disciplined, open passion, he has helped to bridge for others the division he had to fight, alone. For the rerun generation the fight may not even be necessary. They may take it as given that a man can be a man and still express any sensitivity he feels. They've seen it on the bridge of a starship.

For William Shatner the quest for excellence, for the thing which is done "supremely well," remains a significant part of his life, far beyond the point where he has had anything to prove. Even within the last few years he has pushed it further, competing on "Battle of the Network Stars," or "USA Against the World" (as a Canadian—in the last minutes of the show winning for his team). Someone saw him competing in go-carts on a special, and asked him to drive in a Formula I race, the toughest form of automobile racing. He went to a school to learn race driving and competed in a grand prix in Long Beach—suddenly realizing, he says, as he shot through the course at 110 miles per hour, "You know, I could get hurt. Killed."

There are those, starting with a house on a hill, who could wish that would occur to him a little sooner.

On the other hand, there are also those, starting in the same place, who would not want to change that, or him, too much.

And the revolution owes him one, on that count, too.

William Shatner never intended to be a revolutionary —at least not in that particular revolution. He would have considered himself an unlikely candidate to become the champion of a cause which had no name. He would not have cast himself for the role. The infamous sense of humor would have had a field day with that one. "Who, me?"

But he did sign on for that revolution when he chose to try to become both an actor and a man on that level where "anything done supremely well is an act of sex."

He has kept that commitment on a dozen levels, among them a level of energy and of keeping on keeping on which is the despair of anyone who tries to keep up with him.

Almost everyone has a story of that energy.

Jesco von Puttkamer, from the days when he worked with Bill on *William Shatner's Mysteries of the Gods:*

"Bill would sit on the plane and carry on a perfectly normal conversation—sometimes with Marcy sleeping on his shoulder—his arm around her—and all the while he's holding his script and muttering under his breath the lines for his one-man show. It's a two-hour show he has to do, alone. He learned the lines in three days—*while* we made the film. And he would joke, laugh, carry on a serious conversation, plan how to handle the interviews of scientists for the film—all at the same time."

Jesco also tells the story which is possibly our favorite Shatner story.

Jesco, you must understand, is an authentic baron, transplanted here by the lure of going to the moon, which he worked on with Wernher von Braun's Apollo team. Jesco was deeply involved in the NASA fight for the orbital shuttle program which led to the Orbiter *Enterprise.* He is a principal architect of the real space program—NASA's Program Manager for Advance Long Range Planning—who has developed a long-range plan for where-no-man which has been accepted by NASA.

It is perhaps a bottom line on the influence of STAR TREK and the value Jesco places on the STAR TREK

fan movement that he wrote an introduction stressing
the connection between the dream and the reality for
Star Trek: The New Voyages II. But what is still more
unusual is that the book also contains a *Star Trek* nov-
ella, written by that same NASA baron.

After that, no one should have been surprised to find
Jesco becoming technical adviser to the STAR TREK
movie—on everything from hardware to philosophy.

Earlier he had helped Bill coordinate scientific interviews for *Mysteries of the Gods,* and was interviewed
for the movie himself as a NASA expert.

Bill (on film): What is the probability of the existence
of intelligent life in space?

Jesco: One.

Bill: One? (A slight take—not quite following Jesco's
cryptic delivery.)

Jesco: Certainty. 100%. A mathematical probability
of one.

Bill does a double take.

It's a funny moment in itself, which moves on to become a serious interview. All of the interviews, Jesco has
told us, are spontaneous, unrehearsed. Shatner wants a
fresh reaction. But the behind the scenes story of this
one is the favorite story Jesco tells us:

"You have to be very tight, you know, for the interview, for the closeups—very close together—nose to
nose. We had been working on it and I was not used to
it. I was a little stiff or something. He wanted to loosen
me up.

"All of a sudden Bill leaned forward and *He kissed
me!*"

There's a moment of silence from Jesco. Then a laugh.
"Well, you know, from *him* I take it. Nobody else."

They laughed then until there were tears in their eyes.
Then they got the scene.

That also is perhaps a bottom line on the decade.

Or on Shatner. There is that aspect in him. Always the

unexpected. Which is very often the effective, sometimes the outrageous—something only he could get away with.

There is a respect he commands which makes it possible.

The humor, the effort to keep people going with it, are still apparent on the STAR TREK movie set a decade later. Jokes, puns, little Bill-Leonard routines.

It's a little tougher this decade. He keeps on. It's a little more subdued than in the STAR TREK years. And then again once in a while it goes a little wild.

Ask him to tell you sometime what happened when the Captain threw a plate of chow mein at the Vulcan, in full costume, with ears. . .

There's an aspect of gallantry to some of that keeping-on-keeping-on which Shatner himself perhaps does not notice or consider. We've seen it sometimes during the writing of the book:

We go with him when he films the "$10,000 Pyramid" with Leonard Nimoy as opposition—the only exception the show makes to a rule of male and female celebrities.

They are fast and fierce competitors. More often than not both get seven out of seven. If one misses it's a galactic crisis.

In the midst of it all they do an improvised Kirk-Spock/Bill-Leonard routine on emotional openness—clearly taking it as so well known that it needs no explanation and can be a subject of well-understood humor.

Leonard goes into the Spock voice, long-suffering:

"I *have* tried to teach him to control his emotions."

Bill/Kirk: "Well, you know, if you bottle things up inside, what happens is—you get sick. A little healthy emotional display—"

Leonard/Spock: "Is not always healthy for those closest to it."

The audience does understand, cracks up.

But also, Bill is always coming up with one-liners, puns, etc., spinning off of whatever is going on. Once he has to give clues for dances—does it with his body, coming half out of the chair—Charleston, twist.

His jokes are almost always funny. Once in a while they are funny as groaners. Once in a while something doesn't come off, people don't get it.

Shatner takes that risk.

It's only a game show?

Yes. Nevertheless, he's putting out everything he has to be fast, funny, light, amusing.

In some sense, he's walking the wire. As much as on a Shakespearean stage. Maybe more. This is tougher. He can do it. But it's still tougher.

What no one knows is what we saw over breakfast with him that morning. He's exhausted. For once he even lets it show, to us. For weeks past he's been under enormous stress. Rehearsing for a two-role play in which he is on stage all of the time (*Tricks of the Trade*). Mountains of dialogue. It opens in two or three days. He hasn't got it as he wants it yet. He's doing dozens of interviews, publicity appearances, etc., trying to help the people who made his last film. He doesn't have to, but does. He feels obligated to help. He's got other projects going on, phone calls to make, problems to solve. He's wound tight as a wire. He knows the kind of toll that stress can take. For a moment he lets us see that knowledge.

On stage he schools the stress out of his face, his body. But it is still there as a kind of electric tension.

He's told us that the filming of the five "Pyramid" shows—changing costumes to simulate five days of a week—means running up and down five flights of stairs —each time.

It's against that background that he does the jokes, the dances, the Kirk-Spock routines.

Nothing says that he has to do it. He could walk

through it, make it easy on himself. Nobody would really fault him for being a little subdued one time. Much, anyway.

Or so he could tell himself.

He's not built that way.

Finally he wins a chance at the $10,000 pyramid for his partner—a woman who has come close to it all "week."

He carries it through to the last answer—still plenty of time—

He blows it.

He says part of the word. Probably it's the very wired-tight level of effort he is putting out. It's the kind of mistake that's made a thousand times—but not by him.

He is stunned, appalled.

Suddenly he's on his feet, the feeling visibly looking for some way to burst out of his body.

He picks up his chair and—heaves it over the rail, smashing it down.

It starts as an absolutely spontaneous gesture—and you can see him somewhere in the middle of it choose to turn it into a further acting-out of the "express your emotions" routine.

That's a risk, too. There's a chance the audience won't understand, won't accept it. It's startling. It's not done. The audience is shocked for a moment, then hysterical.

But everyone can see the actual emotion. And he allows them to see it.

Behind the scenes as they cut to a commercial, Leonard breaks up completely, then commiserates. Bill just keeps shaking his head. Can't believe it. Expresses profound regrets to his partner.

The camera cuts back, opens on Leonard and Bill. Leonard holding the chair—in two pieces. Another routine between them. They wind up with arms around each other's shoulders as the camera cuts to black.

It's all in a day's work, for Shatner. The keeping on,

no matter what else is happening. Giving his best. Taking the risks.

Turning even a bad moment into one which we hear people talking about months later, with affection—delighted that he would show them that.

To some fairly large extent, many people do understand and appreciate the risk involved in what he does—even without knowing fully what is behind it or what it costs.

Perhaps that is the bottom line on the reason for a very special affection which a great many people do have for him.

He is admired for many things.

Those who love him, love him perhaps most of all for that.

There are actors who play it safe. He is not one of them.

It's an aspect of gallantry which he would not even recognize as such. He would look at you with that innocent look of, "Who, me?" or "What else?" It seems normal to him.

But on another level he does know what it costs and takes. It is a source of pride to him, a commitment he has made to himself:

"You can always do it. Unless you're unconscious or dead. I don't care how sick you are. If you had to get out of a burning house, you could do it. You can always get up and go and say some words."

That is what he has done, whether his life was burning or not, through the crucible years—"shaking" or not, "insane" or not, sick, tired, alone. Whatever. Never saying "no."

For the most part he has always been alone.

Commitments to keep, responsibilities to carry, children to love—but no one really to open himself to, for decades.

He has had to learn to maintain his own central vision

in a profession which is as tough, perhaps tougher than any in this or any other century.

There are wolves here, always "trying to draw some essence from you." He has had to learn even how to maintain the wolf within himself, a certain toughness, a certain loneness.

Sometimes the decisions are soul-searing, especially for a man who set out to follow a dream.

And whatever the cost of that or anything else, he has done it, alone, keeping on.

He has never missed a performance.

The enormity of that statement—after knowing these years, perhaps tells you more than words.

This is a man who has worked, giving his best, whether his world was breaking, or his heart. . .

That also is a bottom line, perhaps the bottom line on what this book has come to be about.

We started with questions.

What we found was a man—a complex, real man. Tough, bright, tender, vulnerable.

We found a boy who had cried out his inchoate longing and love on a stage, and moved people in that way which was always to be his. The boy learned not to walk alone. The man learned to walk alone perhaps as much as anyone ever has: the private man, the shellmouth, who did his work, carried others along on the force of his humor, his will, his energy—and revealed himself to no one.

It was that man who projected the legend of emotional openness.

It was that man who ultimately fought for it in his life.

We found a man who questioned himself, and who was willing to explore those questions with us, and who had the courage to stand on what we saw and what we said, before all the world.

Something should perhaps also be said about what we did not find. We probed for the negative, and what you see here is what you get in that respect, too. A moment of temper, an edge of toughness, an impatience with unprofessionalism, a moment of hurting someone without intention, some of the faults, if they are faults, which he shares with Kirk, some of the desperation of the crucible years, some of the consequences of closing himself off emotionally. That's about it.

There are doubtless people he makes angry, sometimes with reason, and people he makes nervous, or envious. Shatner is doubtless not all things to all men, nor is anyone.

But whatever he has and is, the house on the hill, the love of the woman, the worship of three fine daughters —is bought and paid for with the coin of his life.

We began with the question of a man's encounter with legend. What has emerged is the story of the legend's encounter with a man.

He affected it, profoundly, shaped it, fought for it and with it, virtually reshaped himself by the bootstraps of his projection of that legend of man as he might be.

The revolution returned to affect him.

And he embraced it.

We began with the question of whether the man Shatner had won his own fight for emotional openness.

The book stands as our answer.

Readers will form their own estimate.

We think that the picture which emerges is one of a man who stands not at an end, but at a beginning.

And not only of a new STAR TREK, but of the new great roles which are certain to emerge from the ongoing revolutions.

Shatner would not call any of what he has done or accomplished—not even the keeping on—gallant, would not use a word like "heroic."

It is not something which a man can or should have to say about himself. It is not, in the last analysis even something anyone can say for him.

He says it with his life, or he doesn't.

But if he is William Shatner, you probably cannot even catch him standing on his record.

He will be off kissing some NASA baron, coming up with the one-liners, planning an unheard of format for a new kind of show, sparking an idea, writing a chameleon story in one minute in a sunlit room.

Walking some wire. . .